San Diego Christian College
2100 Greenfield Drive
El Cajon, CA 92019

Myth, Symbol
and Meaning
in *Mary Poppins*

Children's Literature and Culture
Jack Zipes, *Series Editor*

Children's Literature Comes of Age
Toward a New Aesthetic
by Maria Nikolajeva

Sparing the Child
Grief and the Unspeakable in Youth Literature About Nazism and the Holocaust
by Hamida Bosmajian

Rediscoveries in Children's Literature
by Suzanne Rahn

Inventing the Child
Culture, Ideology, and the Story of Childhood
by Joseph L. Zornado

Regendering the School Story
Sassy Sissies and Tattling Tomboys
by Beverly Lyon Clark

A Necessary Fantasy?
The Heroic Figure in Children's Popular Culture
edited by Dudley Jones and Tony Watkins

White Supremacy in Children's Literature
Characterizations of African Americans, 1830-1900
by Donnarae MacCann

Ways of Being Male
Representing Masculinities in Children's Literature and Film
by John Stephens

Retelling Stories, Framing Culture
Traditional Story and Metanarratives in Children's Literature
by John Stephens and Robyn McCallum

Pinocchio Goes Postmodern
Perils of a Puppet in the United States
by Richard Wunderlich and Thomas J. Morrissey

Little Women and the Feminist Imagination
Criticism, Controversy, Personal Essays
edited by Janice M. Alberghene and Beverly Lyon Clark

The Presence of the Past
Memory, Heritage, and Childhood in Postwar Britain
by Valerie Krips

The Case of Peter Rabbit
Changing Conditions of Literature for Children
by Margaret Mackey

The Feminine Subject in Children's Literature
by Christine Wilkie-Stibbs

Ideologies of Identity in Adolescent Fiction
by Robyn McCallum

Recycling Red Riding Hood
by Sandra Beckett

The Poetics of Childhood
by Roni Natov

Voices of the Other
Children's Literature and the Postcolonial Context
edited by Roderick McGillis

Narrating Africa
George Henty and the Fiction of Empire
by Mawuena Kossi Logan

Myth, Symbol and Meaning in *Mary Poppins*

THE GOVERNESS AS PROVOCATEUR

Giorgia Grilli

FOREWORD BY NEIL GAIMAN

Translated by Jennifer Varney

Routledge
Taylor & Francis Group
New York   London

Routledge is an imprint of the
Taylor & Francis Group, an informa business

This book was originally published in 1997 as *In Volo, Dietro la Porta* by Società Editrice "Il Ponte Vecchio" (Cesena, Italy). Translation has been provided by Jennifer Varney.

Routledge
Taylor & Francis Group
270 Madison Avenue
New York, NY 10016

Routledge
Taylor & Francis Group
2 Park Square
Milton Park, Abingdon
Oxon OX14 4RN

© 2007 by Taylor & Francis Group, LLC
Routledge is an imprint of Taylor & Francis Group, an Informa business

Printed in the United States of America on acid-free paper
10 9 8 7 6 5 4 3 2 1

International Standard Book Number-10: 0-415-97767-3 (Hardcover)
International Standard Book Number-13: 978-0-415-97767-8 (Hardcover)

Visit the Taylor & Francis Web site at
http://www.taylorandfrancis.com

and the Routledge Web site at
http://www.routledge-ny.com

For Neil

CONTENTS

SERIES EDITOR'S FOREWORD

Dedicated to furthering original research in children's literature and culture, the Children's Literature and Culture series includes monographs on individual authors and illustrators, historical examinations of different periods, literary analyses of genres, and comparative studies on literature and the mass media. The series is international in scope and is intended to encourage innovative research in children's literature with a focus on interdisciplinary methodology.

Children's literature and culture are understood in the broadest sense of the term *children* to encompass the period of childhood up through adolescence. Owing to the fact that the notion of childhood has changed so much since the origination of children's literature, this Routledge series is particularly concerned with transformations in children's culture and how they have affected the representation and socialization of children. While the emphasis of the series is on children's literature, all types of studies that deal with children's radio, film, television, and art are included in an endeavor to grasp the aesthetics and values of children's culture. Not only have there been momentous changes in children's culture in the last fifty years, but there have been radical shifts in the scholarship that deals with these changes. In this regard, the goal of the Children's Literature and Culture series is to enhance research in this field and, at the same time, point to new directions that bring together the best scholarly work throughout the world.

Jack Zipes

FOREWORD

I encountered Mary Poppins, as so many of my generation and those who followed it did, through the film. I saw the film as a very small boy, and it stayed in my head as a jumble of scenes, leaving behind mostly a few songs and a vague memory of Mr. Banks as a figure of terror. I knew I had enjoyed it, but the details were lost to me. Thus I was delighted to find, as a five- or six-year-old, a Puffin paperback edition of *Mary Poppins* by P. L. Travers with a picture of pretty Julie Andrews flying her umbrella on the cover. The book I read was utterly wrong—this was not the Mary Poppins I remembered—and utterly, entirely right.

Not until I read Giorgia Grilli's book on Mary Poppins did I understand why this was. I am not sure that I had given it any thought previously—Travers's Mary Poppins was a natural phenomenon, ancient as mountain ranges, on first-name terms with the primal powers of the universe, adored and respected by everything that saw the world as it was. And she was a mystery.

Mary Poppins defies explanation, and so it is to Professor Grilli's credit that her explanation of and insight into the Banks family's nanny does nothing to diminish the mystery, or to lessen Mary Poppins's appeal.

The patterns of the first three Mary Poppins books are as inflexible as those of a Noh play: she arrives, brings order to chaos, sets the world to rights, takes the Banks children places, tells them a story, rescues them from themselves, brings magic to Cherry Tree Lane, and then, when the time is right, she leaves.

I do not ever remember wishing that Mary Poppins was my nanny. She would have had no patience with a dreamy child who only wanted to be left alone to read. I did not even wish that I was one of the Banks children, at the Circus of the Sun, or having tea on the ceiling, and perhaps that was because, unlike many other children in literature, they did not feel permanent. They would grow, Jane and Michael, and soon they would no longer need a nanny, and soon after that they would have children of their own.

No, I did not want her for my nanny and I was glad the Banks family, not mine, had to cope with her, but still, I inhaled the lessons of Mary Poppins with the air of my childhood. I was certain that, on some fundamental level, the lessons were true, beneath truth. When my youngest daughter was born I took my two older children aside and read them the story of the arrival of the New One. Philosophically, I suspect now, the universe of Mary Poppins underpins all my writing—but this I did not know before I read Professor Grilli's work.

It would not be overstating the case to suggest that Professor Grilli is the most perceptive academic I have so far encountered in the field of children's literature, and I have encountered many of the breed. She understands its magic and she is capable of examining and describing it without killing it in the process. Too many critics of children's literature can only explain it as a dead thing in a jar. Professor Grilli is a naturalist, and a remarkable one, an observer who understands what she observes. We are fortunate to have her, and we should appreciate her while she is here, before she too walks through a door that is not there, or before the wind blows her away.

Neil Gaiman

PREFACE

My debt to Pamela Lyndon Travers stretches back to childhood, when I was given her Mary Poppins books to read during bouts of illness. Thanks to these books, I began to see those periods spent away from school as intensely precious and intimate. They were personal experiences that I owned entirely, even if stuck in bed. Once I had finished reading the particular book (or had finished its hundredth rereading), I would find that I was well again. Of course, this was probably the result of having spent a number of days resting in bed, but I could never quite convince myself that the figure of Mary Poppins and my mysterious return to health were not in some way connected. When I grew older, I resolved to analyze in more depth the character of Mary Poppins and her obscure capacity (not at all an easy or consolatory one) to "make one feel better." Moreover, I wanted to try and right the wrongs of the Disney film, which, while making this governess very popular, reduced her intriguing nature to a spoonful of sugar and much frivolity.

One of the most important observations to arise from a study of this kind concerns the way in which Mary Poppins sheds light on the conflicting drives and desires that underpin the life of an individual. Resulting from a dialectical play between two extremes, this conflict manifests itself in our desire for adventure while also seeking security, or in our desire for freedom while also craving the stability that a disciplined routine will bring. Indeed, it can also be seen in our desire for the unpredictable while at the same time we always seek to keep each and every aspect of our lives fully under control. Our deepest hopes and desires are, in fact, inherently ambiguous. And yet it is here, in the midst of this paradoxical shift between two quite natural though opposing extremes, that we find the character of Mary Poppins. She, as governess, is entrusted with the task of teaching discipline and good behavior, and her ability to set things straight brings a sense of immense security. She prepares the children for entry into the social order, introducing them to all the various demands that such an order will make on the individual. And yet she is, at the same time, the source of magical experiences and, as provocateur, provides access to a deeply subversive world in which individuals are given extra-ordinary possibilities that are not only unmentionable but even unthinkable before her arrival.

The importance of this character, therefore, lies in her ability to accommodate our contradictory needs and aspirations. She speaks as much to our desire to find a socially acceptable position within the social order, as to our need to feel that we are free, light, open to change, and not determined by preexisting models. Likewise, she gives voice to our need to be considered "normal" whilst acknowledging our need to remain unique, authentic, and full of personal integrity, an integrity that is, of course, lost when the individual seeks passively to adapt to the socializing exigencies of the external world—rigidly rational and abstract exigencies that form the basis of any complexly organized system. And this leads us to another important consideration. Contemporary Western societies have reached such a level of complexity in terms of their social organization that not only has the individual become alienated from his/her most intimate needs, he/she has also become alienated from all recognition and even memory of such needs.

What struck me most about my adult reading of the Mary Poppins books was the fact that, on closer study, these fantastic adventures can be seen to contain the echoes of something far more archaic and primitive. It would be reductive to describe these adventures as being simple inventions aimed at distracting and entertaining children; rather, they signal a set of surprisingly precise visions, beliefs, rituals, modes of behavior, and thinking strategies that will appear "strangely familiar" for the books' readers and characters alike. Indeed, a phrase repeated throughout the books is: "I think I remember something…." Entering into contact with Mary Poppins means to enter into contact with what Freud called *das Unheimliche,* or the uncanny in life. The disturbing situations Mary Poppins brings about are so surprising not because they are entirely new, but because they recall some remote or highly intimate experience that, for some reason, has been erased from everyday consciousness and subsequently forgotten.

The figure of Mary Poppins acquires iconic status because she is relevant not only to each individual's past, but to the collective past of the whole of humanity. In this sense, too, the adventures of Mary Poppins are only apparently fantastic; on a deeper level they function according to more ancient structures and practices that, when juxtaposed against modern—as well as adult—living, have an undeniably subversive and deeply undermining effect. There are, of course, many examples in the history of English literature in which apparently harmless, entertaining nonsense is revealed to contain rather deeper philosophical reflections. But what is so striking about the Mary Poppins books is their unsettling ability to involve the reader at a very deep level, rendering even more powerful the above-mentioned strategy. The governess continually takes recourse to the rules and requirements of the external world which is then subverted. Though the results are often expressed through humor, the adventures we embark upon in the presence of Mary Poppins often point to some very "real" and serious preexisting form of living that precedes contemporary life and our modern outlook. One such primitive form of living whose traces can certainly be found in Pamela Travers's books is the ancient matriarchal one wherein human life is viewed as being intimately bound to the forces of the cosmos as a whole. According to this vision of the world, the individual perceived him/herself as being a living part of an organic whole and the world as being powered by an ungraspable and invisible form of energy. Individuals communicated, thought and acted according to intuition, and trusted in the transforming powers of magic. The Mary Poppins books can be said to speak a matriarchal language in that they require of the reader a similar reliance on instinct, insight, and trust. During their adventures, the Banks children learn that animals, people, imaginary characters, and stars are all made of the same substance, and that all elements in the world can in fact communicate with and understand each other—they can mix and exchange roles, proving that all notions of category and distinction are but arbitrary constructions. This matriarchal vision of the world is enriched by another of the echoes found in the Mary Poppins books, that is, by the Dionysian element. The figure of Mary Poppins is in many ways informed by myth, and the myriad episodes in which life seems to explode with an almost ecstatic intensity when acted upon by the governess find a parallel in the myth of Dionysus. According to this reading of the books, Mary Poppins can be likened to the Bacchantes, those priestesses who initiated disciples into the rites and mysteries of the cult of Dionysus, god of creativity, and she represents this creative force, which reveals itself as natural and necessary but is usually curbed by the constraints of culture and the social order. So, in the presence of Mary Poppins, the books' characters and readers alike are encouraged to adopt a form of self-perception and a perception of the world that mirrors those contained in the myth of

Dionysus as well as in ancient matriarchal societies. On close examination, this outlook, which according to anthropologists characterized primitive visions of the world, also in fact characterizes the life of the newborn child. In what Freud has called the pre-Oedipal phase, preceding entry into language, the child does not yet perceive him/herself as being separate from all that is outside or "other" to him/herself and thus feels deeply involved in the continuity of life and the world. We are encouraged to experience life in a similar way, with a similar sense of continuity, when in the presence of Mary Poppins, who reveals the extent to which everything is united and intertwined and who, in her stimulation of the senses, encourages us to concentrate on the body as being the primary receptor of all experience. Furthermore, because of the way in which Mary Poppins mediates between the everyday world and a world that, for the adult inserted into a highly rational and rationalizing social and historical context, has become "other," unthinkable, and impossible, the governess can be likened to other liminal or threshold figures.

One particular threshold figure that springs immediately to mind when considering Mary Poppins is that of the shaman. Partly human and partly belonging to a world beyond ours, the shaman can certainly inform our reading of Mary Poppins, who belongs to our world (or at least the very recognizably English society of a certain historical period) but hails from somewhere in the sky, and who is at home in the London park where, together with the Banks children, she spends many an afternoon, but also demonstrates impressive elegance and ease by conversing with the sun, flying through the air, or talking to animals and stars. Like the shaman, Mary Poppins administers strange medicines; she sets a perfect example to her charges by instructing them how best to live in the "here" and yet is fatally and inextricably bound to an "elsewhere" that, were it not for her intervention, would remain out of bounds to "normal" people, and once glimpsed, throws into question the everyday world of day-to-day living. Therefore, although she teaches good manners to her charges and is always impeccably well-dressed and composed, she provides access to experiences that counter what is considered conceivable by a particular social context, and it is for this reason that she can be considered a provocateur. Thus, in the course of these books, Travers draws parallels with many other complexly ambiguous figures from myth and history, as, for example, the trickster, and that provocateur *par excellence*, the dandy. These are but a few examples of the way in which Mary Poppins can be located in a very precise thematic continuity that spans anthropology, mythology, psychology, and philosophy and proves that this figure is very much more than the simple protagonist of a children's story. Indeed, Mary Poppins is undeniably richer and more complex than the Disney film would have us believe—Disney's version is an endearing, tamed, and very superficial depiction that drained the character of her very essence, which is as obscure and disturbing as it is fascinating.

The last section of this study draws on the mythological, anthropological, philosophical, and sociocultural interpretations outlined in the preceding chapters, and seeks to demonstrate that a character like Mary Poppins could have occupied no other role than that of governess. If we analyze the figure of the governess in the late Victorian and early Edwardian period, it becomes clear that Travers chose this occupation for her protagonist precisely for the profound ambiguity inherent in this profession—an ambiguity that had the power to subvert society from within. The role of the governess was underpinned by a series of very real contradictions that rendered highly paradoxical her relationship with the society in which she operated. Given that she hailed from "outside" the family, the nineteenth-century governess was always considered "other" and was somewhat unknown. As such, she was potentially the source of wonder and amazement in the closed confines of the private and protected family space. Because of this she was considered threatening and a potential source of danger, and yet at the same time, she represented a form of status symbol for the family that employed her and was thus considered not only a legitimate but also a vital presence within middle-class society. The fear or threat connoted by her presence at the very heart of the family (though she was never really considered *part* of the family) was mitigated by assigning her a very precise and definite role: she was to teach good manners to the children and in so doing would preside over the cultivation and transmission of a publicly approved and recognized ethos. And yet behind the apparently recognizable and paradoxically exemplary activities of the governess, her identity remained profoundly mysterious—not least because she was necessarily a financially independent woman who earned her own living, who was without family responsibilities or constraints of her own, and whose authority made her an incredibly powerful figure within the sphere in which she operated. The governess was thus seen as a contradiction; she was a destabilizing, indefinable, and potentially subversive figure precisely because she stood in contradistinction to, but was demanded by, the Victorian image of the perfect woman that required middle-class women to be domestic creatures (which she was), but, as such, also to be passive, fragile, and economically and emotionally dependent on their husbands (which she wasn't).

Mary Poppins merely exploits to the full what was for the governess a very real situation; that is, despite living at such close quarters with the family and having such a great influence over middle-class children, she was nevertheless inherently ambiguous and not entirely containable by the social context in which she existed. She was entrusted with the implementation of an "educational program" that swung between indoctrination and subversion, between that which was rigidly socializing in aim and that which can be considered emancipatory or alternative, if only for the fact that this program was put into practice by a figure who, despite occupying a central role in the household, was never anything more than "strangely familiar." Travers pushes the strangeness of the governess to the extreme and exaggerates her paradoxical sense of familiarity by enriching it with the disturbing echoes of myth and antiquity. It is through a figure like Mary Poppins that Travers manages so successfully to express the notion that we can only really feel at home in the "here"—the everyday social context that forms the backdrop to our lives—if we open ourselves to contact with what is "beyond" and "other." After all, this "other" is possibly nothing more than a piece of ourselves that we have lost or have forgotten and that has been banished and forced to exist on the other side of the threshold.

Giorgia Grilli

ACKNOWLEDGMENTS

I really want to thank:

Professor Antonio Faeti, for being the old master I had been seeking for many centuries; Jack Zipes, whose great learning I've been honored to translate into Italian; Aunt Nadia, who opened fateful doors for me; Tori Amos, who knows what the bee knows and I think saved my life on a few occasions; Terrence Malick, who makes art out of the deepest truths; Adam, Alex, and Corey Finkelman, my own personal Banks children; Mirella and Ruggero, who have always put up very sweetly with the fact that I am a small solitary insect much more than their own daughter; Ireland where it all began, and Skye where conclusions were drawn (the drizzles, the wind, the cliffs, and the moss).

1

THE STRANGELY FAMILIAR MARY POPPINS

THE MARY POPPINS BOOKS

The name Mary Poppins is universally recognized, yet few people have actually read or even know of the books in which this character first appeared.[1] Mary Poppins achieved fame with the 1964 Disney film and is one of those familiar figures that seem to belong to the collective imagination. Her image is immediately recognizable and feeds into a certain common denominator of shared knowledge, meaning that children might dress up in Mary Poppins costumes at Halloween time or that commercials might profit by borrowing from her iconic status in order to sell products. In whatever context she appears, we find those same defining props: the parachute-like umbrella, the handbag, gloves and flower-adorned hat; and those same defining characteristics: the ability to solve all problems and soothe all worries.

Mary Poppins is present on a broadly popular and informal level as the typical and yet very particular English governess from the world of British fiction. Even those who are not entirely familiar with the precise details of the Mary Poppins books will nevertheless be aware of her defining qualities and will remember what this character is capable of doing. The Mary Poppins books were published over a period of fifty years, from the 1930s to the 1980s, and their creator, Pamela Lyndon Travers, could never have envisioned, as she sat down to write the stories, just how fascinating readers would find her protagonist.

Mary Poppins is a mysterious, fleeting character, but she is also "strangely familiar"[2] (III, p.19) to the children and adults who become acquainted with her. However, the captivating fascination and popularity of this character are not the result of a spontaneous, immediate identification on the part of the reader, as is the case with much traditional narrative. What is continually highlighted in the six books that carry her name is the sense of her being unusual, of her being someone or something quite special, unique and distinct from her surroundings. In leading us toward that world to which we would never gain access were it not for our imaginations, Mary Poppins is at the same time familiar and entirely Other and becomes the emblem not of our actual selves, but of our dreams, reflections, and projections. We understand from the very outset that Mary Poppins represents something to which we as readers will probably never get, and yet she seems so intimately related to us precisely because she taps into a sense of suspension or tension that is integral to our selves, even though it is somehow unconscious, forgotten, or as yet unrevealed.

Mary Poppins represents hope, flight, and—contrary to what may be superficially thought—not just a funny and gratuitous fantasy, but rather a set of deep needs that would be unspeakable unless one turns to "fantastic" metaphors. She symbolizes the experiences of fusion and confusion that, despite being deeply necessary to our existence, have for some reason been withheld or deemed illegitimate. And if she is, on the one hand, the perfect incarnation of certain shared values (Mary Poppins is the impeccable English governess of the early twentieth century whose favorite book, as frequently mentioned, is *Everything a Lady Should Know*), she can also be read as a fairy-tale character, or on a deeper level, as a mythical figure.

The Disney film significantly altered the character of Mary Poppins in its portrayal of her. To put it simply but effectively, we might refer to what Caitlin Flanagan says in her interesting article, "Becoming Mary Poppins. PL Travers, Walt Disney, and the Making of a Myth," in which she captures the essence of the changes made by Disney by asking "Why was Mary Poppins, already beloved for what she was—plain, vain and incorruptible—transmogrified into a soubrette?" Flanagan also points to Travers's private letters in which "she mercilessly criticized Disney's lack of subtlety and what she called his emasculation of the characters."[3]

Travers's books present her as a very solid and somewhat disturbingly dark character, and the illustrations by Mary Shepard (daughter of the better-known Ernest Shepard) reinforce this image. She is the powerful woman with arms raised, encircled by animals and taking part in some strange ritual under the moonlight; or she is that ungraspable character in the raincoat with the half-closed eyes and fleeting look that suggests that what she sees is in some way different from what we might see; or again, when shown playing her gypsy-like accordion, surrounded by those insidious cats and croaking ravens of the witching-world, she becomes the solemn yet ambiguous representative of a well-defined tradition of female characters. It is interesting to note, however, that the Mary Poppins books do not actually encompass their protagonist, nor do they give the impression of in any way claiming responsibility for her creation. There is no sense that these books seek to explain the character and her story in their entirety, in terms of a beginning, middle, and end. Rather, the character is as if "borrowed" for a moment from that unknown place where Mary Poppins has always existed. It is suggested that she may have acted as governess to other fictional children before coming to the Banks household, she is considered by animals to be a sort of "a distant relative," she is friend to the gods and so on. She is whisked through the air one stormy day by the Easterly wind and becomes, though for a limited time only, the leading light in the Banks household, which she apparently sets in order but in fact revolutionizes.

Mary Poppins descends on a very "English" England, or rather a very English city, brightened somewhat by the greenery of the inevitable London park, which, carrying a name no more inventive than that of "The Park," acts as allegory for the archetypal park. She comes to take charge of a household characterized by domesticity and all its attendant stereotypes, including that room or *sphere* known as the nursery where children and the childhood world are habitually confined. The details of this stereotypical environment define the field of identification in which the subsequent adventures take place. Yet, if the space of the story is clearly defined, the time in which it takes place appears suspended, halted in some way, imprecise—it is as if the characteristics of a particular way of life, which certainly do belong to a specifically recognizable if only vaguely delimited moment in time, were perceived as symbolic, robust, and deep-seated enough to be emblematic, capable of projecting meaning well beyond the confines of the specific age in which the stories are set. Certain specific social characteristics, with all their intrinsic contradictions, point to a sort of archetypal "reality principle," the dimension against which, regardless of time or place, the ontological and psychological struggle for freedom, authenticity and individual possibility takes place. The stories then are set against the backdrop of an England caught between the end of the long and burdensome Victorian era and the beginnings of the more frivolous Edwardian age, a moment characterized as much within the pages of narratives as without by a sought after compromise between an inevitable sense of intellectual adventure and an equally un-relinquishable traditional morality (bordering on exasperation and liable to transform itself into a rather interesting and highly dramatic rigor of form): this *past that refused to pass* defined the period going from the end of the nineteenth century, through the years preceding World War I and extending up to the threshold of World War II.

Mary Poppins arrives like a blessing and neatly inserts herself into the daily routine of this middle-class family in which the mother, Mrs. Banks, is beside herself with the responsibility of having to take care of her children and run the household at the same time. Mary Poppins is a model of competency and efficiency, the perfect governess come to help a family that, despite being quite normal (and maybe precisely because it is so normal), would otherwise find itself in grave difficulties. The mother of the family corresponds to the stereotype of the fragile, hysterical, and hesitating woman; the four children are boisterous, argumentative, sincere, and yet quite unmanageable—and there is another child on the way. To all this is added the various vagrant, annoying, and inept figures such as the servants, all of whom must be accounted for by the hardworking and bad-tempered father who spends all his time at the office. These characteristics signal the type of society focused on by these narratives, by these "simple" children's stories.

This burgeoning Edwardian society proved itself already to be resolutely heading in the direction of modern capitalism, which, in turn, affected the way that people and their lives were organized. It was already, broadly speaking, a "money society," even though its tastes, customs, fears, and ostentations still reflected a reluctance to accept competition, entrepreneurship, merit, and astuteness as ways of attaining social status. Society in general was not yet willing to admit that much personal and social action was the fruit of vulgar utilitarianism and the search for material gain. It still preferred to believe that action was driven by noble, disinterested, high aims, and the middle classes in particular were disturbed by their inability to boast "birth" or "blood" as natural justification for the important social positions they were beginning to conquer (by way of the money that they were making).

This scenario provides the backdrop to Travers's books. From the very first volume in the series, we are told that each morning the father of this respectable middle-class family leaves the house (with a hurried pace all too familiar to us) and heads for the city with the sole purpose of "making money." We are given no further details about his job and so are not entirely sure whether he literally "makes money" at the Royal Mint, whether he makes money in the figurative sense that he earns it (as we adults immediately think), or whether, whatever the case is, and as the children would have it, he simply spends his days away from home in the service of the money demon.

For his book, *The Edwardians*, the social historian Paul Thompson interviewed a number of elderly people who were alive during the first decades of the twentieth century, and his book provides some useful insights into the period in which the Mary Poppins books were set. In one particularly relevant passage the men of the middle-class districts come under scrutiny. The character of Mr. Banks clearly springs to mind:

> When the gentleman of the house arrives he is usually grumpy [...] He sinks into his well-cracked, saddle-bag, gent's arm chair as one who has all the cares of the world upon him. He inquires why it is that 'the damned dinner' is never ready, despite the fact that there are three women in the house...[4]

Given the high levels of tension present in the Banks household, Mary Poppins's arrival is seen as a blessing. Efficient as she is, she is able to set the situation straight (an immediate image for which is her straight back and perfectly erect posture). Mary Poppins acts as a sort of *norm*, or rather, she trains the children to respect what are considered to be norms (i.e., the corpus of manners one had to learn and adopt in order to be considered "normal" and thus acceptable by that particular context). And yet paradoxically Mary Poppins also represents something quite strange, inexplicable, and abnormal. She projects a sense of surprise and the promise of adventure; she embraces the unknown, the unexpected, and the incongruous; and she continually provokes a sense of strangeness, of novelty, overturning recognized and established codes such as those governing "good manners."

The name Travers gives her character is equally interesting—the name itself is always reproduced in full, that is, the governess is never referred to simply as "Mary" or "Miss Poppins." This clearly points to the fact that no other character is permitted to enter into an overly intimate relationship with the governess, nor will she answer to any title suggestive of her social position or marital status. She is what she is: just herself. The surname "Poppins" is suggestive not only of the fact that the governess, as we shall find, will literally "pop in" to the lives of the Banks children (she will suddenly become part of them, but only for a short time), but also points to the little explosions and subsequent shocks heralded by the verb "to pop." What we find therefore is a situation in which the name signals explicitly what the character will do and the effect she will have on those with whom she comes into contact. Indeed, it is in the company of Mary Poppins that the children are able to give expression to their flights of imagination and to the fantasies of which they are not yet even aware. The most unthinkable adventures are now possible, adventures toward the *Other, other*wise, in places *other* than that in which the children habitually live, with its normal characters and normal routines. Situations formerly seen as uninteresting, lacking in curiosity, unable to provoke a response or to involve the children in any valuable or stimulating way, are now, thanks to Mary Poppins, the sites of possible adventure.

Mary Poppins is neither fairy, magician, nor witch in the classic sense. The unexpected situations she creates are the result neither of tools, nor of enchanted formulae, nor of magical ingredients. We never see her plotting or preparing in advance the fantastical situations that open up a whole different world for the Banks children. Rather, she is an ungraspable presence (or graspable only insofar as she makes herself socially recognizable) for whom anything and everything is possible, even without her intervention. Life, which had become sluggish, crystallized, and, in some way, latent, in her presence awakens; her approach seems to suggest that only if our (senti)mental capacity to really be aware of the life around us is restored, can we live the potentially epiphanic relationship between our sensations and intuitions on the one hand and the aesthetic, sensitive, and stimulating qualities of the object world on the other. It is not so much a question of our watching Mary Poppins give life to the impossible or the fantastic, as experiencing a real awakening of our consciousnesses that, now released, can interact with a brand new world that reveals itself to us as if for the first time.

Because she remains on the sidelines and gives no hint that she is in any way responsible for the fantastic events that take place, we only perceive the links connecting Mary Poppins to these experiences when we are well into the adventure. The policemen and other law-abiding passers-by who accuse Mary Poppins of being involved in the events have no evidence to support their intuitive suspicions. Our governess is in no specifically rational sense the cause of these strange happenings (even though they only take place in her presence): the intimate associations and allusions of co-implication between herself and the strange events or characters that we meet are not the result of some magical spell cast by Mary Poppins to bring into existence something that heretofore did not exist; the links of complicity result from a sense of Mary Poppins as being intimately related to and in harmony with the *possible* rather than the *actual* (which she often virulently opposes).

THE NARRATIVE STRUCTURE

The same narrative structure is repeated in the first three books of the series, *Mary Poppins, Mary Poppins Comes Back* and *Mary Poppins Opens the Door*. Mary Poppins appears somewhere in the first chapter and disappears suddenly in different and unexpected circumstances during the last. The main part of each of the books deals with the strange situations and adventures that lead the Banks children, and we readers, toward marvelous and startling encounters. We could use the word "fantastic" to define these situations, a word that refers to a specific literary genre whose main elements can certainly be found in the Mary Poppins books, starting with the way in which normal, quotidian, everyday life is essentially intertwined with the alternative dimensions of the unexpected. This intertwining would remain obscure, unexplained, lacking in any sort of logical connection were it not for the fact that this glimpsed "beyond" (i.e., that which was until now unthinkable or unknown) imposes itself as "real": clues pointing to the fact that these particular situations did in fact take place within the narrative abound, such as the snakeskin belt that Mary Poppins sports the morning after the children experience a dream-like adventure, or the scarf belonging to Mary Poppins that Jane finds inserted into the illustration on the side of a vase. This "beyond" and its relationship with the "here" are condensed into that image of the Door, which opens and closes on difference, and allows nothing more than momentary access to that difference. That alone, however, is enough to upset what is officially recognized as "real" inside the house.

The next three books, *Mary Poppins in the Park, Mary Poppins and the House Next Door,* and *Mary Poppins in Cherry Tree Lane* do not follow the chronology of the story established by the first three books in which Mary Poppins arrived and left, before eventually returning in the sequel. In the first of these books, Mary Poppins is brought and then snatched back by the wind; in the second, she appears on the end of a kite string and is taken away again by a fairground ride; and in the third book, she descends from the sky in a rain of fireworks, only to disappear behind a reflection of the children's bedroom door at the end of the book. The fourth, fifth, and sixth books (according to the writer herself) recount other adventures that should be understood as having taken place in the time frame of one of the first three books when Mary Poppins came to fill the Banks home with her presence and the liberated potential of all things.

As in the first three books, Mary Poppins makes the Banks children enter and exit the various adventures in an equally unorthodox fashion.

Yet the narrative structure framing the adventures is predominantly linear and mirrors the movement of a linear mental scheme which is interrupted, dismantled, or proved insufficient. The exit from what we would call "reality," inspired by the "otherness" of the governess, takes place in two distinct ways. The first demands that we adopt an alternative thought process and abandon our usual rational approach to the world so as not to miss a certain incongruence present in the furtive phrases and gestures of Mary Poppins herself or one of the characters to whom she introduces us. We recall, for example, the way she very elegantly slides up the banister or the way she removes impossibly large objects from a handbag that seems far too small to have contained them (though of this we can no longer be sure), or the way she seems to talk to animals, or the fact that she can fly, that she appears and disappears at whim. A similar abandoning of our normal rationale is required when Mary Poppins introduces us to other characters so that we do not miss the statues, stars, or toys moving as if they were human, or the fact that some of them seem to be able to remove their own fingers; or again when the children find their desires instantly turning to reality, or their names unexpectedly written on balloons, or see candy walking sticks begin to fly. The second way in which we exit "reality" as we know it is via a move toward a spatial Elsewhere. Examples of this include flight through the air, underwater sea adventures, or the way in which the nocturnal park becomes a setting for the strangest and most unsettling upheavals. Rather than challenge a belief system or a limited way of thinking, this form of exit involves the physical displacement of the body as a moving, feeling, and living entity.

The return to "reality" after these various exits is defined on all occasions by the same words, which act as a sort of chorus repeated through the different books: the children find themselves back within the four walls of their home, these walls allow them to confront certain truths now enriched with the intuition (stronger for having been experienced) that different possibilities exist, they do not yet understand how they have participated in this, and are left "still wondering." Having entered the spiral of the in-between space, they are now disoriented. This spiral, gap, or "in-between space" between two opposing "realities" is an important metaphor and one to which the Mary Poppins books frequently return. The "incredible" always occurs in an "in-between" time or space. An adventure unfolds in the space between night and day, or in that instant between the end of the old year and the beginning of the new, or on the legendary Midsummer's night, or again on Halloween when the relationship between the living and the dead is renegotiated, or quite simply when the character is seen to be suspended, swinging between the sky and the earth, belonging to both dimensions and to neither:

> Up, up, she went, till her black straw hat was higher than the trees, then down she came with her neat black toes pointed towards the lawn. Her eyes, as she rode her flying swing, shone with a strange, bright gleam. They were bluer than Jane had ever seen them, blue with the blueness of far-away. They seemed to look past the trees and houses, and out beyond all the seas and mountains, and over the rim of the world.
>
> The five swings swung together. [...] [The children] were wrapped in a dream with Mary Poppins, a dream that swung them up and down between the earth and the sky, a rocking, riding, lulling dream… (III, pp. 199–200)

Whatever happens "beyond the door," and whatever form these events take, these exits always mark a sense of upheaval from everyday, normal life.

So Mary Poppins leads us to an Elsewhere and in so doing we are led to question the stability of situations, values, and abstract concepts, and to challenge the rational, obvious perspective. The presuppositions on which this rational approach is based can no longer be considered unquestionably true, and the hierarchy of values underpinning it must be reconsidered.

This Elsewhere is above all suspended beyond the laws of time and space and defies all attempts to measure or quantify that which takes place ("Tuppence, fourpence, sixpence, eightpence—that makes twenty-four. No, it doesn't. What's the matter? I've forgotten how to add!" IV, p. 243). The events happening "beyond the door" are qualitative; they are, primarily, sensory experiences enriched by a heightened perception of taste, smell, color, and touch; and on a more profound level, this concentration on sensory experience leads to the awareness of a spirituality, or aliveness, inherent in the atmosphere and energy characterizing this alternative dimension. In this Elsewhere, the children's bodies become light and take flight, the children become happier and want to laugh; their bodies feel more flexible and they begin to dance or feel less tired ("I expect you're over-tired [...]" "I expect I am," [he] said. "But it didn't *feel like that*…" IV, p. 250). There is a general sense of well-being ("Never before, they told themselves, had they felt so light and merry." III, p. 41) that calls to mind other flights from everyday life as analyzed by Carlo Ginzburg in his moving study of the Benandanti.[5]

Each individual book varies in terms of detail, and yet within the form and substance of the books as a whole a game of repetition and parallels is established. The fascinating balance of structural repetition and content variety recalls the structure of the epic, where the narrated action gains universal value and attains a sense of the Eternal. The relatively modern setting of the books is indeed overridden by a sense of the mythical. If we study the books as a whole, we find a precise design and an almost fatalistic sense of repetition and recurrence. For example, each book contains a rather amusing and farcical episode in which Mary Poppins takes the children to see an eccentric relative of hers, on the auspices of following Mrs. Banks's orders to have repaired some broken household item. As always, the strangest events take place. In the first book the children meet Mary Poppins's uncle, Mr. Wigg, and end up drifting up into the air simply by thinking of something funny. In the fourth chapter of *Mary Poppins Comes Back,* we find ourselves drawn into an upside-down world where everything must exist upside-down, including the characters themselves. In the third book, when the children meet Mary Poppins's cousin, Mr. Twigley, they are transported by a strange music that causes them involuntarily to dance. And in *Mary Poppins in the Park* they meet Mr. Mo and shrink to miniature in order to enter a world of plasticine figures. On these occasions, Mary Poppins is entirely herself, and as such appears unique, exceptional, and very different from the other characters whose bodies undergo extraordinary change or are exposed to strange situations that cause some form of physical mutation, setting the body well beyond the rational control of the mind.

The children's bodies gain a sense of autonomy once removed from the norms of weight, stasis and habitual postures, which in turn exposes them to new experiences. This however is accompanied by a sense of disassociation, denying them the possibility of willfully deciding when to initiate or end the experience, or the form that this physical victory over the laws of nature will take. So these experiences are always accompanied by a moment of disorientation, surprise, or confusion. Mary Poppins, on the other hand, is never in the least bit flustered or disturbed by what happens—she participates in the very same unsettling physical experiences though without so much as creasing her clothes or disturbing her perfectly positioned hat; these sudden chaotic experiences do nothing to alter her impeccably neat appearance or irreprehensible (and thus all the more strange) composure.

Returning to the question of repetitions within the works as a whole, another element we find reflected in the design of the episodes is the recurrent appearance of certain extraordinary figures (extraordinary only to those who are able to see them as such, or only for a moment) who are presented as lifelong friends of Mary Poppins. Along with the children, these are the only other figures who trust her implicitly and who, on certain occasions, act in a similar way to Mary Poppins herself. These figures are otherwise quite normal, always belonging to the working class or a subordinate social group, alienated from any sense of stable power, and marginalized from society. When these characters appear, they are as if awarded the chance to take their marvelous revenge. The matchbox man (also a street artist), the little woman selling balloons outside the park, the woman who feeds pigeons, the old and decrepit Mrs. Corry, Robertson Ay, the shoeshine, and the humble though charming chimney sweep are all characters who communicate a sense of permanency, who seem to exist well beyond the temporal boundaries of a single life. Unlike the other adult characters in the books, these figures are able immediately to understand Mary Poppins and thus follow her, fully enjoying and trusting in the alternative possibilities she gives rise to. Specific chapters are devoted to these figures ("The Bird Woman", "Mrs. Corry", "The Story of Robertson Ay", "Balloons and Balloons", "Peppermint Horses"), who, in effect, are allowed the opportunity to become "heroes for one day," assuming the role of protagonist and leading the fantastic action. At these times Mary Poppins is involved in the action only insofar as she might exchange some strange look or gesture of understanding with the protagonists which the children and we readers cannot fully comprehend.

Another feature repeated through the structure of the works as a whole is the presence of one unexpected chapter that fully immerses us in the world of traditional fairy tales. These episodes begin with the classic "once upon a time" and contain the requisite kings, queens, princes, and counselors. These narrative moments that whisk the listeners away are the only occasions on which Mary Poppins makes any sort of concession to the wishes of the children to listen and understand; otherwise, she is almost always mute, breaking her silence only to issue orders, call into line or reprimand the children with all the severity normally associated with the figure of the governess. Staring into space, concentrated on the evocation of some other dimension, Mary Poppins assumes the role of storyteller with the children sitting at her feet, as attentive to the story as they are to the need not to interrupt her or disturb her in any way in case she might stop.

Examples of these fairy tales include the story of the star that became entrapped in the horns of a cow, making the cow dance and dance until she finally decides to present herself at Court and ask for the wise advice of the King, ("The Dancing Cow" in *Mary Poppins*), or the story of the cat who wanted to see the King, in which the two pit their mental powers against each other, rational reason battling it out against subversive intuition ("The Cat Who Looked at the King" in *Mary Poppins Opens the Door*), or again the story of the incredibly rich but equally stupid King who was unable to learn any school subject, despite the help of the best teachers in the land (who were beheaded for failing in their duty to teach him anything), until one day a Fool arrived at the Court and taught the King that the lessons learned in school are useless and that the ability to invent stories and listen is the key to all knowledge ("The Story of Robertson Ay" in *Mary Poppins Comes Back*). These stories represent the typically popular and hence anti-bourgeois themes of wealth, power, wisdom, and foolishness and are based on the concrete, visual, and tangible descriptions of objects such as the glamorous costumes, magnificent castles, the shiny lancets of the castle guards, the numerous tomes in the royal libraries, and the sparkling crowns and scepters. As is the case with all fairy tales, such objects belong to another world (an Other world) that is however rendered so tangible as to gain symbolic status.

Another of the correspondences in the texts links the chapter in *Mary Poppins* in which we encounter the two twins, John and Barbara (who here act as protagonists but would usually occupy a secondary role or would not in fact be involved in the adventures at all), with the chapter in *Mary Poppins Comes Back* that focuses almost entirely on the newborn baby named Annabel. In these specific cases, childhood is treated as a romantic and almost mystical theme where being a child means to be in intimate contact with nature and the cosmos.[6] A further recurrent theme is that of the subversion of the boundary between fiction and reality, between "facts" and artistic creation, articulated, for example, by the way in which the children enter into paintings, or meet fairy-tale characters, or play with statues miraculously come to life.

Another textual feature that points toward a certain cyclical organization within the works as a whole is the frequent recurrence of certain adventures defined as profoundly "other" to the "real" world; here the tone of the narration becomes solemn, grave, whilst the action revolves around cosmic figures or forces that on some level stand for the whole of creation, with Mary Poppins at the center of a sort of apotheosis. In the first of these episodes, "Full Moon," in the book *Mary Poppins*, the children hear a voice in the dead of night—difference almost always comes to life at night—bidding them to get up and follow it. With the characteristic trust and enthusiasm of children, Jane and Michael leap out of bed and follow the voice down streets and through parks until they reach the zoo, lit by a full moon. Signs abound suggesting that this is no normal night. The zoo is, in fact, no longer a zoo, but some other place belonging to some other world. In keeping with the tradition of literary and mythical entries into "beyond" places (for example Aeneas's entry into the Underworld), the children must pay a toll or make some other similar form of payment. The Banks children are instructed to show a ticket given them at the entrance by a uniformed bear, only to find that all the zoo animals are out of their cages and wandering free. One of the animals challenges the two humans who have entered a universe not their own, but the children are described as "Special Visitors—Friends of—" (I, p. 156) and are given access to this Elsewhere. The device by which access to an Elsewhere (and conversation with those who do not belong to our dimension) is granted by influential protectors is by no means new—think of Ulysses, Aeneas, and Dante, who, in traveling through their own other worlds, all met with similar circumstances. The links with the *Aeneid* and the *Divine Comedy* come to the fore when Jane and Michael find that in this nocturnal world of the zoo, which is the opposite of the daytime world, the cages contain not animals but people. Here a Dantesque logic seems to preside: Admiral Boom for example is kept in the tiger's cage precisely because he acts like a tiger toward other people in the daytime world. For their part, the animals seem to be reliving a scene from the earthly paradise in which they live peacefully side by side in this brief repose from the natural laws of aggression. The presence of the serpent is another feature that calls to mind paradise. The snake is the king of this Elsewhere place and is venerated by all. In one solemn scene it wriggles from its own skin intending to offer this as a gift to Mary Poppins. The animals begin dancing in a circle, then form a chain in which their various separate forms and the boundaries between their bodies grow indistinct. In his notes for the ending of *Heinrich von Ofterdingen*, (subsequently compiled by Tieck), Novalis devises a strikingly similar scene:

> People, animals, plants, stones and constellations, elements, sounds, and colors all come together in one great family, acting and speaking as one single species. Flowers and animals speak. The fabled world becomes visible and the real world begins to seem unreal.[7]

With his romantic notions about imagination and the ability of Eros to liberate the creativity that lies at the heart of the world and of humankind (once it has learned to defend its authenticity), Novalis paves the way for Mary Poppins's exploded world.

The epilogue of the episode described above sees the children returning home to their beds and takes place just as they are opening their eyes as if from a dream. They are convinced, though cannot be sure, that the incredible events took place; but Mary Poppins is no help to them, blocking all their attempts to explain, question and speak about what happened, and calling their stories absurd. Jane and Michael are just about to surrender when all of a sudden and at the same time (and in those familiar surroundings which are so well-known as to neutralize the possibility of the strange) they stumble across proof that what they remember did, in fact, take place. The evidence needed to open a whole world of possible otherness now rendered "real" is provided by the snakeskin belt the silent Mary Poppins is wearing about her waist. This is an example of what Emanuella Scarano calls in an article entitled "I modi dell'autenticazione" (means of authenticating)[8] the "mediating object—or that which confirms the authenticity of the journey beyond the threshold.

In *Mary Poppins Comes Back* we find a scene similar to this taking place on Mary Poppins's free night. As in the previous example, the governess is particularly keen to put the children to bed. It is thus in this warm, cozy, protective atmosphere that the ensuing adventure begins. During the night, Jane and Michael once again leave the house, this time in pursuit of a voice issuing from a star. Once again they find themselves at the zoo. Someone gives them money for the entry ticket (this time the money is made of a stellar substance), and they enter the zoo to find that the animals have been replaced by a series of constellations that, in this new dimension, have attained tangible form. A circus ring forms the center of attention in which each figure performs, until the arrival of the sun who is the absolute ruler of this realm, just as the snake was of the first. The climax of this episode takes the form of a celebration during which the Supreme Being makes an offering to Mary Poppins. Once again, the participants form a circle and begin the "Dance of the Turning Sky," only the second in a long succession of scenes involving music and circular dancing that populate the books.

A third cosmic celebration held in honor of Mary Poppins takes place in the chapter entitled "High Tide" in *Mary Poppins Opens the Door.* As with the previous two examples, the children leave behind their bedroom and the "real" world only when night has fallen. A mysterious being accompanies the children to a party held on the seabed, and here, once again, they meet Mary Poppins. It is only when Mary Poppins herself is the center of these celebrations or guest of honor that the children must travel unaccompanied by their governess, seeking by themselves her whereabouts in some strange new world.

Deep below the surface of the sea Michael and Jane meet all sorts of strange sea creatures. This time they are given coins made of sand to pay for their entry into this world, a gesture that ritually marks the opening of the adventure. Events at the bottom of the sea are just as muddled as they were in the nocturnal zoo: fish go fishing for humans, using pieces of strawberry cake for bait, thus attracting the humans to the water's edge before they are pulled under. The sovereign of this underwater world is the old Terrapin, whom the ocean's inhabitants treat with great respect. The Terrapin, like the other sovereigns before her, also makes an offering to Mary Poppins—a starfish—that on the following morning turns up in the Banks home, the familiarity of which would seem to deny all possibility of the children having really experienced the underwater world of the previous night. The conversation between Jane and the old Terrapin turns to ideas about creation and the common features linking and unifying all creatures. They discuss the incredible similarity of life at the bottom of the sea and life on land and the correspondences or relationships of likeness linking the characters from the two different dimensions. Again we are presented with the circular dances in which the confines of distinct bodies disappear, signaling once more a cosmic unity populated with Baudelairean correspondences.

Other episodes have an equally foreignizing effect, even when they take place in the familiar park or involve everyday characters who might experience something quite extraordinary, though what makes the above-described episodes quite different is the extent to which the subversion of the schemes used to structure reality can have an educational effect at a deep, existential level. These episodes highlight the teaching value of such adventures, where an active, involved learner gains knowledge not through the passing on of any sort of dogma but through an epiphanic revelation of truth. These brief, momentary trips "beyond the threshold" hold revelation for those who are accepted into the new world as guests but are not to remain there.

MARY POPPINS'S AMBIGUITY

It is the singular identity of Mary Poppins that makes these strange and revealing scenes possible and even inevitable, and yet her gestures, opinions, and reactions (though never her faultless manners) are profoundly ambiguous. And what makes Mary Poppins even more attractive and fascinating as a character is the fact that she never allows the perfection, normality, or obviousness of what she is and does to be doubted or put into question. In the Banks household, she continually gives out signs of incongruence, foreignness, and ungraspable singularity—she continually amazes, stuns, and disorientates those around her, though without actually acting as accomplice to this disorientation. She claims not to understand this puzzlement nor wants to hear talk of it, and goes about her business with the utmost conviction that she is merely doing what needs to be done, considering offensive any suggestion that she, or anything she does, is strange. The children in her care, however, cannot help suspecting something is up.

It is precisely this complexity that renders Mary Poppins so fascinating. She is at once perfect yet rather funny, impeccably mannered and yet capricious, she is beyond judgment yet easily offended and difficult to cope with. She admires her reflection in every window she passes, and whilst we readers may appreciate her elegance, we also detect in her a certain rigidity; she is authoritative but also rather wooden. In a very British manner (in keeping with the stereotype), she is always extremely serious, direct and practical, almost amusingly austere, decisive and certain even in the face of the most absurd, incongruous and paradoxical situations. There is nothing sentimental or sweet about Mary Poppins, and this lack of sentimentality finds a parallel in the backdrop to the books—a social and cultural context that made this stiffness one of its most appreciated values, especially among the middle classes seeking respectability. It would seem that nothing can disturb the sense of containment, solemnity, and almost ritual perfection actually required of a governess and to which Mary Poppins corresponds. She remains solemn and composed at all times: when she and those around her take flight and soar into the clouds, when their bodies grow in size or shrink, when statues come to life, when stars descend from the skies to take on human form, or when animals dance, sing, take humans as prisoners or even fish for them, and when the characters from paintings or books step off the canvas or page into the "real" world.

Yet despite Mary Poppins's continual composure and sense of coherence, normality, and certainty, the children she looks after and leads in an almost inevitable manner into these strangest of situations react with amazement, excitement, and disbelief. And, even more important, what Mary Poppins denies to be "magical" or even strange or abnormal does in fact mark the children. These experiences are not just significant, they are meaningful, as would be any element that differs from the norm, disturbs the "typical" in life, or disrupts the repetitive and self-identical character of the "known".

Mary Poppins's actions function as a catalyst for Jane and Michael, the two elder siblings of the Banks family. In steering them toward experiences of *Elsewhere* and *Otherwise*, she casts them in the role of protagonists in a ritual rite of passage characterized by solemnity and a sense of the sacred. The children emerge from these experiences with a greater understanding both of themselves and of the world that surrounds them—not just in terms of its surface reality, but of something deeper, more complete. This is made possible because, although

Mary Poppins initiates these flights from normality (as physical as they are mental), her strict severity and constant presence prevent the children's fascination for this Elsewhere from tipping over into an excessive euphoria resulting in a risk for the children of losing themselves. Such a loss could be produced by the children becoming disorientated by the confused or upturned circumstances, but could also be the product of the loss of one's sense of self or personal identity, once in the Other world. Here, however, identity seems to be emphasized and enriched by these alternative experiences. In fact, in the Mary Poppins books, the adventures often take place during special events (i.e., they are special to the individual) such as birthdays, or during those moments in which they can drop their social and professional roles and "be themselves" (i.e., on their days off work), or when their truest identity is affirmed, such as when the children are given balloons with their own names written across the front (and subsequently take flight).

Perhaps the most fascinating and fleeting of Mary Poppins's qualities is the way in which she rigidly imposes *order* with a view to allowing those around her to experience *disorder*. Mary Poppins gives access to a disordered world in which life is led on a qualitative basis, no longer according to the most common mechanisms of the quotidian, where everything is taken for granted and where there is no place for amazement, for genuine ecstasy, for childlike incredulity or creativity, these states having effectively been outlawed by a certain type of upbringing and imposed way of thinking about and emotionally reacting to the world.

There is, however, a sense that the difference or alterity continually encountered in the Mary Poppins books is to some extent controlled; difference is always consciously depicted with a daringness that on close examination is not entirely released, as would be the case if the otherness depicted were seen as completely indomitable, uncontainable, and unruly. In fact, otherness is controlled to the extent that via the elegant intervention of Mary Poppins, that otherness is brought closer to us and domesticated; we can meet and begin to know it without running the risk of never being able to return. We cannot therefore consider a writer like Pamela Lyndon Travers as being straightforwardly *for* or *against* what we could call pedagogical narratives; rather, Travers is the sort of writer who aims to liberate her readers from all overly strict and reductive pedagogical claims, from a very specific civilization process and its standards, and from narrow-mindedness in general. Yet at the same time, her narratives suggest that she believes that, in order to grow and develop as authentically as possible, certain lessons must be learned and certain rules must be respected, or at least recognized. (The point being that the lessons that are to be learned, or more deeply so, in the Mary Poppins books, are the ones of Life, rather than those of the specific society we find ourselves living in. The latter have to be respected too, but in what is a personal way: (i. e. not to the point of not realizing that, if adopted mechanically and passively, they can run counter to the possibility of living, finding out, and expressing what is more deeply true.)

Mary Poppins's behavior and her codifiable actions (seemingly above suspicion, but that nevertheless grant access to the Elsewhere) in some way act as absolutes and remain unchanged with each new dimension she enters; or rather, her very controlled disposition is highlighted and rendered even more distinct precisely because such a mode of behavior contrasts starkly with the disordered, subverted situation in which she sometimes finds herself (and to which she transports her charges). What is interesting is the fact that before her arrival, the Banks children were boisterous, unruly, and badly behaved youngsters who refused to accept the ways of adults and who sought to rebel against them, yet to no avail: their childhood world was in no way an alternative to the adult world. Under her care, however, these children become surprisingly eager to obey each and every one of her commands, and suddenly lose their desire to divert from the socially acclaimed exigencies of order, cleanliness, and efficiency. They do so not because they blindly accept these values but because these values suddenly take on new meaning: they are no longer seen as oppressively burdensome tasks to be fulfilled in the service of some unnatural duty; rather they are now seen as the lighthearted and cunning rules of an exciting game, and become a form of disguise. The children keep themselves clean and tidy; they walk with their heads held high and their shoulders squared even though they would rather slouch, rather not worry about whether their outward appearance meets the required standards, and rather not be bothered with the need to learn good manners; and they decide to make the effort to behave correctly because they realize that merely by behaving well they can create a favorable impression on those around them and will thus be left alone to search for deeper and more meaningful alternatives than the one of a simple saying "no" to rules not followed by the realization of something new. And these alternatives offered by Mary Poppins, provided that they behave, are profoundly creative and prove more interesting than the punishable and rather sterile refusal to comply with unnatural constraints or the staging of an act of disobedience. The children's opposition to the world of the grown-ups becomes, with Mary Poppins, less overtly obvious (and is thus unpunishable) but far more radical.

As already suggested, even the exploration of the Elsewhere that takes place beyond the door (now revealed to be pure convention, a "mental" invention to keep alternative experiences on the outside) and the embarking on adventures during which anything might happen do not result in pure chaos or the destruction of the rational world. Mary Poppins's characteristic severity never disappears, and its purpose soon becomes clear: it is a device through which the impossible can become possible without becoming too overwhelming. Her demands for containment may seem exasperating, but are a way of approaching the irrational that allows the individual to experience this at a deeper, more intense, and meaningful level.

The gift Mary Poppins brings is the gift of a greater, fuller life, and as such she might be defined as a sort of archetypal mother figure; and yet, at the same time, her rules, discipline, and strict views on behavior she imposes with extreme rigor and absolute authority link her to the figure of the father. What results, both for the Banks children and for the reader, is a sense of infinite richness of experience in which so much is lived and absorbed but nothing is lost (especially not the self)— she allows, by means of her duality, a wonderful balance between the instances of fusion with the whole and of one's own identity, the only balance that can allow for a true understanding both of the world and of one's self.

The kind of understanding called for here is not one based on an intellectual and logical examination of the causes and connections underpinning life; indeed, the Mary Poppins books subtly criticize logic as a way of thinking about and seeing the world, as well as strictly logical thinkers. Given that the word "logic" comes from *logos*, a term that unites the themes of thought and speech, it is interesting to note that none of the adventures that in some way defy all logic are allowed to be discussed, explained, or in any way narrated once the children are back in their home. Mary Poppins is particularly strict when the children want to discuss and relive their adventures on that side of the door; she forbids the recounting of the adventures because back in the realm of logic and order, any narration would give those fantastic experiences a compromised and imperfect form. The children must imitate her solemn silences and become, like her, the guardians of a sacred knowledge which must be experienced and lived rather than narrated, a knowledge that is immediately linked to the development of certain practical strengths or abilities which transform the children and make them aware of possibilities and skills that they had not previously recognized, such as flying, talking to birds, or meeting characters they had thought belonged only to the realm of the imagination (now revealed to be as one with the realm of what is "real").

THE WONDERFUL REAL WORLD

The adventures that take place beyond the door might prove entertaining but they are never escapist and can never be defined in terms of a vague, gratuitous flight from life. If Mary Poppins, with her severity, prevents the Banks children from interpreting the adventures as such, the reader is equally encouraged not to view these flights from normality as purely escapist. The stimulatingly flavorsome style adopted by Pamela Lyndon Travers acts as a remedy for the temptation to read the novels as representing an escape from reality; the writing might be extroverted and audacious, but it is always deeply rooted in concrete sensations that bring the real world into focus. Paradoxically, then, Travers's concentration on immediate and sensually powerful descriptions grants the reader a truer and more disinterested vision of reality than would have been the case had the world been depicted and narrated according to some abstract ideology—including the one of "realism" when this is only concerned with representing something plausible on the level of content but forgets to pay attention to the small details of life involving both the characters' and the readers' five senses. Travers's writing, because of her surprising, constant, childlike attention to one's—first of all physical—sensations, stages transgression towards "official" proposals of world views, towards more abstract ways of looking at and understanding the world, the real world. So even if it is classified as children's literature in what is somehow always a dismissive sense, it cannot be labeled as simple or simplistic, but rather as an altogether philosophical alternative vision.

Mary Poppins is inextricably linked to the smells, tastes, sounds, and colors that abound in the books—from the smell of shoe polish, to clean sheets and freshly baked toast; from the sweet taste of candy-floss, peppermint, and gingerbread, to the jingling bells of ice cream carts or the call of peddlers and the cries of children playing (equal in volume to the cries of adults intent on stopping them); from the delicate colors of the nursery to the bright colors of the merry-go-rounds and golden hues of fairs and parties, from the attractive reds and purples of cake toppings (often appearing in adventures) to the green grass of the park (resplendent against a grey cityscape backdrop) that pulses with life and sees a whole world of children's games and English afternoon outings take place within its boundaries. Moreover, through Mary Poppins we sense the presence of the natural world as a world with its own rhythms and life; she is down to the very last detail immersed in the cyclical (though never linear—the characters never seem to age) passage of the seasons, and so we pass from winter shoes, coats, and colds to sunhats and daisy chains; and she is equally immersed in the cyclical rhythms underpinning each individual day so that, led by the governess, we pass from the smell of warm bread in the morning to the soft, reassuring warmth of covers tucked in at night.

There is no escape from the "real" world since it is precisely the familiar world that suddenly becomes attracting and wonderful. Mary Poppins awakens a diffuse vitality and latent creativity; she represents a releasing force that frees elements from a previously mute or forgotten identity. The incredible or fantastic is not simply pulled out of a hat, but is revealed to be the inevitable result of a curious and trustingly open attitude and a childlike, creative ability to see, hear, and perceive. Given these premises, adventure becomes inevitable. What the children take from these fantastic adventures as a whole (and what indeed changes them) is the sense that it is always possible for the impossible to happen; indeed, what they gain is the ability and openness necessary to expect and face unknown situations in general, even the most unthinkable.

Mary Poppins makes no promises; unlike the typical fairy tales whose efforts to guarantee happiness distance the narrative from the reader's actual experience, the governess never speaks of eternal happiness, ("You can't have everything for always, and don't you think it!" III, p. 177) and does all she can to dissuade others from basing any sense of personal stability on the conviction or hope that eternal happiness is attainable. What her actions and the resulting situations actually seem to imply is that stability can only result from an understanding that all things change. Such an understanding should not however lead to resignation, but to a heightened awareness, renewed curiosity, and a more invigorated sense of commitment. What she seems to imply is that the children should learn to accept that nothing lasts forever and that she herself will one day have to leave them in the same way that she arrived, brought by a gust of wind to a family that would like her to remain but that must ultimately come to terms with her loss. Her total self-sufficiency and the temporary nature of her stay with the Banks family are symbolized by the apparel she is never without: the camp bed (through some strange magic she manages to slip it back into her bag every morning), the umbrella (she uses to fly), and the travel bag (containing all that she could possibly need).

From a stylistic perspective, although a solemn and dramatic tension underpins many of the important scenes, including descriptions of the most significant Elsewhere places, a great deal of what Pamela Lyndon

Travers narrates is meant to have a comic effect and as such to enter-tain readers as well as to make them think. Much of the representation is paradoxical, absurd, or exaggerated (aided by the subtle caricatures of the illustrations), and gives rise to irreverent or liberating laughter, especially when dealing with those characters who refuse to blur the boundaries between true and false, credible and incredible.

Travers seeks to express parody and subvert the "common sense" of a society governed by absolute fixations and exasperated manias, in which robot-like citizens are characterized by absurd attitudes, futile com-mitments, insane hang-ups, and prejudiced views of reality (leading to their having a blinkered view of the world, limiting their appreciation of what can in fact be considered as "real"). Travers was clearly a child of the society she depicts, and although she holds it up to ridicule, her deep understanding of how it worked shows that she, after all, felt for it. Her brilliant, lively intelligence works its way through a social order whose raison d'être is to toil, often ridiculously, to eradicate all that might con-tradict it, and to paralyze any outward-looking or creative enthusiasm, hope, or intuition. A social order of this sort (and all social orders must to some extent be like this) would seek to destroy all hope in the possi-bility of an alternative truth, an alternative in which this writer believes and to which she gives voice through her narratives.

Travers's achievement is all the greater precisely because, although she perceives and describes the official interpretations of the world (and ways of behaving in that world) as being absurd, abstract, limiting, and even unnatural, she neither sidesteps it (as if it did not, in fact, exist) nor forcibly erases it by simply depicting a whole different reality. Rather than seek—out of a spirit of polemical rebellion—to destroy that false, limited social order, Travers opts to retain it; in fact, that social order that she subjects to surprising tricks, explorative undermining and cunning subversions becomes, for the children who act as interlocutors (and whose adventures provide a promising epistemological introduc-tion to how to resist standardization and passivity) something that is no doubt real, and with which they must come to terms, but that is also open to question and reassessment.

The derisive, undermining tone of these narratives creates a culture of opposition in the Mary Poppins books. This culture of opposition does not really seek to establish a concrete alternative to the social order of its readers—it seeks though to express faith in the possibility of assuming a more autonomous and daring perspective. Travers's writing is permeated by many examples of this contradiction inherent to the social order but that can undermine that order only when highlighted and insisted upon.

Late Victorian society started a trend that favored realist narratives and saw texts refusing to respect the norms of realism as lacking in value. Well, any desire on the part of that social order—like of any other order—to remain self-identical in fiction is effectively thwarted by books such as Travers's ones (Travers did not intend to have her work classified as children's literature, defying any attempt to depict the books as lacking in significance or commitment). Figures with which realist readers are used to identifying—normal, average middle-class citizens—are flanked by the antiheroes of a counterculture whose entry disrupts any reader unprepared for difference, and whose power resides precisely in the fact that these characters seem so powerless in the "real" world. Travers's narrative strategy reinforces the individuality and depth of these marginal characters but provides a purely stereotypical description of the officially acceptable, normal characters; her narratives are seemingly unable to turn the latter into anything beyond a set of social roles to be filled (the park keeper, the policeman, the husband and the wife, and above all the father and mother) and, in their effort to be consistent with their roles, these characters never acquire true personalities. In other words, those characters deemed socially acceptable will never lay claim to the uniqueness, power, freedom, and mythical qualities of their antihero counterparts whom Mary Poppins counts as personal friends.

2

PAMELA LYNDON TRAVERS

SELL YOUR CLEVERNESS AND BUY BEWILDERMENT

Pamela Lyndon Travers began writing when still at a very young age and wasted no time pondering about style; it is perhaps for this reason that the style she uses is so distinctive, so captivatingly confident and immediate. Too inexperienced to feel threatened by the fear of bad reviews, she developed an irresistibly attractive self-confidence that persisted throughout her career, despite the fact that the content of her books is often more than a little provocative. Travers was a poet, novelist, journalist, essayist, writer of short stories, co-editor of a quarterly journal on myth and tradition, writer in residence at various American universities, and a prolific letter writer. From when she first emerged on the literary scene, in the early 1930s, to the 1990s, Travers continued to demonstrate the arbitrary, relative, and purely functional notion of boundaries—not least those perceived to separate different literary genres.

Her career spanned the twentieth century, and her approach to writing was often frank and carefree. She spent little time worrying about the context, circumstances, target and very often even the titles of her writings, which remained untainted by what was generally thought to be appropriate or by what might be expected. It was less important for Travers to please an audience or even to express the opinions that she herself held than to give voice to that which she felt *needed* to be said. Favoring allusions, metaphors, suggestions often bordering on the cryptic, ambiguity, and open-endedness over any didactic claims, her writing is openly daring and yet inspires trust, even from those readers who might not be as independent and adventurous as she herself was.

25

Travers narrates like an old bard. She had lengthy essays as well as disarmingly short articles published in important newspapers and magazines (e.g., the *New York Times*, the *New English Weekly*, and *Parabola*), spoke at conferences and gave countless readings at various different universities without ever giving the impression of trying to please or reinforce common views on the various subjects she wrote about. Readers of Travers will be rewarded if they allow themselves to be swept along by the disorienting yet potentially liberating wave of words, suggestions, connections, and references that astonish in the way that any unexpected event might. And this sense of astonishment is magnified by the fact that what we read sounds in some way familiar; it reawakens within us a sense of "home," one that somehow manages to exist beyond the well-known walls and beyond all usual expectations, one that manages to be so, even though it has nothing to do with the very practical, everyday world.

Travers is alien to any tendency to explain or render completely understandable to minds accustomed to a quotidian reality those events or objects that could be classed as "Other." She finds and criticizes, in the works of authors such as Tolkien, precisely this type of approach. Indeed Travers does not agree with the idea that Tolkien actually succeeds in *creating* myths. What he does, in her view, is to determinedly substitute with an effort of the intellect and in full awareness that which is in fact a very deep process, one that cannot be plucked from anywhere but life itself. Myth is something that "drops down on us":

> Of course, you may ask—indeed people are always asking—who invented the myths? And do you think they are true? Well, true? What is true? As far as I'm concerned it doesn't matter tuppence if the incidents in the myths never happened. That does not make them any less true, for, indeed, in one way or another, they're happening all the time. You only have to open a newspaper to find them crowding into it. Life itself continually re-enacts them…
>
> The myths and rites run around in our blood; … [and] when old drums beat we stamp our feet, if only metaphorically. … There is a wonderful Japanese phrase, used as a Zen koan, which says 'Not created but summoned'. It seems to me that this is all that can be said of the myths.[1]

In an article appearing in the journal *Parabola,* there is a dialogue between Travers and the writer Laurens Van Der Post that traces the fatal sterility of the imagination, typical of our age, back to the Cartesian *"Cogito ergo sum."* Of course, it would be trite to deny that we do indeed think, yet at the same time those flights of the mind to which we are all susceptible are also moments in which thoughts, images, and figures think themselves through us. This is the stuff of myth, one of life's most deep-set processes. This pure form of creativity energizes and orientates; if we learn to use our minds and imaginations, and if we learn to be silent and to listen—which, in turn, gives way to a deeper, more authentic form of perception—we can access this creativity.

Travers's essay entitled "Only Connect"[2] gives a clear idea both of the author's personality and poetics and sets out Travers's ideas on the rights and duties of humanity. We are like alchemists, she says, who mix the elements we find at our disposal, who piece together the different messages we receive, waiting for that lightning flash of inspiration that will explain the connections between the disparate elements. We are neither author nor creator of this work, but an essential part of the process. Only if we are able to gradually mute the knowledge of life we gain through formal education, will we be able to gather real stimulus. In an essay entitled "On Unknowing," Pamela Travers states:

> It is not ignorance. Rather, one could say, it is a particular process of cognition that has little or no use of words. It is part of our heritage at birth, the infant's first primer. And the young child lives by it, gathering into its young body and aboriginal heart a cosmography of wonder. ... But soon the chattering mind takes charge and obscures Unknowing with information.[3]

We hunger for "factual truth," for the obvious (whether relevant or not); we have names if not meanings for everything and unscrupulously employ the phrase "I know."

> But what if, in a momentary lapse in its knowing, it should stumble upon Unknowing? On Jalal-uddin Rumi, for instance:
> *Sell your cleverness and buy bewilderment*
> *Cleverness is mere opinion, bewilderment is intuition*
> [...]Will it have the courage, or even the wish, to pay the price? Throw overboard all the information that Unknowing does not need? Let go and set itself to listen so that the condition of simplicity may arise? [...] Unknowing, if one can be open and vulnerable, will take us down to the very depths of knowing, not informing the mind merely but coursing through the whole body, artery and vein—provided one can thrust aside what the world calls common sense, that popular lumpen wisdom that prevents the emerging of the numinous.[4]

Travers is well aware of the fact that we cannot simply wash our minds of knowledge as we might wash our faces, because, paradoxically, we need that knowledge. It is an essential part of life and should not be held in contempt. But if we allow the intellect to usurp knowing, then all possibility of discovering the unknown will be lost. For Travers, there are no answers, only questions:

> Fallible creatures that we are and being ourselves in question, we inevitably demand answers to ease the lack within us. All things must be capable of explanation, every effect must have a cause, each problem a solution. It is thus that we arrive at conclusion, for conclusion brings about the ending that we mistake for an answer. 'That's finished,' we say, mendaciously. 'We can go on to something else'.
>
> But nothing in life—nor perhaps, in death—is ever really finished. A book, for instance, is no book at all, unless, when we come to the last page, it goes on and on within us.[5]

Travers extended these ideas to discussion of her books and her famous character Mary Poppins. In fact, when asked how she came to create such an immediately successful character, she would frequently reply that she did not like to speak about things she "didn't know." Travers was relentlessly elusive when confronted with the usual dull and inevitable questions, though on one occasion she was pleasantly surprised by an interviewer who stated that her books were interesting precisely because they were not invented; she replied that of course they weren't—bicycles and atomic bombs were invented. However, when the interviewer pushed her for an answer on the question of where her ideas had come from, Travers confounded his expectations by replying "where on earth do ideas come from?" The interviewer decided this was frivolous, and asked, "Well, have you ever met anyone like her?" To which Travers neatly replied, "What? Someone who slid up banisters? No, never. Have you?", thereby underlining her refusal to join in the search for definitive, univocal conclusions in matters of the imagination.

BIOGRAPHICAL HINTS

The essay "Only Connect" is possibly the only text in which the author willingly refers to her childhood and the place in which she grew up. Clearly this text does not present any definitive explanations, but it does provide some useful insights into what might have contributed to the creation of a character like Mary Poppins.

Travers's Irish mother married her Scottish father, and the two emigrated to Australia. In such a deserted place (geologists believe it to be the oldest of the continents) and so far from the civilized world, the predominant, ever-present voice was the voice of the earth itself. Travers claimed that the sense of the primitive was so strong that not even a child could ignore it. Equally strong in the Travers household was the exaggerated sense of tradition, commonly found in expatriates seeking to recreate their own customs in a foreign land. Travers remembers that her family was not well off, and because contact with their distant neighbors was rare, the children had to amuse themselves with their imaginations. Each event or meeting that was out of the ordinary therefore became highly meaningful and gained almost monumental status. The Travers household may not have been filled with furniture, but it was certainly filled with books—from the classics of English and Irish literature to the more popular books containing heroes and villains who reproduced in their own small way the grand gestures of great mythological figures. Travers began her lifelong passion for reading in childhood and each week would impatiently await the arrival of the next *pennybook:*

> You could buy a fairytale for a penny—that's how their lore went in to me. And just as good, perhaps even better at that age, you could buy a *Buffalo Bill.*[6]

She read *Alice in Wonderland* at an early age and was familiar with the Brothers Grimm, who, for Travers, were particularly awe-inspiring, though not for the usual reasons. Travers tells how as a young girl, not yet ten years old, she confused the authors "Grimm" with the word "grim." "Grim" was the elusive word used by adults to describe certain events that were clearly not for the ears of children, but only made the Travers children all the more curious to secretly listen in on such conversations. For Travers, "grim" was more than a simple adjective; in her mind it became associated with a whole genre of illicit storytelling. It was therefore quite fitting that the big red book she came across in her father's drawer was penned by the Brothers Grimm. The book was *Grimm's Fairy Tales*, a collection of stories not dissimilar to the banned adult stories she had avidly listened in on, and not at all like the sugary fairy tales she had read so far.

Travers's imagination was also fed by her father's eccentric personality and nostalgia for Ireland, and it was her dream, from a very early age, to return one day to the Emerald Isle.

> My body ran about in the Southern sunlight but my inner world had subtler colors, the grays and snows of England [...] and the numberless greens of Ireland which seemed to me to be inhabited

solely by poets plucking harps, heroes lordily cutting off each other's heads and veiled ladies sitting on the ground keening.[7]

She continues:

I think, perhaps, if there was any special virtue in my upbringing, it lay in the fact that my parents, both of them, were very
allusive talkers. Neither of them ever read anything that didn't
very quickly come out in conversation and from there pass into
the family idiom. If my father discovered a poem he liked, even a
piece of doggerel, it would presently be, as it were, on the break-
fast table. Many a phrase, as ordinary to me as the daily porridge,
began its life, as I later learned, as a quotation from a poem or a
snatch from a ballad. As an instance, my father, who was a great
lover of horses—and tricky, dangerous horses at that—would
call out, whenever he returned from riding or driving, 'Bonnie,
George Campbell is home!' And my mother from somewhere in
the house would always answer 'Thank God.' But who has come
home, I used to wonder, for my father was neither George nor
Campbell. It was not until much later, when I began to read the
Scottish ballads, that I understood.[8]

The "Ballad of George Campbell" recounts how one tragic evening George Campbell's horse returned home without its rider; so in
the Travers household, heaven was to be thanked whenever a George
returned home safe and sound. Travers goes on to say that:

Then, too, there were the maxims galore and proverbs and apho-
risms. I was so often told—being a passionately lazy child—to 'Make
an effort, Mrs. Dombey,' that I began to think that Mrs. Dombey
was one of my names. How could I know it was out of Dickens?
  Then, there were other, closer, connections with myth. In
those lucky days there was always help to be had in the house.
Such people are wonderful meat for children. The life they live,
from the child's point of view—because to him it is strange and
unknown—seems to be filled with the glamour that his own
dailiness lacks. One of them—Bella, or was it Bertha?—had a
parrot-headed umbrella. This fascinated me. On days out, it
swung beside Bella's furbelows—she was far more elegant, I then
thought, than my mother—and was carefully put away in tissue
paper on her return, while she told us the always fantastic story of
what she had done and seen. Well, she never *quite* told—she did
more, she hinted. 'Ah', she would say, looking like Cassandra, 'if
you could know what's happened to my cousin's brother-in-law!'

But all too often, when prayed to continue, she would assure us, looking doomed and splendid, that the story was really beyond all telling and not for the ears of children. Oh, those inadequate ears of children! We were left to wonder, always mythologically —had he perhaps been chained to the mast because of someone's siren voice? Was his lover slowly being eaten by some bald-headed local eagle? Whatever they were, the things she didn't tell, they were always larger than life. [...] In a world where there are few possessions, where nobody answers questions, where nobody explains—I say this with joy, not sorrow—children must build life for themselves.[9]

In an interview that appeared in the *New York Times* in 1965, Travers was asked to speak about fantasy, a subject she did not like and refused to discuss. The interviewer, not to be deterred, then pushed her to respond to the question: "How can we, in our technological age, foster the imagination in children?" Travers responded:

I would just say feed and warm them and let the imagination be— though wonder, I think, is a better word. [...] Does it *need* fostering, anyway? And is technology your only villain? What about education? We learn very quickly from books and teachers not to respect our childhood wisdom. [...]

Yet it's all there, the bud is the clue, you have to go back to that. No: back is perhaps, the wrong word. You need to be there as well as here—simultaneous experience—to recapture what was. And to know that it is.

As to preserving this experience, I can only speak for myself, of course, but I have always been grateful that nobody, as you put it, fostered my imagination. It was not deplored, neither was it ... given room. It was taken as a matter of course—another fact, like whooping cough, another fact, like daylight. Every child has it as a natural inheritance, and all the grown-ups can do is leave him alone with the legacy. It is the child's own communicable experience—perhaps the only thing that is truly his own—and should not be spied on or disturbed.

This, I think, is what AE, the Irish poet, had in mind in 'Germinal' when he imagined a child playing in the dusk—that magical moment between day and night—and the grown-ups calling him in from his dream. [...] He knew that it is in the crack between opposites—dark and light, yes and no, here and there—that the real thing happens.

My childhood was full of such moments—wasn't yours?—and all that I am now somehow relates to them. Of course, (and this is inevitable), I was called home from them to supper and bed and the life of the lighted house. But a clever child, a quick, cunning, foxy child, learns to smuggle them in with him and keep them alive in some inner secret cupboard.

'Children, it's late!' my mother would cry, in a voice full of clocks and water-heaters. (Not 'What are you doing—let me share it!') And my father would come striding, giving his impersonation of Zeus in a rage that we never could quite believe in. [...]

I am grateful now, though I wasn't then (gratitude is a late growth) that I grew up in an atmosphere in which tradition was still part of life, laws few, fixed and simple, and children taken for granted; not 'understood' in our modern sense, not looked upon as a special race but as growing shoots of one whole process— being born, living and dying. My parents never played down to children, nor, on the other hand, did they treat them as equals; we were all just lumps in the family porridge. My parents had, I see now, what WB Yeats called 'a sort of radical innocence', as though, through some thin spider thread they were linked with their own youth. When they joined a game it was not at all for our sakes, but for their own enjoyment.

Altruism—that impure emotion—had no part in their natures. If he lost the throw in a game of chance, my father would stalk off in a huff, saying someone had cheated. And beating my mother at Old Maid was like slapping a Goddess in the eye; a most dis-courteous act. In our family life it was their moods that were to be respected, not ours. It was clear that they had their own exis-tence—busy, contained, important. And this, as I now see, left us free for ours. There is no greater burden for a child than parents who want to live *his* life; contrariwise, when they are content to be simply landscape and leave the child to make his own map, there is no greater blessing. His mind can turn in upon itself (and I don't at all mean introspection), wondering, pondering, absorb-ing the world, re-enacting in himself all the myths there are.

[...] I remember how, for a long period in childhood, I was absorbed in the experience of being a bird. Absorbed, not lost, knowing, had I been faced with it, that I was also a child. Brood-ing, busy, purposeful, I wove the nests and prepared for the eggs as though the life of all nature depended on the effort. 'She can't come, she's laying,' the others would say, arriving for a meal with-out me. And my mother, deep in her role of distracted housewife, would come and unwind my plaited limbs and drag me from the nest: 'If I've told you once, I've told you a hundred times, no laying at lunchtime!'

Not, 'You are mad. I fear for your future. We must find a psychiatrist.' Simply, not at lunchtime! Could she, too, once have been a bird, I sometimes wonder now? Not that one ever could have asked her, she would have thought it fanciful. But her homes were always a bit like nests, warm and well-fitted to her shape.

[…] She had, too, flashes of inspiration, when the streak of poetry in her Scottish blood broke up the daily pattern. Picnic breakfasts miles from home; or a table-cloth spread out on the carpet and supper on the floor. The sudden lively moments! She would have called them merely moods, but they seem to me now a kind of wisdom, as though she knew instinctively that nothing brings so much energy as the breaks in the regular routine. Full of the saws and customs that are handed down from the generations, innocent, honest, predictable—it was from her we learned, far more than from our less dependable father, to be ready for the unexpected, even to the point of knowing that truth can be juggled with.

'Is this Mrs MacKenzie?' asked my father, pointing with a carving knife at a chicken on the dish. (The fowl fattened for the table were called after friends and relations.) 'If it is, I'm not hungry. I was fond of her.'

'No,' said my mother, 'it's Nancy Clibborn.' And fixed us with a hypnotic glance as though we were serpents and she a snake-charmer.

'Good!' he exclaimed, slicing a wing. 'I never could abide that woman—far too thin and scraggy.'

And we, who that very morning had assisted Mrs MacKenzie to the chopping block, were left to sit in silent judgement. The facts, indeed, had been distorted. But we knew somehow that this was a matter less of morals than expediency. Men—it was simple—have to be fed, otherwise everyone suffers. So we sat there like the three wise monkeys, seeing, hearing and speaking no evil. It is fortunate for grown-ups that children understand them so well.[10]

Remembering her father, Travers writes:

I remember his melancholy, which was the other side of his Irish gaiety, and know that it was catching and inheritable. When he had taken a glass, he would grieve over the sack of Drogheda in 1649 till everyone around him felt personally guilty. We, not Oliver

Cromwell, were responsible for the blood and slaughter. He was Irish, too, in argument, determined to have the last word, even— or perhaps specially—with children. [...] Criticism he did not like. And from his own flesh and blood—really, it was too much. [...] Arguments, yes. But no explanation. I cannot remember that he, or anybody else, ever explained anything. It was clear from their general attitude that our parents had no very high opinion of our intelligence, but at the same time, apparently, they expected us to know everything. We were left, each on our desert (but by no means unfruitful) island, to work things out for ourselves.[11]

Travers goes on to explain how the children once took their father to task for having said something that he denied having said. It transpired that he had been using a figure of speech, something the children had not understood:

'Jumpin Jehosephat!' he cried, rolling his eye at Heaven for help. 'Haven't you heard of figures of speech?' And he threw the newspaper at our heads and went calling, as usual, for our mother.

Well? Figures of speech were Greek to us, and we were left with the suspicion, already familiar, that we still had a lot to learn. But this, in itself, was a kind of education. Had he explained, we would have been furnished with an indigestible piece of knowledge but very little the wiser. As it was, another question was laid down in us to row and breed and seek its meaning.[12]

It is clear that the character of Mary Poppins is in part inspired by her parents. She shares with Travers's mother an ability to create an atmosphere of security and authority imbued with surprises; and like her father, Mary Poppins is insufferable and self-centered, formidable and amusing in equal measure, and unable to accept criticism. Indeed, Travers's parents greatly influenced her writing, and maybe because of their premature deaths, they never aged in their daughter's mind and retained forever their youthful idiosyncrasies, irrational manias, and capricious behavior that clearly resembled that of their own children. But the character of Mary Poppins also contains much of Pamela Lyndon Travers. The writer never had children of her own, and it may be for this reason that she was able so shamelessly to retain her childlike qualities, though she did come into contact with and entertain many, and like Mary Poppins, she was employed as a nanny. In her writings, Travers discusses the way in which as children, she and her sister would quite naturally greet all strangers with a spontaneous sense of fascination and wonder, qualities Travers valued throughout her life. Children crave the incongruous, the nonfamiliar, the fracturing of routines. If this contrast with the ordinary one day presents itself in the flesh—a stranger who taps into their sense of surprise—then children will be undeniably drawn to this character who effectively brings to life what they could previously only have wanted to believe in. They will pursue this character with curiosity, ready to leave behind an adult world inadmissive of incongruence and the unpredictable, and governed by indisputable logic and rules that must be respected and in which any deviance must take place, if at all, in private. In her writings, Travers suggests that these qualities belong as much to her as they do to her fictional character:

> To find out the truth about any author you must look for him in his books. They alone are his true biography.[13]

And at the end of an autobiographical piece she was asked to write, she concludes:

> And in the meantime, if you are looking for autobiographical facts, Mary Poppins is the story of my life.[14]

This, of course, has meant that the name of Pamela Lyndon Travers has become, in the minds of her readers, inextricably linked to that of Mary Poppins. Her other works, including the poems she wrote in the 1920s and the books she wrote apart from the Mary Poppins saga (written over a fifty-year period, the first appearing in 1934, the last in 1989) are practically unknown and have certainly never reached the same level of success.

Although Travers was essentially an autodidact, she very quickly (when she was still in her twenties) came into contact with the luminaries of the international intellectual and cultural milieus. She sent her writing to AE (George Russell), who was at that time the editor of *The Irish Statesman*; the envelope she sent contained several poems and a stamped addressed envelope without a cover letter of any sort. The envelope soon came back. In place of the poems was a check for three guineas and a letter from AE asking if she had any other poems and proposing that if she ever came to Ireland, they should meet. Pamela Travers didn't wait for a second invitation:

> That was how I came under the wing of AE and got to know Yeats and the gifted people in their circle, all of whom cheerfully licked me into shape like a set of mother cats with a kitten. As you can imagine, this was blessing far and beyond my deserving [...] It was strong meat, the first introduction to my father's country, among

the poets and the makers of history. Perhaps it was just as well that my first contact with my Irish relatives should take me down several pegs. I needed it [...] Irish to the marrow, full of local lore and story, lovers of horses and the countryside, they weren't at all sure that life depended on poetry and they took the Celtic Renaissance with more than a grain of salt. 'I don't like you gallivanting around with men who see fairies', said one [...] 'And you'll meet such frightful people', he said. [T]here's one who lives down the road a way—old, now, of course, but a terrible great boastful fellow. If you meet him, be courteous, but do not pursue the acquaintance. His name is Shaw. George Bernard Shaw.' Gradually I learned to dissemble my enthusiasm for all that the elderly relatives of my father's generation found so reprehensible.[15]

So Travers's enthusiasm was hidden but not spent. She tells of how on one occasion she found herself near the island often described by Yeats in his poems, Innisfree. Despite the stormy weather, she had a boatman row her to the island. Surrounded by the grey clouds and claps of thunder, Travers was struck by the endless sorb trees growing wild there, whose berries shone like jewels. She suddenly decided to make a present of these to the great poet, and so before her romantic resolve could leave her, she began gathering an armful of branches. She made her way back to the mainland and jumped on the first train to Dublin, but the wind and rain had taken their toll on her offering. When she reached his house in Merion Square, both she and her gift were withered and soaked. She hoped Yeats might not be at home, but after a few moments the door opened and there was Yeats, staring at her in shock. In fact, so shocked was he that he could not even speak to her at first, fleeing back into the hall and shouting for someone. Humiliated and embarrassed, Travers was taken in by the maid who dried her off and gave her a seat by the fire. Just as Travers was deciding never again to show her face in the poet's company, the maid arrived saying that "the master can see you now." Travers was beside herself with fear and embarrassment but could not refuse. On receiving her, Yeats acted as if nothing had happened, treating her as a kind visitor. Feeling calmer, she could not but admire his manners:

> He was always the Bard, always filling the role of the poet, not play-acting but knowing well the role's requirements and giving them their due. He never came into a room, he *entered* it; walking around his study was a ceremonial peregrination, wonderful to witness.[16]

And so here we find what might be the source of all those descriptions regarding the behavior and comportment of Mary Poppins, her perfect posture and that way she has of expertly assuming the role, in this case, of governess. The above episode is interesting from another perspective: feeling better and ready to take her leave, Travers glanced down at the poet's desk, where she spotted a vase containing a twig from the sorb trees, adorned with its red berries:

> I glanced at him distrustfully. Was he teaching me a lesson? I wondered, for at that age one cannot accept to be taught. But he wasn't; I knew it by the look on his face. He would do nothing so banal. He was not trying to enlighten me and so I was enlightened and found a connection in the process. It needed only a sprig, said the lesson. And I learned, also, something about writing. The secret is to say less than you need. You don't want a forest; a leaf will do.[17]

ONLY CONNECT

This lesson is evident in many episodes of the Mary Poppins books. For example, after participating in some strange adventure and still reeling from enthusiasm and euphoria, the children are eager to speak about and question the incredible events they have just witnessed. The governess, however, remains impassive and refuses to give in to any form of uncontrolled emotion; she remains as composed as ever, initially frustrating the children, and feigns incomprehension, acting as if nothing were amiss. What then happens, however, is that all of a sudden she lets slip some sign, she reveals some clue or object which then appears all the more surprising for its paradoxical familiarity. These clues form the missing link and the children realize that their governess is, in fact, fully aware of all that has happened; like them she has lived, felt, and believed in the adventure. What the children then seem to understand is that the adventure is a very intimate experience, a form of intuition, and that any attempt to reduce and capture that experience with language would be to violate, to falsify, and would ultimately prove impossible. This highly meaningful, vital, though unsettlingly strange experience can indeed be acknowledged, but only through a silence punctuated with exchanged glances, gestures and clues that reaffirm the reality of the experience lived (if not quite understood) and recapture its quality and essence.

> "I had such a strange dream last night," said Jane, as she sprinkled sugar over her porridge at breakfast. "I dreamed we were at the Zoo and it was Mary Poppins's birthday, and instead of animals

in the cages there were human beings, and all the animals were outside—"

"Why, that's *my* dream. *I* dreamed that, too," said Michael, looking very surprised.

"We can't both have dreamed the same thing," said Jane. "Are you sure? Do you remember the Lion who curled his mane and the Seal who wanted us to—"

"Dive for orange-peel?" said Michael. "Of course I do! And the babies inside the cage, and the Penguin who couldn't find a rhyme, and the Hamadryad—"

"Then it couldn't have been a dream at all," said Jane emphatically. "It must have been true. And if it was—" She looked curiously at Mary Poppins, who was boiling the milk.

"Mary Poppins," she said, "could Michael and I have dreamed the same dream?"

"You and your dreams!" said Mary Poppins, sniffing. "Eat your porridge please, or you will have no buttered toast."

But Jane would not be put off. She had to know.

"Mary Poppins," she said, looking very hard at her, "were you at the Zoo last night?"

"At the Zoo? Me at the Zoo—at night? *Me*? A quiet, orderly person who knows what is what, *and* what isn't -?"

"But *were* you?" Jane persisted.

"Certainly not—the idea!" said Mary Poppins. "And I'll thank you to eat up your porridge and no nonsense."

Jane poured out her milk.

"Then it must have been a dream," she said, "after all."

But Michael was staring, open-mouthed, at Mary Poppins, who was now making toast at the fire.

"Jane," he said, in a shrill whisper, "Jane, look!" He pointed, and Jane, too, saw what he was looking at.

Round her waist Mary Poppins was wearing a belt made of golden scaly snake-skin, and on it was written, in curving, snaky writing:

"A present from the Zoo." (I, p.174–176)

Travers speaks with admiration of all the poets who were important for her (and for Mary Poppins) and who belonged to the so-called Irish Renaissance:

These men—[AE], Yeats, James Stephens, and the rest—had aristocratic minds. For them, the world was not fragmented. An idea did not suddenly grow [...] all alone and separate. For them, all things had long family trees. They saw nothing shameful or silly in myths and fairy stories, nor did they shovel them out of sight in some cupboard marked Only for Children. They were always willing to concede that there were more things in heaven and earth than philosophy dreamed of. They allowed for the unknown. And, as you can imagine, I took great heart from this. It was AE who showed me how to look and learn from one's own writing. "Popkins" he said once—he always called her just plain Popkins, whether deliberately mistaking the name or not I never knew. His humour was always subtle— "Popkins, had she lived in another age, in the old times to which she certainly belongs, would undoubtedly have had long golden tresses, a wreath of flowers in one hand, and perhaps a spear in the other. Her eyes would have been like the sea, her nose comely, and on her feet winged sandals. But this being Kali Yuga, as the Indus call it—in our terms, the Iron Age—she comes in the habiliments most suited to it".

Well, golden tresses and all that pretty paraphernalia didn't interest me; she could only be as she was. But that AE could really know so much about it astonished me, that he could guess at her antecedents and genealogy when I hadn't thought of them myself—it put me on my mettle. I began to *read* the book. But it was only after many years that I realized what he meant, that she had come out of the same world as the fairy tales. [...] The true fairy tales [...] come straight out of myth; they are, as it were, miniscule reaffirmations of myths, or perhaps the myth made accessible to the local folky mind. [...] One might say that fairy tales are the myths fallen into time and locality. [It] is the same stuff, all the essentials are there, it is small, but perfect. Not minimized, not to be made digestible for children. [...] Or it may be that you will categorize all this as "old wives' tales." But I am one who believes in old wives' tales. Old wives have the best stories in the world, and long memories. Why should we treat them with contempt?[18]

And in connection with this, Travers quotes from a Rupert Brook poem:

There's wisdom in women, of more than they have known,
    And thoughts go blowing through them, are wiser than their own.[19]

Brook's words clearly rang true for her; she gives the following example:

I was reading recently how Aeneas came to Campania—which is now in Naples—seeking some means of getting into contact with the ghost of his father, Anchises. [...] You know the story. [The Cumean Sybil] tells him to break from one tree in the forest a small golden branch. With that in his hand he will be able to descend into the depths. So, holding the branch before him as an amulet, he begins the dreadful journey. [...] And I remembered, as I thought about this, how Aeneas had begged the Sybil to speak her oracle in words and not, as was her usual practice, to write it on leaves that would blow away. That struck a chord in me, for I knew a story where this had actually happened. In this story, the wind blows leaves into the hands of two children. And on each leaf a message is written. One says 'Come' and the other says 'Tonight'. Now, the story I am talking about is 'Halloween'. It is in *Mary Poppins in the Park*. And there is the Sybil disregarding Aeneas by writing the oracle down on leaves! And I thought I had invented it![20]

The episode referred to here describes a party in the park where the shadows of people and things are released from their owners (who had instead been left at home) and are now free to roam the park and enjoy themselves. The only shadow to refuse to leave its habitual owner is, of course, that of Mary Poppins.

This episode both originated and did not originate with Travers; it is by no means accidental that the author has a party take place on the evening of Halloween, and that the party is attended by shadows, or shades. At the time of the ancients, Halloween was, of course, the day of the dead; it was only in more recent times that the church eliminated all pagan rituals from the calendar, replacing this particular celebration with the commemoration of martyrs and saints. Yet, despite this attempt at erasure, the original myth has lost none of its mystery or force. In pagan times it was thought that people needed to ritually celebrate the dead and to find a way of escaping the anguished fear that the spirits of the dead could come back to haunt them. They wore masks or painted their faces and, in order to confuse the spirits, would cover themselves from head to foot in black. For us, their distant descendants, black clothes have come to symbolize mourning. The Irish wake, for example, derives from this ancient ritual and gives mourners the opportunity, through feasts, singing, food and dancing, to embrace life once more. It creates a suspended moment in time experienced on the level of ritual: it presents a sense of fracture through which elements of the unknown are revealed to the conscious self. These days, Halloween seems to have regained something of its pagan origins, especially if we consider the way children celebrate the day. Dressed up figures come knocking on our doors proffering tins to be filled with money and out-stretched hands to be filled with sweets. The night swings between trick and treat, angels and devils, fiction and reality; it is a night of ghosts and shades, a night linking present to past, and a night during which we just might find ourselves faced with the opening of the door that separates known from unknown.

Having reached the Banks home from a distant and obscure place of abyss-like depths, Mary Poppins, whom we now find ensconced within the four known, familiar and cozy walls of the children's nursery, represents this sense of possibility. Such a suggestion, together with the various other suggestions I make in this book concerning Mary Poppins's symbolic meaning and value, were inspired by—or were a way of taking literally—Travers's conclusion to her critical essay, in which she urges her readers to "Only Connect":

> In making these connections, I do not want to assert or impose. But, in fact, all things are separate and fragmentary until man himself connects them, sometimes wrongly and sometimes rightly. As far as I am concerned it is all a matter of hint and suggestion, something seen in the corner of the eye and linked with another thing equally fleetingly. You remember Walt Whitman's poem, 'On a Beach at Night'. 'I give you the first suggestion, the problem, the indirection.' Isn't that wonderful? Turn your back on it and you'll find it! It's like Shakespeare's 'By indirection find direction out'. And with these quotations I connect Swift's dictum 'Vision is the art of seeing things invisible'.[21]

3

THEMATIC CONTINUITY OF MARY POPPINS

LIMINAL FIGURES AND THE THRESHOLD

The Mary Poppins books, and especially their main character, can be inserted into a broader thematic context that extends beyond the confines of literature. If we reject a purely scientific stance seeking "mathematical" demonstrations in favor of one that is more interested in hints and examines the circumstantial evidence available, we find that the Mary Poppins books and the character herself embody a certain thematic continuity that transcends literature in a narrow sense (even though it is the latter that most frequently gives expression to these themes) as it has clearly to do with the way in which human beings have, from the beginning, perceived themselves and have seen, or lived in, the world. In fact, it is to studies of anthropology, mythology, psychology, and philosophy that we shall now turn in order to try to understand the meaning of this character.

The two principal qualities found both in the figure of Mary Poppins and in the situations she creates, and that become themes on the level of narrative, are those of the *liminality* and *lightness*. These qualities find their most intense expression in the metaphor of flight beyond the threshold.

A series of real, literary, and mythological figures and situations focus our attention on these themes that are revealed most clearly by the metaphor of flight. Through flight we transcend the "real" or the purely "realistic" definition of the possible, and gain access to a double or a plural identity (belonging, for example, to earth and sky, or to human and suprahuman), which subverts the logic founded on binary structures and noncontradiction—principles that in the Western world and culture have been considered to be absolutes and underpin identity itself.

That of the liminal, or marginal, is a concept immediately capable of subverting or disturbing. The liminal necessarily implies a *threshold*, and if we can conceive of a threshold, or are forced to acknowledge its existence by dint of some epiphanic experience, then we must also acknowledge and accept the existence of some *beyond*. The beyond is unknown, and as such it evokes in us simultaneous forms of conflict such as fear and fascination, threat and attraction. Moreover, philosophically speaking, the existence of a threshold, door, or precise demarcation between our world and a beyond suggests that contact between the two different realities and passage from one to the other should not be continuous and cannot be taken for granted or overlooked. Any movement between these two worlds should be dense with meaning and value. The passage between the two is framed by the door, a symbolic boundary distinguishing outside from inside, and shall take place within a solemn context of ritual that marks the participants and can be neither forgotten nor evaded.

Becoming aware of a threshold, and thus the beyond, can be a sudden event that occurs thanks to the presence of some concrete form, or liminal figure that symbolizes, alludes to, and evokes the beyond. These paradoxical figures exist in different dimensions without ever really belonging exclusively and definitively to any of them and as such signal to the fact that we are not governed by one single reality or sole possibility of existence. These liminal figures can be found "here," but can also pass over to the "beyond" where they are equally at home. These two dimensions, the here and the beyond, correspond to diverse ways of being at a qualitative level, and because of this it is neither space nor time—both of which are measurable (i.e., quantitative) concepts—that actually separates them. These liminal figures who constantly cross the threshold and make us aware of it escape definition and precise identification. They are ungraspable, disruptive, and tend to throw into disarray any attempt to "give" them any fixed meaning.

Anthropology and tradition see these threshold figures entering life in order to help, enrich, and bring value to those who live within the world of fixed definitions. Yet, given their ambiguity and indefinability, these figures of passage represent alternative possibilities and as such have the power to upset, frighten, and throw into potential crisis those who cling to normality. Given that to define means to create order, or rather to create a single order, these indefinable and marginal figures imply disorder, subversion, and demystification.

This is nowhere more evident than on the level of narrative—especially within the fantastic, considered as a very broad genre, but by no means exclusive to this (and with the exception of what we call 'fantasy', if it takes place, as it often does, completely and only in the "beyond")—where the reader is usually first made to witness their cyclone-like arrival, then is encouraged to engage with their essence, only to be subsequently abandoned and left alone to pick up the disorienting pieces of both that "other" world and the "real" world that is now seen to be cracked and damaged by the brief "popping in" of these figures.

In literature, the significance of these liminal figures (both on a level of narrative and individual reader response) is unpredictable and cannot be fixed; yet, anthropology has taught us that those liminal figures belonging not to fiction but to the real world, such as for example witch doctors and shamans, are purely functional. These figures are deemed marginal because of their relationship to a dimension to which "normal" people usually have no access, but are assigned the privilege and approved mission of establishing contact with the "other" world, with other forms of knowing and powers that are "other" with respect to material, everyday modes of living and thinking.

The reason why these figures cannot be defined as being entirely "social" is that the adventure into the disordered regions of the mind, or into those regions that are inaccessible to the mind (e.g., experiences involving ecstasy, or magic, implying abnormal powers) is necessarily an adventure beyond the confines of society and is accompanied by the risk of nonreturn.[1]

From the Red Indian "medicine man" or "witch doctor," depicted by Hollywood westerns and cartoons as wearing bearskin to represent his contact with the nonhuman Other (be it the animal or the divine sphere—considered to be one and the same by the primitive mind), to our modern image of the Celtic Druid as depicted, for example, in popular comic books such as those of *Asterix* (in which the old druid is also the "wise man" capable of preparing the magic potion that leads to invincibility), what we find are figures who have a recognizable contact with suprasocial dimensions and who by dint of such contact are entrusted with the knowledge and power to protect the well-being of a society that cannot see beyond its own confines. This, however, by no means reduces the ambiguity of such marginal figures, and their functionality in no way neutralizes their threshold (and as such always somehow mysterious) position.

THE SHAMAN

The idea of the shaman has been present—though in different forms and with different names—in an incredibly wide number of cultures, peoples, places, and historical eras. As a threshold figure, the shaman has been the focus of anthropological analyses, and it is to this figure that we must now turn in order to enrich our reading of the Mary Poppins books.

The shaman is a paradoxical figure in which scientific studies have identified qualities considered to be in absolute difference with respect to that which is considered "normal." The shaman's "abnormality" is often erroneously likened to, though resists comparison with, psychological disorders such as epilepsy and hysteria. Indeed, the shaman's difference lies in his ability to reach, and to help others reach, a state of ecstasy—yet such an experience is in no way pathological; it is merely an alternative way of experiencing the self and the surrounding world.

Mircea Eliade's exhaustive comparative study of shamanism[2] shows how the shaman's shocking lucidity and ability to control his movements even when in a state of ecstasy are evidence of a fully functional nervous constitution. Eliade also presents the shaman as possessing an above-average memory and sense of spirituality as well as a strength of character tested both by the shaman's training and activity that demands a very particular form of energy and ability to dominate—above all himself. It is interesting to note that these qualities—displayed as such by Mary Poppins—can be found in, or were required from, a character which was equally marginal within its own context (though closer to our own society)—that is, the governess (as I will seek to explain in the last chapter of this book).

The shaman is a threshold figure whose vocation implies that the individual must leave behind the social space of the village and embrace a marginal, errant existence, a choice that cannot later be revoked. The shaman can never return to the social world and its internal hierarchy, nor can he live within the confines of the village or community. He puts up his *Yurta* on the edge of that space (just as Mary Poppins refuses to sleep anywhere other than her own camp bed) between civilization and the wild natural world, between the external and internal worlds, and occupying an in-between space—he himself embodying the confines between human and nonhuman, between proper and improper (both in the sense of ownership and acceptability).

The shaman becomes a border creature: emptied of self and of his own personal history (and here we find a further parallel with Mary Poppins, who is so silent about her own past as to seem not to possess one), he acquires through the ritual of initiation a new identity, one that in its diversity is indefinable, fluctuating, founded on a freedom of movement and identification that his separation from society and all social roles allows him. In short, his identity is founded on *lightness*.

The shaman's lightness is fundamentally a voyage—as is that of Mary Poppins, who can, like him, take flight. We find thus a departure from the "here," but also a return, though neither the shaman nor Mary Poppins will ever remain in the social sphere and will never become "like" those who inhabit the social sphere. To us, the shaman's voyage seems purely metaphorical, figurative, or intrapsychic, yet for the individual concerned such experiences are perceived as real, objective, and extrapsychic. The word ecstasy means to "be beyond" something. The shaman's voyage is toward an invisible world, invisible, that is, to the waking world that tends to use its sensitivity and perception in the service of logic and rationality. The initiated shaman is like a dead man among the living, or rather, a living soul dead to the ordinary world and its ordinary roles. Moreover, the shaman enters into contact with the whole of the natural world and the entire cosmos. In the same way, Mary Poppins engages with all that is around her—she talks the language of birds, receives gifts from snakes and tortoises, is kissed by the sun, and converses with the stars.

Everything about the shaman is ambiguous, even his gender. The shaman is simultaneously masculine and feminine, embodies contradiction and straddles supposedly irreconcilable dimensions. To the well-organized community (which undoubtedly must negate or deny something in order to gain that status of being "well-organized" and to define itself in contradistinction with all that is Other), the shaman will certainly appear as a strange figure—yet it nevertheless recognizes its need of this figure because only through entering into contact with the difference symbolized by the shaman can it negotiate its own social identity. Through his ritual manipulation of the experience of the beyond (of which he is a messenger for the people of the village), the shaman neutralizes the fear and sense of danger and chaos that such an experience could provoke. In his experience of the beyond (beyond the mental and social reality of his fellow men), the shaman remains completely lucid and in control. His mind never loses control of his visions and is able to direct his physical and psychic energies. And even if the ecstatic experience is essentially one of disorder—where anarchic energy challenges norms—the shaman is by no means undone: for him, this sense of multiplied potentiality is in no way uncontrollable, but is lucidly directed towards his specific ends. The shamanic vision of the world (which itself becomes a reality) is a vision in which all is based on the notion of "trans," where all is suspended and can—and will—at any moment become Other to itself and to expectations.

During the shamanic experience, the air becomes electrified and filled with indecipherable energies escaping linguistic description. In the presence of the shaman, we find ourselves in a permutable, permeable natural space traversed by energy currents that the shaman's hands can transform into healing powers. The shaman works principally on a symbolic level and his job is to reinstate a sense of order to a community or individual, even if the shaman himself represents disorder and chaos. The shaman uses the principle of myth to help those thrown into disorientation—by some intangible perceptive experience—creating a system of narrated symbols and signs that provoke unswerving belief and faith because that which is narrated organizes reality and the entire cosmos into a manageable structure. Recourse to myth is in itself such a deep-rooted device in the human process of making sense that it has always, more or less explicitly, been used and is for example very evident in the work of twentieth-century writers and poets (e.g., T.S. Eliot, *The Waste Land*; James Joyce, *Ulysses*) who sought to give new meaning to an inexplicably alienating present. Likewise, Travers also uses myth, though with the difference that she rejects myth's static structures in favor of a ritual dynamism that she accomplishes by tracing the movement for example of flight, dance, circular patterns, and the "Grand Chain of Being" that parallels Lovejoy's theories of a unified cosmos, developed during the same period.[3]

"See you later at the Grand Chain, I hope…" (I, p. 161)
    "Do I hear the signal for the Grand Chain?…" (I, p. 168)
    "Grand Chain. Grand Chain! Everybody to the Grand Chain and Finale." (I , p. 169)
    "As they drew nearer, [the children] could hear the animals singing and shouting, and presently they saw leopards and lions, beavers, camels, bears, cranes, antelopes and many others all forming themselves into a ring around Mary Poppins." (I, p. 170.)

Anthropologists such as Levi-Strauss have studied the way in which shamans work with trauma and pain. Analyzing the way they work with women in labor, they found that shamans used mythical symbols, signs, figures, and narrative structures to counter the highly disordered and disorienting experience of giving birth. Through song, narrative, sound, and image (though without direct physical contact), the shaman organizes in an essentially meaningful way the symptoms of the disturbance; through myth, he manages to explain (and unexplain), creating relationships and parallels that succeed in uniting the woman's personal experience with a cosmic reality that counters the sense of dislocation from any form of meaningful context. These difficult births come to form, thanks to the shaman's intervention and presence, just one leg of a lengthy journey littered with obstacles and conflicts that the shaman (in the company of other heroic figures) must undertake in order to win the battle against the forces of evil.

The mythical system is a stable, objective, and ordered structure in which everything, whether good or bad, has its own place and its own raison d'être. The shaman uses this structure to cure the suffering individual. But rather than passively absorb the narrative, the individual directly experiences the mythical code by participating physically and mentally (with the help of the shaman) in the structure, which is no longer perceived as external but becomes part of the individual him/herself. The shaman thus liberates the individual and her experience from her own perception of herself and from all conventional codes of meaning. He exposes her to the idea that individual experience (including the experience of the body and the experience of pain) is not necessarily an immutable given but something that fluctuates, something that can be revised and reorganized. The shaman, therefore, changes, even if only for a short time, the way in which the individual feels and experiences life in order to heal her of whatever suffering inflicts her, especially when that suffering is the result of some unforeseen and unforeseeable event. The cure takes the form of a flight away from the usual, communally accepted perspectives that work according to exclusion, precision, and evaluation. The experience and rediscovery of the self brought about by the shaman's "trans" is a purely original experience, free of all definitions and expectations that are in any way more limiting than those of myth. The individual's experience of self is no longer fixed and takes no precise or definite form. It is in a state of "becoming"—no pre-established value can define it. The individual radiates the energy of the universe. Exposed to this form of energy, the self seems capable of anything, in the sense that the distinctions between the possible and the impossible, between nature and culture, and between body and spirit seem to collapse. Pain is replaced by a sense of well-being, and the body seems to become light enough to dance, to fly. During these moments of ecstasy or "trans," those who believe in the powers of the shaman and his cures are as trusting as they would be before any normal everyday experience, despite the fact that what lies beyond the waking state nevertheless remains enigmatic and indescribable by common systems of meaning.

According to Eliade, the defining characteristic of the witch doctor and the shaman is his capacity for flight, a "magical flight." Indeed, the shaman's chief quality lies in his ability to "fly" from one region of the cosmos to another, from earth to heaven and down into hell. Flight upwards expresses the autonomy of the soul (whose mythical symbol is the bird). The myth of the soul contains the seeds for a metaphysics of spiritual freedom. The nostalgia for flight seems to be an essential part of the human psyche, as demonstrated by numerous studies on the "imagination of movement."[4]

It is important to remember that the myth and rituals of the shaman's magical flight proclaim and confirm the transcendence of the shamans themselves over the human condition, which is, by dint of these myths, revealed as one of decadence. Numerous myths allude to a primordial time when *all human beings* could fly up to the heavens at any given moment. The myth and symbolism of magical flight therefore go beyond the shaman and precede its figure, belonging more specifically to the ideology of universal magic. Eliade notes how the levitation of saints and magicians is present in both Christian and Islamic traditions. Incidentally, in the Mary Poppins books, as soon as the governess arrives at the Banks household and is asked something about the bag she carries, we find what might not be a chance allusion to the *Thousand and One Nights*, or rather, to what was considered in the traditional Arabian folk imagination as the most typical device enabling flight:

> But when she bent down to undo her bag, Michael could not restrain himself.
> "What a funny bag!" he said, pinching it with his fingers.
> "Carpet," said Mary Poppins, putting her key in the lock.
> "To carry carpets in, you mean?"
> "No. Made of." (I, p. 16)

But the flights of the shaman are particularly interesting to the present argument because of the surprising coincidences that link those flights to the flight of Mary Poppins. Eliade's study on shamanic figures around the world describes how the shaman's ascent towards the heavens is represented by a ladder or staircase which is a symbol present in Christianity, Islam, and the tradition of alchemy. The symbol of the ladder is also present in the Mary Poppins books, for example in the episode taking place on the night of the spring equinox when Mary Poppins climbs the rungs of a ladder hanging from the sky in order to set the stars in order. Unusually, the Banks children do not participate in this scene and must watch Mary Poppins's ascent up into the night sky from their bedroom window. (I, chapter 8) The ladder is one of the many symbols of ascent present in Mary Poppins and what is surprising to note is that each of Travers's representations of flight or ascent finds a parallel in Eliade's study of shamanic flight. Clouds and rainbows are the vehicles of flight according to the famous anthropologist, as they are in *Mary Poppins and the House Next Door* and *Mary Poppins in the Park,* respectively; or sometimes the vehicle might be a string signaling the connection of earth and heaven, and in *Mary Poppins Comes Back,* Mary Poppins comes back down to earth on the end of a kite string.

Where flight is symbolized in myth, the flyer is often a hero, king, or wizard and the flight often takes place following a breakdown in communication between the here and the beyond. What we find in these instances is the suggestion that "the elect" are granted the possibility of returning to the origins of time to find that mythical pre-Fall moment where communication between heaven and earth was still intact. Shamans belong to this category of the elect because of their ability to enter into a state inaccessible to most people, distancing themselves from the human world in order to establish a more direct relationship with the sacred and its manifestations. Once more we find a parallel with Mary Poppins, who is often described as belonging to the category of the elect:

> "There was never a human being that remembered [...] Except, of course, Her." And he jerked his had over his shoulder at Mary Poppins.
>
> "But why can she remember and not us?" said John.
>
> "A-a-a-h! She's different. She's the Great Exception. [...] She's something special [...]" (I, p.110)

In the shamanic myths we often find that the figure of the shaman is intimately connected with supreme beings or supreme forces. Such is the case in the myth of the First Shaman, who was sent down to earth by the celestial being to defend man from evil spirits and diseases. If a parallel can be drawn between the shaman as a figure and Mary Poppins, it might not be by chance that when the governess first enters the children's bedroom, she extracts from her bag a bottle of strange medicine that she doses out to her charges. Indeed, there are many other episodes in the Mary Poppins books where the protagonist seems to mirror the role of the shaman. Eliade notes how from Siberia to America to Africa, the figure of the shaman is frequently linked to the same set of elements. The serpent, for example, commonly features in the shaman's rituals and is a protagonist in one of Mary Poppins's adventures toward the beyond. Here the snake is represented as a divine being, adored by all and ministering wisdom. The skin of the serpent is carried through to the following episode, where Mary Poppins is found wearing the magnificent snakeskin belt given to her by the serpent (I, chapter 10). Another element common to Mary Poppins and the sha-man is his way of ritually leading others towards ecstasy by means of the drum. In chapter 11 of *Mary Poppins Opens the Door*, a magic drum sets Mr. Twigley and the children whirling around the room as if pos-sessed by some irresistible force. (III)

Another object closely linked to the shamanic ritual is the mirror, which on a metaphorical level represents the need to look beyond the accepted, "realistic" image of life and self. Mary Poppins is often found looking at her own reflection, yet this is only apparently an instance of vanity; these shiny surfaces reflect the image of the self and the occa-sions on which Mary Poppins seeks her own reflection are often ritual-istic in nature.

> Mary Poppins put her hat straight at the Tobacconist's Shop at the corner. It had one of those curious windows where there seem to be three of you instead of one, so that if you look long enough at them you begin to feel you are not yourself but a whole crowd of somebody else. Mary Poppins sighed with pleasure, however, when she saw three of herself, each wearing a blue coat with silver buttons and a blue hat to match. She thought it was such a lovely sight that she wished there had been a dozen of her or even thirty. The more Mary Poppinses the better. (I, p. 32)

The shamanic ritual of healing is highly dramatic and this height-ened sense of drama is equally present in the Mary Poppins books. The dramatization of the shamanic experience is highly elaborate and what results is an unusual spectacle that Eliade describes as follows:

> The fire tricks, the "miracles" of the rope-trick or mango trick type, the exhibition of magical feats, reveal another world—the fabulous world of the gods and magicians, the world in which *everything seems possible*, where the dead return to life and reap-pear instantaneously, where the "laws of nature" are abolished and a certain superhuman "freedom" is exemplified, and made daz-zlingly present [...] The shamanic "miracles" [...] stimulate and feed the imagination, demolish the barriers between dream and present reality, open windows on worlds inhabited by the gods, the dead and the spirits.[5]

By way of an open-ended conclusion, Eliade wonders how much of our artistic heritage—from the epic, through legends and fables to the-ater—has been inspired by the figure of the shaman and his experience of ecstasy.

It should be of no surprise that the shamanic Mary Poppins refuses to speak about the children's experiences of the beyond that she herself has brought into being. The author herself speaks about them for her readers, who, together with her protagonists, journey through supernatural worlds surrounded by supernatural forces and beings. Of course, it would be hard to negate the suggestion that these elsewhere spaces—like all elsewhere spaces ever conceived by human imagination—conjure up allusions to death. Yet, for readers, because of the nature of any fictional "going beyond," to read of it means to be involved not in a mortal adventure, but in an intensely enriching aesthetic one.[6] In being so elaborately described, these adventures, which contain potentially terrifying unknown worlds (since whatever is unknown comes to be associated with death and causes anxiety) are, in fact, populated by very specific and tangible types, and this structures the experience for the readers, allowing them to come to terms with what may usually be frightening but can, when represented through an artistic channel, become wonderful instead (or as well)—as is the case with the Mary Poppins books.

The shaman is but one example of the threshold figure who exists on the margins of society. Other liminal figures, however, are often seen in a negative light. Given the fact that their essential ambiguity threatens to bring disorder and disorientation, there is the tendency on the part of societies to try to hide or eliminate these figures. The witch, historically speaking, has been an example of the marginalized threshold figure, in contact as she was, or was considered to be, with extrahuman, animal and satanic forces, dealing in transformations and residing in the metamorphic realities conjured into being by her own spells and magic-making. This dealing with, or residing in, metamorphosis is a quality common to many marginalized figures who are for this very reason excluded from society. Society—any society—necessarily makes of "stasis" and of fixity, of clear-cut definitions and of immutable labels given to people and things, a fundamental value (in contradistinction to metamorphosis), as it is by means of this precise defining that any social system keeps, or believes it can keep, everything in order and under control. Instances of this attitude and of those who are considered outsiders for not conforming precisely in this respect are endless. We might take as an example even as popular and apparently frivolous a Hollywood film as *Pretty Woman*, in which we find the rise of the female protagonist from prostitute to "lady"—from a marginal to an accepted woman—in a modern-day *Bildungsroman* whose plot revolves around the themes of metamorphosis and polymorphism as qualities that have to be lost in order to gain access to the social world of good manners and of respectability. The character is granted the freedom to move and to be a multifaceted being characterized not by coherence but by change and changeability, where she is unrecognizable and as such fleeting and ungraspable (she wears wigs, changes looks, has no fixed abode, and is always embarrassingly unpredictable in her behavior) only as long as she is, as a prostitute, somehow an outsider. With the "privilege" of being accepted into what is socially acceptable, she acquires the new and significantly fixed identity of a predictable lady, one who has learned to behave "well," that is, in the way she is expected, on every occasion, to behave.

It is also interesting to point out that, as was the case with witches, in terms of gender identity, these marginal figures who threaten disorder and are thus considered dangerous and unacceptable (unless they undergo a strong "civilizing process") have often been feminine rather than masculine in the course of history in the Western world.

THE DANDY

Another figure considered "other" by the society in which he lived and by its conventions is the dandy. Distinguished by a particular sensibility, perception, awareness, and attitude, the dandy could not be contained by any conventional social role and rejected the blind acceptance of socially construed identities in order to consciously identify himself at every turn. The dandy was a product of the nineteenth century, whose heyday was the final decade of the Victorian period. Openly critical of bourgeois values, he was an antisocial character and was ostracized from society by various accusations, the most frequent being that of homosexuality (which might have been a strategy aimed at making the provocative messages and challenge to the given social order—indeed patriarchal in its essence—seem as if they were coming from a man who was not really "a man" after all). The dandy openly conveyed his exasperation at the artificial nature of nineteenth-century life and the way in which society's conventions were taken for granted and went unchallenged. His provocative attitude was indeed antisocial, but in a rather peculiar way: it manifested itself, paradoxically, as hypersocial behavior.

Dandyism was therefore a way of life, or a sort of eccentric philosophy that challenged norms and conventions through an exaggerated adoption of these norms and conventions in a way that hoped to reveal, because it was so excessive, how artificial the lives of people actually were—something people tended not to see or be aware of. The dandy opposed bourgeois homogenization and the conformism it demanded with individuality, temperament and personality, but did so from the inside, from a position internal to the structure he was seeking to subvert, behaving not in a way that was opposite to the bourgeoisie, but following the manners they considered proper to the extreme, thus making them appear absurd. And Mary Poppins employs the same strategy, presenting herself always as "practically perfect," but different, as such, from everyone else. What lay at the heart of the dandy's commitment to noninvolvement was the value of "difference," which found expression in divergence, autonomy, in an intuitive attraction for the new, for the indeterminate, for risk and paradox (and its eventual noncommunicability), and which challenged the prescriptivism of accepted behavior and thought which sought to privilege certainty and communicability—a communicability which condemned to silence all that could not be conventionally named and spoken about.

The dandy replaced convention with a uniquely individual form of behavior, and if society thought of itself and of its own ways as normal, or even natural, the dandy chose for himself the "unnaturalness" of a mask, the mask of impassibility. This mask was a method, it was a question of style and reflected his critical attitude toward society's obsession with role and convention. Also, given that he was not committed to anything or anybody but to himself, this mask allowed him a truthfulness that was absent from bourgeois social discourse. The Other, or what others did, was by no means considered a norm: the only Other for the dandy was present in his own narcissistic relationship with himself.

> "What, Mary Poppins!" exclaimed Mrs. Banks. "Your best fur-topped gloves! You gave them away!"
>
> Mary Poppins sniffed.
>
> "My gloves are my gloves and I do what I like with them!" she said haughtily.
>
> And she straightened her hat and went down to the kitchen to have her tea…
>
> (I, p. 85)

In many other ways Mary Poppins can be said to recall the figure of the dandy: in the attention she pays to her impeccably perfect appearance and in the way she dresses, for instance, focusing even on the slightest of details, a habit typical of the dandy. We have already seen how she stops to admire her reflection in every mirror and shiny surface.

> "Just look at you!" said Mary Poppins to herself, particularly noticing how nice her new gloves with the fur tops looked. They were the first pair she had ever had, and she thought she would never grow tired of looking at them in the shop windows with her

hands in them. And having examined the reflection of the gloves she went carefully over her whole person—coat, hat, scarf and shoes, with herself inside—and she thought that, on the whole, she had never seen anybody looking so smart and distinguished. (I, p. 148)

But she glanced at the window as she went so that she could see how her new shoes reflected in it. They were bright brown kid with two buttons, very smart. (I, p.96)

The dandy established a distance between himself and the somewhat distasteful world of those surrounding him by exaggerating his apartness, sometimes even refusing all physical contact and often expressing disgust.

"Mary Poppins, are we *never* going home?" [Michael] said crossly. Mary Poppins turned and regarded him with something like disgust. (I, p.98)

"I wish we were invisible," said Michael, when Mary Poppins had told him that the very sight of him was more than any self-respecting person could be expected to stand." (I, p. 125)

"Ah! Mrs Banks. Then these must be -?" Mr Twigley waved his hands at the children. "They're Jane and Michael Banks," she explained, glancing at them with a look of disgust. (III pp. 36–37)

In order to increase his distance and difference from society, the dandy copied the behavior of his fellow men, but in an inimitable manner. Poised between reality and game, between vanity and suggestion, the dandy concealed a serious nature behind his mask of frivolity; at times appearing almost solemn, but this solemnity was not that of the moralist, philanthropist or educator. Despite the artifice inherent in his appearance—his walking stick, gloves and buttonhole—there was depth to his superficiality and commitment in his inconstancy. (Mary Poppins displays the same seemingly unjustifiable and inexplicable moods that continue to puzzle the children). The dandy's elegant way of dressing aimed to surprise, to throw the on-looker off guard. It was a form of ceremony or ritual: the dandy's art was himself. As Baudelaire comments:

Contrary to what many ignorant people believe, Dandyism is not about being obsessed with one's *toilette* or with material elegance … It is not about garments as such, but rather, the way in which such garments are worn. Dandyism is a human, social and spiritual undertaking.[7]

Dandyism was no mere aesthetic attitude; it was a moral undertaking, the essence of which verges on the stoic and is reminiscent of the commitment of classical heroes and saints. Indeed, in a world in which the bourgeois values of capitalism and competition held forth and where a specific social order had to be maintained at all costs because it served those ends and the material gains to which they lead, the dandy was a sort of hero whose task it was to subvert such small-mindedness. With his unpredictability and impertinence, he challenged that ready-made world of predictability and control. He sought to invert the order of accepted values, and as such, can be likened to the revolutionary or the illusionist; he recognized no value in utility or progress and sought to undermine them. Illustrating a similar point, Cowper Powys said that Oscar Wilde opposed the impertinence of society with the impertinence of the artist and met the impudence of the world with the impudence of the genius.[8]

The dandy refused to play long with society, preferring to play his own game, and yet as Wilde asserts, the dandy played with his own life and was on excellent terms with the world.[9] This attitude towards the world is also reflected in the character of Mary Poppins who, we are often told, is on excellent terms (and the formality of this expression is fitting) with the world around her.

The dandy saw life as a choice between two extremes: life is either equated with art, or with an existing in reality. Wilde, again, claims that "To live is the rarest thing in the world. Most people exist, that is all."[10] Art reveals to the creative self the beauty, secrets, intensity and value of the world. Commitment to art and especially to an artistic way of living cannot be made to obey the exigencies of passive or unconsciously mechanical imitation, reproduction, and repetition. Art creates life; life should thus be seen as a work of art in which all emotions, thoughts, dreams and expressions should be lived as fully as possible. Such is the dandy's philosophy; he negates all constraining forms of the "real" that demand that the individual adapt to a predefined way of life.

> "That's coral!" she cried in astonishment. "We must be down in the deeps of the sea!"
>
> "Well, wasn't that what you wanted?" said the Trout. "I thought you wished you could see the sea."
>
> "I did," said Jane, looking very surprised. "But I never expected the wish to come true."
>
> "Great Oceans! Why bother to wish it then? I call that simply a waste of time." (III, p. 143)

In Travers's writing, the boundaries between fiction/art and reality are frequently blurred and the imaginary becomes more tangible than the real. Thus, a character like Bert, for example, draws Mary Poppins into one of his own pavement paintings, where the two enjoy a sumptuous meal of tea and cake surrounded by idyllic countryside—something that beyond the frame of his own painting, out in the real world, a character like Bert would never be able to afford to do. This slipping between the boundaries of fiction and reality is a theme present in the two successive books in the series. In *Mary Poppins Comes Back,* Jane steps into a scene painted onto the side of a porcelain vase and meets the children she had so often watched captured in play by the artist. But this experience terrifies Jane. These sinister and somewhat disturbing children want to keep her in their world, and in the end Mary Poppins has to rescue her, bringing her back to the safety of her own bedroom. With this episode Travers suggests how fiction and reality are not only closely linked, but that the one can alter the other irreparably. Jane awakes, safe in her bed, and is convinced that what she experienced was nothing more than a dream. Then she finds that the scene into which the painted children had drawn her has changed. In the foreground of the picture she finds a scarf where previously there had been none. She recognizes it as belonging to Mary Poppins who had inadvertently dropped it when coming to save her. The disorientation resulting from such a realization resembles the sort of romantic irony present in the works of German writers such as Ludwig Tieck and E.T.A. Hoffmann that depict the dissolving of the barriers between fiction and reality. Narratives such as this work by convincing the reader of the reality of a particular fictional world, only to then expose the artificial nature of this world, thus subvert the traditional distinction between reality and imagination.

Travers once again makes use of this form of romantic irony in "The Marble Boy," in the third book. We often find this same premise, whereby Mary Poppins takes the children to the auspiciously peaceful park for an afternoon stroll. Michael and Jane play close to the lake. Mary Poppins sits on a bench, gently rocking the twins in their pram whilst sewing. Opposite Mary Poppins, a man sits reading on a bench placed immediately underneath a marble statue of a boy carrying a dolphin.

> Bang! The Elderly Gentleman closed his book and the sound shattered the silence.
>
> "Oh, I say!" protested a shrill sweet voice. "You might have let me finish!"

Jane and Michael looked up in surprise. They stared. They blinked. And they stared again. For there, on the grass before them, stood the little marble statue. The marble dolphin was clasped in his arms and the pedestal was quite empty.

The Elderly Gentleman opened his mouth. Then he shut it and opened it again.

"Er—did you say something?" he said at last, and his eyebrows went up to the top of his hat.

"Yes, of course I did!" the Boy replied. "I was reading over your shoulder there—" he pointed towards the empty pedestal, "and you closed the book too quickly. I wanted to finish the Elephant story and see how he got his trunk!" (III, p. 84)

The boy makes friends with Jane and Michael and the three play about the park until Mary Poppins finally sends him back to his pedestal. The children discover that the boy's name is Neleus and that he is the son of Poseidon, the Greek god of the sea. Growing tired of his pedestal, the boy had jumped to the ground and although this provokes the disdain of Mary Poppins, she forgives his capriciousness on this occasion. Jane and Michael are taken aback by the fact that the two clearly already know each other:

"Do you know Mary Poppins?" demanded Michael.

"Where did you meet her?" he wanted to know. He was feeling a little jealous.

"Of course I do!" exclaimed Neleus laughing. "She's a very old friend of my father's." (III, p. 84)

As on many occasions, Mary Poppins acts as mediator between the mythical world and everyday reality. In "The Park in the Park" (IV, chapter 5) we find another episode that focuses on the relationship between art and reality. At the beginning of the chapter Jane constructs a miniature world out of branches, leaves, and plasticine figures that then comes to life. The plasticine figures however refuse to believe that they are anything but "real," and Jane, Michael, and Mary Poppins become involved in the adventures of this miniature world. As always happens, the children return to the "real" world, but remain altered by their experience:

Crowned with the gold of the buttercup tree, Jane walked home under the maple boughs. All was quiet. The sun had set. The shadows of the Long Walk were falling all about her. And at the same time the brightness of the little Park folded her closely round. The dark of one, the light of the other—she felt them both together.

"I am in two places at once," she whispered... (IV, pp. 173—74)

This, again, could be described as a threshold position. Indeed, Mary Poppins is a sort of door separating the two worlds, allowing contact between the real and the Beyond. Through Mary Poppins, the real world is able to experience all the possibilities of the Beyond without losing its all-important sense of safety and security.

This meeting of the fictional and real worlds can also be found in the episode entitled "The Children in the Story" which uses the common theme of characters from a picture book coming to life. Jane and Michael are reading a book of stories whose illustrations they themselves had colored in when the characters depicted come to life. The children learn not only that Mary Poppins was once the governess of these fictional children, but that their relationship could only have taken place in a fictional time. The interesting twist that completes this episode comes when Jane and Michael realize that these picture-book children believe that the world of the Banks family is fictional:

> "But—how did you get here?"
>
> [...] "we jumped right out into the story!" Amor concluded gaily.
>
> "Out of it, you mean," cried Michael. "We're not a story. We're real people. It's you who are the pictures!"
>
> Yet the pictures refused to be deterred:
>
> "*You* are the children in the story. We've read about you so often, Jane, and looked at the picture and longed to know you. So today—when the book fell open—we simply walked in." (IV, pp.105–06)

Again, a typically romantic irony, and one that was for Travers much more than just a narrative technique to be used in certain given scenes, given that she claimed, more in general, not to have invented the character of Mary Poppins: "I have never once thought that I invented her. Maybe she invented me…"[11] Staffan Bergsten, who met Pamela Lyndon Travers and wrote about the author and her books, says of the above affirmation:

> Such a remark is more than mere pleasantry and yet less than a solemn theory. Like most of the things said both by Mary Poppins and Pamela Travers it hovers on the frontier between tale and truth, reality and myth. Somewhere in the universal depths of myth the question of literal truth loses all meaning. That which is, that which has been and that which could have been all merge.[12]

As Oscar Wilde has said, the dandy likes to be misunderstood because it gives him an advantage over his interlocutors.[13] The implication is that the dandy (and Mary Poppins, and Pamela Lyndon Travers) will always appear in some way deceitful or untruthful, though only because he refuses to give absolute value to Truth. In art, contradictions reign and there is no place for universal truths; indeed, can one ever tell the truth?[14]

The dandy's world was necessarily equivocal: "In matters of great importance, style, not sincerity, is the vital thing."[15] "Philistine" truth is the product of utility, morality and rationality and equates with bourgeois hypocrisy and control. Lying, on the other hand, traces the movement of "becoming," it is an act that veils and diverts, pointing to new directions, subverting given perspectives, illuminating anarchic and irreverent ways of thinking and possibly of being. Indeed, in the Mary Poppins books we find many examples in which a change of mental perspective goes side by side with a change of the physical reality of the individuals, with their finding themselves in an "other" position or place. This then is a form of prerequisite if one is to be exposed to new experiences.

> Suddenly Jane noticed that they were going in the wrong direction.
>
> "But Mary Poppins, I thought you said gingerbread—this isn't the way to Green, Brown and Johnson's, where we always get it—" she began, and stopped because of Mary Poppins's face.
>
> "Am I doing the shopping or are you?" Mary Poppins enquired.
>
> "You," said Jane in a very small voice.
>
> "Oh really? I thought it was the other way around," said Mary Poppins with a scornful laugh.
>
> She gave the perambulator a little twist with her hand and it turned a corner and drew up suddenly. Jane and Michael, stopping abruptly behind it, found themselves outside the most curious shop they had ever seen. (I, p. 98)
>
> "Here's your ticket," the gruff voice said, and, looking up, they found that it came from a huge Brown Bear who was wearing a coat with brass buttons and a peaked cap on his head. In his paw were two pink tickets which he held out to the children.
>
> "But we usually *give* tickets," said Jane.
>
> "Usual is as usual does. Tonight you receive them," said the Bear, smiling.
>
> (I, p. 128)

Belonging to a social context that was moving toward the substitutability of the individual and looked with suspicion at the figures of exceptionality, the dandy challenged the bourgeois values of standardization and respect, especially when he found himself having to deal with people whose so-called authority rested on the mere fact that they had been given a socially recognizable uniform (and thus a role) to wear. Mary Poppins very often challenges the authority, for example, of the uniformed park keeper.

> The Park Keeper in his summer suit—blue with a red stripe on the sleeve—was keeping an eye on everyone as he tramped across the lawns.
>
> "Observe the rules! Keep off the grass! All Litter to be Placed in the Baskets!" he shouted. [...] "No rubbish Allowed in the Park!" shouted the Keeper as Mary Poppins swept along Lime Walk.
>
> "Rubbish yourself!" she retorted briskly, with a haughty toss of her head.
>
> He took off his hat and fanned his face as he stared at her retreating back. And you knew from the way Mary Poppins smiled that she knew quite well he was staring. How could he help it, she thought to herself. Wasn't she wearing her new white jacket, with the pink collar and the pink belt and the four pink buttons down the front? (III, p. 80)

The dandy radically rejected compromises and was always prepared to put himself at stake. Moreover, he did not feel that he actually belonged to time, or not to a time that passes: the present—and his presence—was all that counted. The dandy's ideal book would be "a book with no plot and a single protagonist"[16]—and that protagonist would, of course, be the dandy himself. But in the end the dandy had to leave that society whose values he succeeded in undermining, as was the case with Melmoth, the wandering Jew of the tradition, whose name Oscar Wilde took during his period of exile, and who left behind him nothing more than a scarf blowing in the wind. This was probably the same scarf that Mary Poppins also left behind, proof both of the fact that she had passed through and that she was no longer there. This left-behind scarf also reveals the attention to detail that is typical of the dandy's philosophy; it is a sign that captures attention, it is the distinctive sign of his *difference*.[17]

Linked to dandyism is the myth of androgyny. The dandy is an androgynous being, capable of infinite seduction, symbolizing the revolt against imposed identity. His search for authentic personal identity undermines the values of a class dominated by a particular vision of the sexes that restricts the possibilities of the individual. The dandy embodies the primordial androgyny of the alchemist and subverts the bipolar structure of masculine and feminine, replacing the sense of lost wholeness with unity, and countering the strict gender classifications of the bourgeois world with a vision of gender that is inclusive rather than exclusive. The character of Mary Poppins is in a similar way androgynous, embodying both recognizably masculine and feminine traits. She dresses and cares about dressing (perfectly, moreover) like the ladies of her time, and yet her posture is at all times rigid and stiff—never does she appear soft, delicate or in any way sensuous. But more importantly, her character is strikingly androgynous: she possesses a stereotypically feminine vanity and capriciousness; yet, at the same time her role allows her a measure of power, authority, and independence more usually reserved for the men of her time.

THE TRICKSTER

This undermining of gender differences, this exposing of masculine and feminine roles as something inherited from society and which may not necessarily reflect the true identity of the individual, is a popular theme in the mythology of diverse peoples and traditions. To reject the limited possibilities offered by gender determinism is, of course, to adopt a more general threshold position where boundaries are permeable and possibilities are multiplicitous. The "normal" characters who come into contact with Mary Poppins are in fact characterized by the limited vision that results from a univocal understanding of reality that produces the belief that only one particular way of life can be considered "real," possible, or even natural. Indeed, their reaction to the inexplicable situations that Mary Poppins brings about is telling:

> "But what on earth is happening?" somebody said close by.
> "But it's not possible!" said another voice. (I, p. 157)
> "But—but! Glog—glog! Er—rumph! Glug—glug!" Speechless with astonishment the Park Keeper blocked their path […]
> "You can't do things like this, I tell you! It's against the Law. And, furthermore, it's against Nature!" (III, p. 20)

Myth is populated by such a wealth of paradoxical figures, figures who straddle order and disorder but who are at home in neither, figures who embody contradictory extremes but who belong neither within nor outside a given system, that these latter could almost be said to constitute a universal theme. The trickster is one such figure who resists precise definition and represents multiplicity, mobility and unpredictability. The trickster undermines the stability, apparent comprehensibility, and structured pattern of the safely organized world because he belongs to the world of disorder. Yet, what he brings about is not, as a paradox, utter destruction: with a slip of the tongue, error or oversight on his part a new world comes into being. He is, to be precise, a creative figure, though he creates by means of subverting, of exposing contradictions, of throwing everything into question. Originating in mythology, the trickster quickly found his way into many literary traditions (e.g., Puck and Ariel are Shakespeare's trickster-fools in Elizabethan drama, whilst Till Eugenspiegel belongs to the German tradition). The trickster is also reincarnated in Travers's works, under the guise of Friend Monkey, the eponymous heroine of the only novel not to feature Mary Poppins, which was published in 1971. The book, titled *Friend Monkey*,[18] is set in London in 1897, Queen Victoria's jubilee year, and recounts the tale of Friend Monkey who reaches London in a cargo ship and is taken in by a middle-class family that resembles the Banks family. The Monkey seeks to help the family, though her zealous enthusiasm for order usually ends in disaster as she creates one catastrophic situation after another. This paradox is, of course, characteristic of the tricksters found in mythology whose involvement in particular situations leads to a re-evaluation of the accepted order of things and introduces the concepts of risk and disorder as possible sites of exploration.

Tricksters in myth are lawless, primordial beings who transgress all physical and moral limitations. They disrupt the most rigid of dichotomies, displaying a total lack of respect for the laws governing distinctions and oppositions: their internal organs might, for example, be visible to the external world, or physically they might be completely uncoordinated; they are the product of incest or menstrual blood or are borne of dead fetuses, depending on the tradition in question. In any case what they bring about, at all levels (physical, ethical, biological) is the impossible—or what was thought to be such.

The trickster is essentially ambiguous, refusing to explain himself and his actions, and works by tricks and deceit. Yet, as we have already said, these tricks often bring about positive effects, displaying the extent to which the true origins of order are often to be found in disorder (from which the well-organized society seeks to keep a distance). The trickster bridges different worlds. In the Haitian Voodoo tradition, for example, the trickster's name is Legba, and his threshold status is highlighted by this name, meaning: "the god who opens the barriers" or "the keeper of doors, thresholds and crossroads." The trickster represents the destruction of a given social order and bridges the gap between the binary opposites on which this order is founded. It is an essentially mobile figure and moves between dimensions (earth, air, water, and fire); he brings with him a sense of the primordial continuity from which culture has developed and his tricks often bring to light the oppositions inherent in every situation, and in so doing allows the transcendence of such opposites. In the Algonkian Indian tradition, for example, the figure of the trickster is a sort of giant whose form stretches across the whole sky, linking North to South, East to West, and thus dissolving the barriers between night and day, hot and cold, black and white, and so forth.

In *Mary Poppins*, this same paradoxical neutralization takes place, not however in the dimension of space but in the temporal one, where time facilitates the perception of the distance covered between two points and thus emphasizes difference. In a single moment (thus collapsing all temporally motivated perceptions of difference), Mary Poppins takes the children on a trip around the world, stopping on each of the cardinal points so that the children can meet the representatives of each of these different geographical areas, the Eskimo, the Chinese man, the African, and the Red Indian.

Psychoanalytic criticism has nominated the phallus as the trickster par excellence, and Carl Gustav Jung and Paul Radin for example have described the phallus as being the most independent and anarchic organ because it cannot be controlled by will or reason. In the same way, we can identify Dionysus, the god of creative strength and fertility, as a trickster. The power of Dionysus is neither measurable nor justifiable and is not exacted over something or someone specific; rather it is a dynamic power for and of itself, it is a form of pure, free energy. Dionysus is a trickster also because of the fact that his specific dimension and destiny is one of wandering. The trickster is, in fact, characteristically nomadic or errant and, as such, is considered transgressive by a social order that has developed itself in the course of history as a dimension increasingly linked to, and dependent on, stability, immobility, rigidity, in both a literal/geographical and metaphorical/psychological sense. Incidentally, this may explain at a deeper level why nomadic peoples or peoples without their "own" land such as the Jews or gypsies have traditionally been persecuted by the settled dominating societies of the Western world, or why, still today, loitering is considered a crime by our legal systems.

Dionysus is a god with no fixed abode who appears out of the blue. He is Kzenos, the stranger, who crosses every known boundary, whether physical or metaphorical; indeed, he is the god who plays with the concept of barriers, gushing forth like wine coursing from a barrel, one of his most common manifestations. He is the god who eradicates difference and unites oppositions.

DIONYSUS AND *THE BACCHAE*

It was not until the fifth century B.C. that the previously fleeting mythological figure of Dionysus came into focus with *The Bacchae* by Euripides. Dyonysus became more than a distant divine entity condensing deep and obscure human aspirations; he became a character of a story, the telling of which helps us grasp its essence. Literature makes myths, archetypes, and deep unspoken truths somehow more "familiar" to us; it is a bridge connecting us, with our language and what is understandable to us, to the beyond from which we come and which lies underneath us, but which we can only vaguely "know." Euripides (born around 480 B.C.) took the conflictual introduction of the cult of Dionysus to Thebes as the basis of his tragedy *The Bacchae*, thus linking a mythological motif to a precise historical moment and place. It is thanks to this play's explicit recounts of who Dionysus was and what he did that we can trace the mythological origins of Mary Poppins to ancient Greece and the Dionysian principle. The play takes its name from the god's female followers who were determined to bring to Thebes their religion. Dionysus, the god of fertility, nature, and ecstasy, is said to have originated in the ancient city of Thrace. Despite being built on the remains of this ancient city, Thebes wanted nothing to do with this mythological figure; it did not recognize itself as being the birthplace of the god and, as such, did not honor him with rites or rituals. Dionysus was the product of perhaps the first mythical union between heaven and earth: he was the divine son of Zeus and Semele, a mortal woman from Thebes. In the play, the king of Thebes refuses to recognize Dionysus as the son of Semele and is thus responsible for the tragedy that ensues. The king's greatest error lies in the fact that he names Dionysus the foreigner, a name that, at the same time, alienates and liberates the threatening potential of all threshold figures, of all figures who are in some way Other and beyond our control.

It is the Bacchante, the women possessed by the god and at one with him, who bring the cult of Dionysus to Thebes and involve the town's citizens in never before seen experiences. Pentheus, the king of Thebes, mistrusts the foreigner's power and refuses to call him "god," opting for the somewhat disdainful term "magician." Despite the king's refusal to refer to Dionysus as a god, he nevertheless recognizes in him superior qualities that irritate the king and undermine his concept of "common sense."

The chorus sings (as the voice of the Bacchante) while the king suffers his drama of pain, anguish, presumption, and illusion in his useless attempts to bring order to the chaos pervading his city. The song recounts the joy of those initiated into the cult of Dionysus, and their newly found lightness and freedom from all burdens, especially from that of social constraint. The chorus describes the rites followed by their cult of ecstasy and invite the people—especially the women—of Thebes to join the followers of this new religion. At the outset of the play, the Bacchante recount how they left Asia (they come from the East, like the wind bringing Mary Poppins to our world) in order to follow the god Dionysus and order the citizens of Thebes to stay indoors in complete silence while they offer up praises to their god. The exhortations of the chorus, like those of Mary Poppins, are highly solemn and ritualistic, reminiscent of the orders and directions that priests or ministers give before undertaking a sacred ritual. The Bacchante, therefore, act as priestesses in the ministering of the mysteries of Dionysus.

Integral to many mystical cults, including the one depicted by Euripides, is the purification of the initiate through tests, teachings, and with the aid of sacred symbols (all of which the Banks children also come into contact)—and, unlike public rituals of worship, these mystical rites must take place in private (at night, in secret places, when everybody else is busy or cannot see, as in the Mary Poppins books).

The Bacchante are always very solemn in attitude and are well aware of the origin and symbolic value of their activities; in this they differ greatly from the citizens of Thebes who follow them (just as Mary Poppins remains different from the people she involves, suddenly and often despite their will, in her ritual adventures), but who have no idea as to what might be happening to them and who do not possess the theoretical knowledge about Dionysus that could save them from the potentially terrible effects of mania. This mania is a force that Dionysus infuses into individuals and that makes them do things they would never before have done—in some (those who are prepared to trust in this force) this proves ultimately liberating, in those who reject this force and refuse to recognize its power (not simply as the power of an external god, but as something to be experienced personally), this mania will have terrible effects.

In *Mary Poppins Opens the Door*, we find an interesting parallel with the idea expressed in Euripides' play. In the chapter entitled "Peppermint Horses" all the peppermint walking sticks sold at the entrance to the park by a strange old woman suddenly take to the air:

> "Be careful, Michael!" Jane called after him. But just at that moment her own stick wobbled and made a long plunge upwards. Away it swooped on the trail of Michael [...] it buckled and reared

like a horse beneath her and she kept her hands on its neck for a rein. (III, p. 103)

The children are quick to learn and enjoy the experience, which is not the case for many of the adults who suddenly find themselves floating in midair:

Help! Help! Murder! Earthquakes!" cried a hoarse, distracted voice. The children turned to see Mr Trimlet riding madly up behind them. His hands clung tightly to the Peppermint Candy and his face had turned quite white.

"I tried to eat my stick," he wailed, "and look what it did to me!" (III, p. 115)

And again:

"Oh! Oh!" shrieked Ellen. "I daren't look down!" (III, p. 120)

While:

…ever before them, showing the way, making a path through the jostling riders, went the figure of Mary Poppins. She sat her umbrella with elegant ease, her hands well down on its parrot's head. The pigeon's wing in her hat flew at a perfect angle, not a fold of her dress was out of place. What she was thinking, they could not tell, but her mouth had a small, self-satisfied smile as though she were thoroughly pleased with herself. (III, p. 120)

A similar scene can be found in the chapter "Mr. Twigley's Wishes." The Banks children are taken up by a magical rhythm emanating from musical boxes shaped like drums and, as usual, they enthusiastically accept all that comes from Mary Poppins—even when this takes them by surprise.

The feet of the children were light as wings as they danced to their own music. Never before, they told themselves, had they felt so light and merry. (III, p. 41)

The policeman, however, cannot accept what is happening, even if it is happening before his very eyes, and is unable to see beyond his own role and the responsibility invested in that role:

The attic itself, like the music boxes, was turning round and round […]. The Policeman took out notebook and pencil.

"Come on! Stop spinning, all of you […] I want an Explanation […] Now, that's enough. You just come down! This spinning and twirling is bad for the 'ealth. And not permitted in Private

Dwellings. 'Ere! 'Oo's that pulling me! Let me go!" The Policeman gave a frightened shriek as he shot off his feet and through the air. A music box broke into noisy song as he dropped like a stone onto it. "'Elp! 'Elp! It's me—P.C. 32 calling!" (III, p. 44)

The policeman's cries for help fall on deaf ears, as do those of Mrs. Clump, who had called the policeman in the hope of having the rather suspicious Mary Poppins arrested:

"Officer!" shouted Mrs Clump. "You do your duty or I'll have the Law onto you too. Get down and arrest that woman!" She thrust a huge finger at Mary Poppins. "I'll have you out behind bars, my girl. I'll have you—Here! Stop spinning me around!" Her eyes grew wide with angry amazement. For a curious thing was happening. Slowly, on the spot where she stood, Mrs Clump began to revolve. She had no musical box, no platform, she simply went round and round on the floor [...] A shudder of horror shook Mrs Clump as she tried to move her large black boots. She struggled. She writhed. She wriggled her body. But her feet were firmly glued to the floor. (III, p. 45)

It is likewise to the same disturbing rhythm of the drum that the Bacchante of Euripides' play conduct their ecstatic rituals. The drum's beat acts on the psyche, provoking frenetic physical movement or collective exaltation, and is used by many communities as the rhythmic accompaniment to their sacred dances. Music here gains a cosmic value and is used to reintroduce balance to the universe and its constituent parts. The Bacchante/chorus assume all the characteristics of their god who, primordial like life itself, wields terrifying power and authority but can also bestow incredibly generous graces on its subjects.

In Euripides' play, Pentheus, the king of Thebes, greets with disdain the way in which the Thebian women have begun to offer up praises to this new, foreign god. Undermining his own characteristic rationality, Pentheus blindly accepts the citizens' claims that the Bacchante are the bringers of immorality and destruction, and it is for this reason (i.e., his willingness to name, define, and affirm that which is totally unknown to him) that the king is seen by the Bacchante and their god as a blasphemous victim of his own preconceptions.

During the play, the king's conviction that he holds absolute authority—bestowed on him by his role and by his powers of reason and supposed ability to distinguish the possible from the impossible—gradually reveals itself to be an illusion. The king is warned by Tiresias, the oracle, and by all those around him to adopt an attitude of humility towards

Dionysus and to recognize his own impotence, one of the prerequisites of initiation into the mysteries of the cult. But Pentheus considers himself immune to what he describes as superstition and madness; and yet it soon becomes clear that in his fear of being contaminated by the mania spreading through his city, the king understands the extent to which the Dionysian cult is almost a physical contagion. Pentheus's increasing frustration at the situation leads him to seek to impose randomly his authority on anyone who happens to pass in front of his palace and his exasperated threats and commands provoke a sense of pity in the spectator. The king's blind need to defend his definition of reality and his vision of himself precedes rather than responds to the attack on his power, which is never overt. In fact, Dionysus does not actually fight against him, nor against anyone else; Dionysus simply *is* (and needs to be recognized). The king behaves as if he were aware—though will not admit it—that the certainties he clings to are but arbitrary constructions, liable sooner or later to be dismantled. And whilst Pentheus rages, the chorus adopts a paradoxical position and sings of the advantages of measure. Clearly, the measure they allude to is not synonymous with the king's arrogant, self-sufficient and presumptuous rationality that leads only to blindness, but equates with a form of joyous acceptance of life as that which is in a state of becoming and which often escapes logical and systematic definition. As we learn in the play, individuals will be in a position to receive the divine only if they adopt an attitude of measured humility and respect, only if they accept the world without imposing judgments and learn to approach life with curiosity and a sense of wonder. This perspective gains credence in Travers's works; indeed, all Mary Poppins's friends and relatives, and all those capable of flight or weightlessness, approach life in this way.

When Dionysus and Pentheus finally meet, Pentheus presumes to take the role of judge questioning his criminal. He begins with an official, dispassionate tone but as the dialogue proceeds the king is unable to suppress his curiosity, hatred, and exasperation until his questions become fired with passion; Dionysus, however, maintains his measured calm throughout.

There are many ways in which this reading of *The Bacchae* can enrich our understanding of the Mary Poppins books. Indeed, the above-described scene in which the agitated Pentheus interrogates the calm and dispassionate Dionysus finds many parallels in the Mary Poppins books. In *Mary Poppins Opens the Door*, for example, we find the park keeper waving his arms around and shouting whilst Mary Poppins maintains her calm, looking like any other perfectly respectable and innocent woman who had accompanied her children to the park. The park keeper points an accusing finger at Mary Poppins:

> "There's the guilty party! She done it or I'll eat my hat! [...] As soon as that girl comes into the park, the place begins to go cross-wise. Merry-go-rounds jumpin' up in the sky, people coming down on kites and rockets, the Prime Minister bobbing round on balloons—and it's all your doing—you, Caliban!" He shook his fist wildly at Mary Poppins. (III, p. 107)

The governess refuses to deny the accusations of the park keeper, but remains silent, solemn, and austere, just as Dionysus maintains his calm before the irate Pentheus. This is an important moment, both in Euripides' play and Travers's book, because the spectator is presented with two opposing attitudes. The first, exhibited by figures holding official power, is the attitude of those who boast authority and do so by means of commanding, shouting and judging. Such figures are shown here to be fragile and precarious, on the verge of collapsing should they find that their world is not what they thought it was. The second is the attitude of someone who, although besieged by a desire to neutralize and negate his/her presence and power, is only apparently lacking in authority. What we are faced with here is a strategy that subtly works against the world of order and reason and against the world of those who care about order and reason more than they care about the authenticity of life. The strategy—here of Dionysus, elsewhere of Mary Poppins—consists in being able, when necessary, to apparently renounce the self. Dionysus understands that to win against his enemy he needs to become as like his enemy as is possible, or rather, he needs to embody and display those same characteristics that his adversary values as ideal.

In the play Dionysus is accused of being the cause of disorder, exaggeration, and undermining of civil control but shows himself to be far more measured, ordered and stable than his counterpart. Dionysus's self-control is directed inwards, he does not measure himself against others, and his behavior is without fault before these potentially destabilizing circumstances. Nobody can reasonably accuse him of disorder, given that he conducts himself so impeccably. In a similar way, Mary Poppins answers to no one but herself and with the wisdom gleaned from her reading of *Everything a Lady Should Know*, acts accordingly. What takes place because of her—disorder and subversion—can never be actually attributed to her, for her ways, in social terms, are nothing short of perfect. This is not just hinted at but openly stated, time and again, in the books. When the governess returns for the third time to the Banks household, for example, she determines to measure the children's development with a strange measuring device that takes account of qualitative rather than quantitative growth and finds that the children have changed for the worse. Tellingly, Mary Poppins subjects herself to the same measuring, and we learn that she is "Better than Ever, Practically Perfect" (III, p. 25).

In *The Bacchae*, Pentheus questions Dionysus about the rites of initiation. His foolish, profane questions reveal him to be afraid of losing the control he has over the status quo and unwilling to open himself to experiencing the Beyond. His questions are an attempt to exorcize his fear of difference and are by no means the fruit of true curiosity or the desire to expand himself through contact with alternative possibilities. However, initiates into the mysteries of the cult are ordered to obey a vow of silence, and Dionysus refuses to break this sacred law. With wisdom and calm irony, he evades all of Pentheus's questions, which only serves to heighten the king's curiosity and anger. Such a scene finds a direct parallel in *Mary Poppins Opens the Door*:

> "But you came down on—I don't know—what! Where did you come from? 'Ow did you get 'ere? That's what I want to know!"
>
> "Curiosity killed the cat!" said Mary Poppins primly. (III, p. 22)
>
> "I suppose you understand what it all means?" [said the Park Keeper to Mary Poppins]
>
> "I suppose I do," she replied smugly. And without another word she gave the perambulator a little push and sent it bowling past him. (III, p. 101)

The schematic logic of the rationalist or moralist collapses under the force of a religious consciousness that seeks not to translate itself into defined and classifiable propositions. The king's arrogant prejudice stands in the way of his understanding this mystical religious phenomenon, and in a display of power and authority he has Dionysus imprisoned. Dionysus is quick, however, to regain his freedom in a scene which sees the palace destroyed by an earthquake. (The metaphor is quite clear: Dionysus, and Dionysian figures, when entering our familiar world, shake it to its foundations. When Travers introduces Mary Poppins for the very first time, the Banks children are looking out of the window and suddenly see a strange figure brought, it seems, by the wind to their front door. In that moment, "the watching children heard a terrific bang, and as she landed the whole house shook." (I, p. 13))

Pentheus and Dionysus once more find themselves face to face—the deluded king's self-deception pitted against Dionysus's calm confidence. The fragility of the king's supposed objectivity is underlined in the scene where the messenger is sent to spy on the citizens' ritual worshipping of the god. When the messenger returns to the king, having experienced firsthand the shocking scenes, he feels unable to speak truthfully of Dionysus's strangely "other" power because he fears a wrathful reaction on the part of Pentheus, known for his rigid and sententious morality and his arrogantly prejudiced self-assurance. Nevertheless, it is this messenger who finally reveals the truth about what happens during the Bacchante's rites. The Bacchante's anthem is the joyous materialization of people's deep and sometimes unspeakable desires, and this finds, once again, many parallels in the Mary Poppins books where the "Beyond places" visited by the children often reflect in some specific way the materialization of their own dreams and desires. What is particularly striking about these adventures beyond the door is that they always stage the notion of abundance in some way—an abundance that often materializes in the form of food, cakes, or sweets, things that the children would be denied, or would never be able to enjoy so fully, at home. And if, today, this might seem a frivolous need, it is in fact so basic as to signal back to a very ancient human condition and to a child's most basic form of survival, the first to be learned and mastered, and its primary source of knowledge about the external world (known as the oral phase of a child's development). The need for food—for magically abundant or different food—is portrayed as such, as a very basic, irresistible and metaphorical need, in fact, in all traditional folk and fairy tales (the witch's house in "Hansel and Gretel" representing figuratively one of the most remarkable examples).

The cult's rites and rituals are unsettlingly strange for the layman. The Bacchante enter into profound contact with nature, and empowered by the primitive forces represented by Dionysus, they raise themselves above normal people and are able to carry out acts of great wonder. The Bacchante and the women of Thebes are in effect fleeing from that narrow, clearly delimited space in which, because of his weakness and fear (hidden behind an attitude of arrogance and power), man has taken refuge. These women refuse to accept the roles given them by this need to define and fix. And to do the same, though without raising the suspicions of those who in Edwardian England would be afraid to detect in her a Dionysian quality (one that the western world has continued to consider dangerous for the specific civilizing processes it wanted to foster), Mary Poppins has to present herself as a governess there. Her coming (from the East) to a "normal" household in these shoes will allow her to conduct her subtle rebellion from inside the institutionalized order and at the same time to escape its limits, the role of the governess being, in the specific society she enters, so full of contradictions as to undermine itself as a socially recognizable and controllable commitment, as we shall see in the last chapter of this study.

Filled with Dionysus's force, the Bacchante fear neither that which is superior nor that which is inferior to them, and the wondrous experiences in which they now participate allow them to enter into a shameless, secure and fearless relationship with the whole sphere of existence. The most important moment in the Bacchante ritual is when the initiates begin to dance, the rhythm of the music sweeping them towards open contact with nature. In *Mary Poppins* we find a similar scene when the children begin to dance with the animals at the zoo:

> "Look!" and he nodded his head towards the moving mass of creatures before them. Birds and animals were now swaying together, closely encircling Mary Poppins, who was rocking lightly from side to side. Backwards and forwards, went the swaying crowd, keeping time together, swinging like the pendulum of a clock. Even the trees were bending and lifting gently, and the moon seemed to be rocking in the sky as a ship rocks on the sea.
>
> "Bird and beast and stone and star—we are all one, all one—" murmured the Hamadryad, softly folding his hood about him as he himself swayed between the children. (I, p. 144)

When the messenger finally tells Pentheus of the rituals, the latter is unable to grasp the true significance of what is taking place and cannot see beyond what he perceives to be the principle danger: the fact that these possessed women rebelling against the rules and institutions of civil life might seek to overpower the city. Dionysus, on the other hand, hates institutions but loves the human life that they contain and offers to his followers the gifts of joy, liberty, inebriation, and love. If an individual accepts the divinely superior powers of dynamic, vital creativity, he/she must learn how to abandon all hope of dominating, controlling, and appropriating life for his/her own ends. He/she must abandon all attachment to material prosperity and learn to appreciate the good to be found in the simplicity of everyday life. Filled with the immanent presence of the god, the world for the initiates into the Dionysian cult becomes filled with marvels and riches.

The classics scholar Kenneth J. Reckford has studied the themes of continuity throughout the history of literature and cites the Mary Poppins books in connection with Dionysian themes:

> The *Mary Poppins* stories are written by a woman who welcomes, yet truly reveres, the power of Dionysus in the world. I say this partly out of gratitude, since my own appreciation of comedy, and of life, is

derived in large part from Mary Poppins and partly because these stories include and illustrate [some] key aspects of the 'Dionysian fairy tale'. The first is that with Mary Poppins, a wonderful transforming energy breaks through into ordinary custom and routine (which nonetheless remain extremely important) into a world of magic where the Laws of nature are suspended. Part of the fun consists, naturally, of recognizing familiar things in such strange and wonderful surroundings. Still more comes through surprise, incongruity and reversal. The fantasies are rich and fulfilling.[19]

At the end of Euripides' play, Dionysus triumphs over Pentheus; his victory assumes the form of sacrificial offering as Pentheus capitulates before the god and appears in front of the palace dressed in women's clothing. The king's so-called madness manifests itself in his seeing "double," symbolizing the destruction of his univocal vision of reality. Yet, paradoxically, in seeing the multiplicitous nature of life, the king is actually able to see the world for what it really is. He accepts his women's clothing and is overwhelmed by a sense of euphoria that erases all his inhibitions and increases his strength. But the king's happiness is only an illusion. The Bacchante are also subject to this "madness," and yet their sensations are guided and controlled by their god, whilst the king's exaltation is imposed as a sort of punishment, and because it goes uncontrolled, it finally leads Pentheus toward the tragic end that awaits all those who in their supreme arrogance seek to defy the will of the gods by severing those essentially harmonizing links between self and the rest of the cosmos.

Dionysus disappears from the stage at the end of the play, though his invisible omnipotence continues to make itself felt through the energy of the women. Here we learn *what* rather than *who* Dionysus is, that is, a force residing as much in man as in nature, and one that needs to be recognized and lived in a way that will make the individual become part of the broader life running through the world instead of a creature who feels alienated and different. Once he recognizes this force within him, man will stop arrogantly considering himself to inhabit the role of artist (of some limited world of his own) and will become part of the work of art—that is, of the mythical world considered as a totalizing, beneficial, and healing experience.

Travers calls this a "reinstating of the lost world" and suggests that this is the task of heroes, or that the act in itself is somehow heroic. The effect, she says, remains for as long as the hero remains. With the hero's disappearance, the effect too disappears, because the normal man will return to his old ways, losing sight of the mythical reality and its demands. Toward the end of *Mary Poppins Opens the Door*, in a scene filled with omen and signs which only later will become clear, we suddenly meet a whole series of strange and wonderful figures from previous books who come to bid their farewells to the governess. The children are worried; they do not yet understand what is happening, and misinterpret these signs as meaning that each of these other characters is about to take their leave.

> "Are you going away too?" Michael demanded as [Mary Poppins] stared at Miss Corry.
> She gave a merry shriek of laughter. "Well, yes, I am, in a manner of speaking! Once one goes, they all go—that's the way of it." (III, p. 179)

What this shows is that, in order to fully participate and trust in the mythical reality, we need a mediator, someone who incarnates and renders tangible that mythical reality so that we might experience it without risk. With such a mediator we will be able to rise above the limitations and constrictions of everyday life (without actually erasing it).

Ecstasy and the notion of "trans," understood as a journey beyond logic and the quotidian, is a fundamental part of the cult of Dionysus. This leaping beyond the confines of the self is a form of "trans-fert" and involves one's body. The Dionysian "trans" begins always with a deambulatory act: not a regular, predictable, rhythmic, but an asymmetric, syncopated physical movement. It is a leap or flight away from "here," toward...

LIBERATED BODIES: THE DANCE

It is interesting to note how this asymmetric movement of the body is present throughout myth, legend, and the atavistic knowing of our collective imagination. Indeed, so frequently do we find examples of this kind of irregular physical movement or "different" gait in literature that we could almost suggest that it constitutes a universal. Those characters whose movement through space does not match the two regular beats characterizing the "normal" way of walking are often special, mysterious, or are liminal, threshold figures.[20] This physical asymmetry of movement that could be labeled as a "defect" is in fact the defining characteristic of a particular character and that which makes it attractively different—we might consider, for example, the dangerously charming pirate Long John Silver, in *Treasure Island*, with his recognizably irregular step, whose difference from the (in Jim's eyes, boring and dull) socialized men is symbolized by this impediment. And in the case of Long John Silver, we find a further impediment: Silver has one blind eye, another very clear metaphorical sign of his being the holder of a different way of "seeing" the world. His blind eye and his limping gait prove his difference from those who hold a balanced, rational, commonsensical view—none of which is meaningful for the young protagonist who, like the children in Mary Poppins and so many children in literature, is attracted to the marginal figure, no matter how mysterious and dangerous he and the experience might be.

These characters have in common the fact that each has ventured toward some dimension that is invisible or inaccessible to others and their norms and laws, towards a beyond that has transformed them, assigning them a greater degree of awareness, charisma, and power.

Oedipus is an archetypal figure and hero, notwithstanding (or rather because of) the walking impediment that characterizes him. His very name signifies "swollen foot," and his impediment gains significance through its metaphorical value especially when Oedipus encounters the Sphinx, who demands that he solve the famous riddle: what being walks on four legs in the morning, two in the afternoon and three in the evening. Oedipus can solve the enigma because his own physical "defect" presents him with the answer: being lame he must walk with a walking stick (i.e., three legs) and so correctly guesses that the answer to the riddle is man himself.

Another mythical figure characterized by a "problem" involving a lower limb is Achilles, whose mother's name (Thetis) means "silver foot" and whose father was crippled. Achilles is immersed in the waters of invulnerability, but the heel of his foot remains weaker than the rest of his body, thus exposing him to future tragedy. The story of Jason too—another mythical figure different from his fellow men as he was raised by simple shepherds and the half-man, half-beast centaurs in a hidden place far from civilization—tells of him wearing a single shoe at the moment of his victory over the would-be usurper of his throne. This same symbolic representation of asymmetric movement can be found in the Dionysus myth, of course, Dionysus being the god of wine—that which, when drunk in excess, causes the individual to stumble and fall.

Impeded mobility often leads to and symbolizes rejection of the individual on the part of society. Perfect physical symmetry and rhythm could be interpreted as being the material counterpart to a vision of the world that seeks order and control through the perfect balance of binary dualism. The asymmetric man, or the man with the uneven gait and incoherent rhythm, is a boundary figure; he is only partly man. That part of him that is rejected by the world of "normal" men belongs to a different sphere, a place where rigid regularity and predictable balance are no longer norms. If bilateral symmetry represents normality—that which is expected, known, and always reiterated—those not respecting this norm will, by dint of their difference, gain in meaning and symbolic value.

Returning to our discussion of the mythical valence of Mary Poppins, it is interesting to note that the governess's umbrella with its parrot-shaped handle is not only a symbol of flight, but that even when apparently useless (i.e., it is not whisking Mary Poppins up into the clouds), folded, and erect like a walking stick, the irregular rhythm it lends to her stride is nevertheless representative of the difference being discussed here. Moreover, in *Mary Poppins Opens the Door* we find the relationship being traced between the metaphor of walking and a certain vision of the world. In the above-mentioned episode where the children mount the candy sticks as if they were horses and take to the air, a strange figure enters the scene and wants to know why the children are sulking:

> Michael shuffled his feet and his face grew red. "We didn't want to go on walking—" he began shame-facedly. But the sentence was never finished. Miss Calico interrupted him with a loud shrill cackle.
>
> "Who does? Who does? I'd like to know! Nobody wants to go on walking. I wouldn't do it myself if you paid me. Not for a sackful of rubies!"
>
> Michael stared. Could it really be true? Had he found at last a grown up person who felt as he did about walking?
>
> "Why, I haven't walked for centuries," said Miss Calico. "And what's more, none of my family do. What—stump on the ground on two flat feet? They'd think that quite beneath them!" She cracked her whip and her pins flashed brightly as she shook her finger at the children.
>
> "Take my advice and always ride. Walking will only make you grow. And where does it get you? Pretty near nowhere! Ride, I say! Ride—and see the world!" (III, p. 112)

Movement and the form it takes are important elements in the Mary Poppins books, and directly connected to this is the theme of dance. Defying and evading logic, dance has been present throughout history as the physical expression of solemn or ritual moments and gives life an aesthetic form that is neither naturalistic (where the mind would seek to scrutinize and analyze the outer world) not utilitarian (which would imply the existence of an "end" and probable material gain). The gravity, seriousness, and purpose of life in dance become weightless, and the world is experienced not as a burden but as something intensely involving and memorable. Andersen's famous fairy tale "The Red Shoes" dramatizes and brings this theme to an extreme (Travers herself was once a dancer).

In Nietzsche's philosophy, dance is the most perfect representation of a circular time, of "eternal return" that stages the meeting of the world in becoming with the world of being:

> Eternity realizes itself in time and in-sists on time as a form of remaining within change; it is like a passing-by that presents over and over again an identical monogram, like some form of divine rest at the heart of becoming.[21]

If this configuration finds expression in dance, then we must make the link between this concept and all those occasions on which dance concludes the Banks children's experiences beyond the threshold and triumphs over stasis, immobility, and all that has become mechanical. And whilst for the children such moments of dance imply chaos and confusion, Mary Poppins appears as the "identical monogram," that moment of "divine rest at the heart of becoming"; she dances along with the others but retains her composure and is neither overwhelmed nor liberated from any preconceived constraints. The books' illustrations underline this idea; whilst the other figures captured in dance are blurred, the character of Mary Poppins is always distinctly and precisely drawn.

Dance is that mutable form of equilibrium that rhythmically remodels the self-in-becoming and expresses the ec-static tension existing "beyond" rather than "within" the self, and drawing it to where multiplicity and possibility reign. Dance is the antithesis of the spirit of gravity that tyrannically demands always that "one must," as opposed to asking what one wants or is capable of. It is a liberating movement which, as Mary Poppins continually reminds us, nevertheless can overwhelm; and yet it is in the discipline of dance that we find Nietzsche's notion of the "return" as that which while liberating the fluidity of movement, is also able to dominate it and leads to a state of "becoming" which is free but not to the point of dissolution or dispersion. Dance represents a moment of harmony in which the world regains authenticity, and all its constituent parts are set back in the labyrinth of chance. Dance becomes, for Nietzsche, that moment in which the Divine can re-enter existence; it prefigures a life which will, eventually, be populated by gods again:

> Where all the becoming looked to me like a dance of gods, a playful divine whim; and the world had neither links nor constraints

and was in itself fleeting: like the eternal fleeing from one another and chasing one another of many gods, like the cheerful opposing, listening and belonging to one another again of many gods...[22]

ITALO CALVINO AND THE CONCEPT OF LIGHTNESS

With a dancing stride, with a leap, with lightness—considered not as synonyms of frivolity but, as we have seen, as an alternative way of being in (and seeing) the world: this is how Italo Calvino hoped humankind would approach the third millennium.

The theme of lightness is the first of Calvino's *Six Memos for the Next Millenium*,[23] in which the writer, on the verge of the twenty-first century, set down his aspirations for the future. Calvino's chapter on lightness presents a series of examples taken from mythology, anthropology, and literature that are all connected with the notion (and possibility) of flight in its metaphorical meaning.

An excess of ambition can be criticized in many fields, but not in literature. Literature lives on exaggerated objectives which seem beyond hope of realization. Only if writers and poets set themselves tasks that no-one else would dream of attempting, can literature continue to have a true sense or purpose.[24]

Speaking of lightness as the quality he has always tried to achieve in his own writing, Calvino states:

I soon realized that the facts of everyday life which should have acted as primary material for my writing and the sudden, incisive agility which I hoped would characterize my style were separated by an abyss. Maybe I was discovering for the first time the weight, inertia and opacity of the world, qualities which burden one's writing if one is unable to flee from them. At times I worried that everything was turning to stone; a form of slow petrifaction that was more or less advanced in particular people or places but which spared no part of life. It was as if no-one could escape the Medusa's inexorable gaze. Perseus was the only man capable of slaying the Medusa; he of the winged sandals. Perseus refused to look directly upon the Gorgon, gazing instead upon her image as reflected in his bronze shield.[25]

This recalls the dandy's negation of the world as a given—being natural and true in itself—and his refusal to be deceived by appearances and his commitment to identifying the artifice in the world. Calvino reminds us that Perseus managed to cut off the head of the Medusa and avoid being turned to stone precisely because he realized that he could not look at her directly, but had to use a filter.

> Perseus is carried along by the lightest of elements—by wind and clouds, and looks upon that which only reveals itself through indirect vision, the image captured by a mirror.[26]

The reference to mirrors certainly calls to mind Mary Poppins's habit of self-approvingly searching for her own image in all reflective surfaces. And we also find references to the wind and to clouds that also signal the flight not only of Mary Poppins but of all her close friends and relatives. These figures are only in the "lightest," vaguest sense social individuals because despite the fact that they are capable of social relations, each of them rejects society's official ethos, flouting norms and conventions and refusing to live according to an essentialist agenda. Thus we find conventions being broken across the board: one character finds himself floating up into the air each time he laughs, another is suspended upside down, another shrinks in size, another is able to remove his own fingers and watch them painlessly grow back, whilst another climbs into his own pavement paintings. Each is in some way capable of the apparently "impossible", and yet all these subversive acts are conducted with the highest regard for and recognition of "good manners"—and frequently take place during that very English ritual of afternoon tea.

In his chapter on lightness, Calvino continues his discussion of Perseus and the symbolism connected to the Medusa's power to turn the individual into a single, unchangeable form by turning to stone all those who look directly upon her.

> Rather than abandon it, Perseus takes the Medusa's head with him, hidden in a sack [...] which becomes an invincible weapon in the hands of the hero; a weapon which he uses only in the most dangerous of situations and only against those who deserve to be turned into statues of themselves. [...] Perseus succeeds in taking control of the head precisely because he keeps it hidden, just as he triumphed over it initially by observing its reflection in the mirror. Perseus' strength lies in his avoidance of direct vision, but this does not mean that he refuses to acknowledge the world of monsters in which he is forced to live, a reality which he accepts to carry with him [...]
>
> The burdens of life inhere in all forms of constraint, in the dense network of public and private constraints that bind the individual with ever-tighter knots. Vivacity and a mobile intelligence might

be the only qualities able to resist this condemnation. And in understanding that the world is condemned to heaviness, I realize that I should take flight like Perseus to another place. I'm not talking about escaping into dreams or irrationality. What I mean is that I must change my approach, I must observe the world from another angle, according to a different logic and different methods of knowledge and understanding. [The world of literature] allows us to discover new paths, it reveals innovative or ancient styles and forms capable of altering our perspectives on the world.[27]

For Calvino, this lightness is a way of perceiving the world, and he stresses the point that such an outlook is by no means vague; it is a precise and constant undertaking that demands concentration and continuity. The same could obviously be said of Mary Poppins. Calvino points out later in the chapter that one of the ways literature can give voice to the notion of lightness is through the creation of an emblematic image:

Some literary inventions are capable of imprinting themselves on the memory more for what they *suggest* than for what they actually *say*. The scene from *Don Quixote* in which the lancet catches on the wing of a windmill which in turn pulls the character up into the sky occupies but a few lines of Cervantes' novel; we could say that in this case the author used not to the maximum but to the minimum the literary resources available to him; and yet this scene remains one of the most famous in the history of literature.[28]

There are myriad episodes in the Mary Poppins books that create precisely this form of emblematic image of lightness; examples include Mary Poppins's cousin who gains weightlessness through laughter, or the very respectable park goers who rise to the skies on the back of peppermint walking sticks, or, again, the scene where the children are given balloons that allow them to float up into the air. Lightness of form, on the other hand, is attained through the stylistic choices made by the writer—something to which Calvino was always committed. The ideal would be, for him, "that special poetical and existential modulation which allows one to contemplate his or her own heaviness as if from the outside, dissolving it into melancholy and humor."[29] Calvino identifies this form of weightless gravity in the work of Shakespeare, who found precisely that special "connection between melancholy and humor:"[30]

Just like melancholy is sadness become light, humor is that form of comedy which has lost its bodily weight [...] and which throws into question the self, the world, and its whole network of relations.[31]

Travers's writing is elegantly ironic and inexorably melancholic. Travers writes with great lucidity and conviction about the comedy or humorous content of everyday life. And yet she does not fail to recognize and express the emotional bond that ties us even heartbreakingly to our everyday lives, making us willing to forgive the inevitable imperfections. This is because we link the trivial and laughable in our lives to memories of who and what we used to be, the places we grew up in, our past, and especially (in books talking about and to children) our childhood, that moment in life when the outside world was the source of wonder and richness.

Discussing what for him is the ideal style, Calvino states that:

> I am not talking about any form of compact or opaque melancholy [...] but a veil of minute particles of humours and sensations, a fine dust of atoms which is what ultimately constitutes the multiplicity of things.[32]

If the writer can conceive of the world on this level, that is, as a complex system of atoms, then his writing will attain a degree of lightness enriched with stimulating, sensual detail. On close analysis, the images that result will appear as if suspended and yet precise, so great is the sense of internal balance created by the accumulation of these tiny details. What results is a work that attains lightness through its embracing of multiplicity and possibility. According to Calvino, the first modern writer to contextualize in his work a similar atomistic idea of the universe was Cyrano de Bergerac:

> In pages where his irony cannot conceal a genuine cosmic excitement, Cyrano celebrates the unity of all things, animate and inanimate, the combination of elementary figures that determine the variety of living forms, and above all he conveys his sense of the precariousness inherent in the processes which have brought these into being, i.e., he reveals how nearly man missed being man and life, life and the world, the world.[33]

This reading can also be applied to the Mary Poppins books, in which Travers shamelessly undermines and subverts quotidian reality using its very elements, though in a liberated way, in a way that sets them free of previous definitions. This is how Cyrano manages to find "bonds of fraternity between men and cabbages," concludes Calvino, in a sense that holds true also for the Mary Poppins books, in which Travers, with unsettling realism, constantly contrasts "normal life," where things are seen as separate, with the flight toward universal fraternity.

THE PRIMITIVE VISION: THE MATERNAL RIGHT

Calvino's literary analysis of the theme of lightness (seen as this precariousness of being, as the possibility for identities to change, to shift, to be something else) leads him principally through the world of modern literature; yet anthropologists (especially those following in the footsteps of Bachofen) have found that such a vision of reality was diffuse in primitive societies. Bachofen's analysis of the concept of matriarchy was not concerned with the study of a specifically female authority, but in a broader and deeper sense centered on cultures whose decision-making activities were influenced less by the exigencies of reason than a more "maternal" form of affectivity. Such a way of life was diffuse in ancient pre-patriarchal societies and remained more or less alive until, in the Western world, the Sophist tradition and Aristotelian philosophy took hold. What succeeded this, that is, the patriarchal organization of life and thought, imposed itself so strongly that modern man has now completely forgotten the previous way of conceiving life, himself and the world.[34] The matriarchal vision (or sensation) of life was founded on the belief that man belonged to the earth and was thus in close contact with the cosmos. Primitive societies believed that all the elements of life belonged to a single system bound together by a sort of magical link, meaning that all that *was*, was somehow linked and united.

We have already discussed the chapter entitled "Full Moon" in *Mary Poppins*, where all the animals in the zoo celebrate a solemn rite worshipping the snake, who in conversation with the children, states that

> We are all made of the same stuff, remember, we of the Jungle, you of the City. The same substance composes us—the tree overhead, the stone beneath us, the bird, the beast, the star—we are all one, moving to the same end. Remember that when you no longer remember me, my child".
>
> "But how can tree be stone? A bird is not me. Jane is not a tiger," said Michael stoutly.
>
> "You think not?" said the Hamadryad's hissing voice. "Look!" and he nodded his head towards the moving mass of creatures before them. Birds and animals were now swaying together, closely encircling Mary Poppins, who was rocking lightly from side to side. Backwards and forwards, went the swaying crowd, keeping time together, swinging like the pendulum of a clock. Even the trees were bending and lifting gently, and the moon seemed to be rocking in the sky as a ship rocks on the sea.

"Bird and beast and stone and star—we are all one, all one—" murmured the Hamadryad, softly folding his hood about him as he himself swayed between the children.

"Child and serpent, star and stone—all one." (I, pp. 143–144)

Such a vision of the world understands all relationships as being ruled by chance and destined to end. We also find this in the adventures of Mary Poppins, where the Banks children are, in fact, very often worried or sad because each time they visit a Beyond place with Mary Poppins, the figures they meet suddenly disappear and are irrevocably lost, leaving the children wondering if they will ever meet them again. Yet, the idea that "nothing lasts forever" was such an important truth in the matriarchal vision, and is such an important lesson to relearn today, that it is one of the very few statements explicitly uttered by this very special governess whose origins seem to reach back to the very beginning of human culture. It was only later in the history of man and his institutions that the notion of biological and generational continuity (and all the social interests bounds up with this) took hold; previous to this, man's relationship was with the earth (being that which contained him). The maternal womb was therefore seen as a secondary, accidental container, and the relationship with the mother was to some degree fragile and not deemed particularly necessary.

The cosmic structure of the world was seen as being more important than familial links, and the mother's task was simply to bring children forth into this structure. Primitive man did not differentiate the world according to the different species, and Mary Poppins expresses a similar perspective; her philosophy is one that admits and accepts all elements into a universe that mixes and inverts them so that all notions of proper or improper are thrown into question. And by implicitly but constantly questioning the role of the family in its bourgeois form, Mary Poppins, who is an outsider to the family and whose very presence and role as a governess displays its futility (at least for the everyday life of the children who have been handed over to her), constantly underlines the greater importance of other kinds of bonds in her adventures and can certainly be considered closer to a primitive vision of the world than to the modern middle-class vision that turned the family into the bulwark of its most important values, hierarchies, and distinctions. So primitive is this vision, in fact, that, as already suggested, it has been forgotten to the point of becoming unknown and "other" in the Western world. The fact that Travers's governess seeks to reinstate this vision should not therefore be thought of as a regression, but rather as an uncanny experience (in the Freudian sense) for modern man—that is, in the end, a potentially subversive and liberating provocation. And if to primitive man, who existed in a form of prenatal symbiosis with Mother Earth, essentially belonging to the cosmos, this could be seen as a source of anguish and provoked a sense of fragmentation (given the many potentially disorienting reference points),[35] Travers seeks both to give her readers access to this salvaged world and to mitigate the potential anxiety caused by coming into contact with the multiplicity and indeterminacy of this world, mediating the experience through the figure of Mary Poppins whose guiding presence lends a sense of security to the reader.

The existence of humans in the primitive vision was in a sense guaranteed by nature or the world, seen as total, all-including entities, as was their cyclical coming into being and passing away. The world and nature were thus experienced as something ungraspable in their complexity and yet, at the same time, deeply reassuring. It was as if nothing could be lost because man belonged to a dimension that also contained the rest of existence—whether visible and tangible or not. And in fact, even if "nothing lasts forever" (in a specific shape or manner), the other somehow complementary truth Mary Poppins likes to state, in her typically paradoxical and sententious manner, is "all that is lost is somewhere."

In her study of primitive cultures, Corinna Cristiani speaks of invisible threads contained in a "prevalent maternal code"—threads that weave together into a single circuit each and every element of the human and natural world. This allowed for the transfer of certain mysterious powers or forces from one dimension to another, from the external to the internal, from the world beyond the village, or door (with its infinite otherness) to the here.

Primitive "knowledge" was cryptic and mystic in nature, founded as it was on a relationship to the world that allowed for "truths" that could neither be modified nor elaborated but merely transmitted. In the Mary Poppins books we find many instances in which the governess and the strange characters she meets seem to be engaged in some form of mysterious ritual activity that superimposes itself over the concrete and verifiable actions they undertake and that the children are not meant to understand.

"How extraordinary!" says Jane on meeting the ancient Miss Corry, who treats the Banks children with kindness but is inordinately cruel to her own. What surprises the children is that Miss Corry and Mary Poppins already seem to know each other:

"Not at all, my dear," said Miss Corry, chuckling. "Or rather, not so extraordinary as other things I could mention." And she winked largely at Mary Poppins. [...] Then she gave Mary Poppins a long look and nodded her head slightly. Mary Poppins nodded slightly in return. It seemed as if some secret had passed between them. (I, pp. 105–106)

On another occasion, Mary Poppins converses with a starling:

The starling stared at her.
    "Ha!" he said suddenly, and turned and looked enquiringly at Mary Poppins. Her quiet glance met his in a long look. [...] Then with a little shake of the head the starling turned away.
    "So—it's happened," he said quietly to Mary Poppins. She nodded. (I, p. 123)

In the chapter entitled "Full Moon" the children are taken to the zoo in the dead of the night where they find everything inverted, the animals are all roaming around freely, engaged in preparing for a secret celebration.

...another seal had emerged from the water and was whispering in his ear.
    "Who?" said the first seal. "Speak up!"
    The second seal whispered again. Jane caught the words "Special visitors—Friends of" and then nothing more. (I, p. 131)

Later, the long-awaited king of the world arrives, and:

Jane said, in a whisper: "He talks as though he were a great Lord."
    "He *is*. He's the lord of our world—the wisest and most terrible of us all," said the Brown Bear softly and reverently.
    The Hamadryad smiled, a long, slow, secret smile, and turned to Mary Poppins. (I, p. 139)

Until the arrival of the Sophists, human philosophy was dominated by a cosmological outlook that saw man as being merely a constituent part of the whole natural world. Pre-Socratic thought sought to trace the unity of the world to the very substance at the base of all of its elements and to the laws governing its "becoming." Substance, as the unifying principle, was both the matter and the force governing all beings and their transformation. It was Aristotle who took the definitive step toward rendering human philosophy and the organization of knowledge significantly "paternal" in nature. Such an outlook imposed a new form of rationality founded on method, experimentation, and scientific theory, and opened up a gap between human thought and the object world, resulting ultimately in the sterilization and neutralization of the latter in order to control it fully (not only mentally but also practically). In this new way of looking at the world, there was no space for occult or more than human considerations, and the ancient natural sympathies linking man and all that was not him were broken. This new context consequently saw the emergence of the intellectual scientist, devoted to expanding (without scruples) his own knowledge, which was considered significantly more important than the "objects" it sought to comprehend and categorize. This formulation, of course, called for preparation, and to this end (and in order to disseminate this new approach), the School was founded, an institution that in its organization was specifically paternal in nature. The school cultivated the intellect and sought to direct it toward a scientific rationality that came to be considered man's most important faculty. It was the school that started to impose new forms of organization on the transmission of knowledge, the most remarkable difference from the past being the separation of learning into the different disciplines. The ancient unity of traditional wisdom that characterized primitive thought was now deemed chaotic, and the new scientific disciplines began to undermine the former system of belief. Man no longer belonged to the perennial flux and indeterminacy of Mother Earth; he was no longer linked to and brother of all that came, like him, from her womb. Rather, he started to define and perceive himself according to that which differentiated him, as man, from the natural world. It is worth noting in this respect that, in the Mary Poppins books, even though time clearly goes by and seasons pass and at least the two eldest children are old enough to attend school, there is, in fact, never any reference to school or schooling.

Bachofen suggests that in the history of knowledge two different perspectives can be traced, which correspond to the categories of "maternal" and "paternal" codes. Maternal systems of thought are characterized by sudden insights and an immediacy of knowledge whilst paternal systems function according to the painstakingly slow and progressive form of understanding that results from a rational approach. Bachofen states that maternal systems of thought give a significantly greater degree of life and color to the world than do paternal systems, which see the world through the rational intellect.[36] The maternal faculty of imagination allows for vital, brilliant results, whilst the rational intellectual approach, deemed limiting by Bachofen, produces results that are lifeless and hollow. The maternal universe is characterized by a great and immediate capacity for communication (and not only verbal communication) between people and things, suggesting the possibility of relationships existing across different species and an ever possible intimacy. Against this universalizing vision, which conceives of no internal barriers and sees existence as a form of brotherhood, Bachofen pits the paternalistic principle which attempts to separate the flux of life into clearly distinct categories. It was as a result of this new vision of life that the family as a distinct, diversified unit came into being.

In her study of the notions of contamination and taboo, Mary Douglas[37] analyzes "primitive" visions of the world and suggests that in primitive societies different styles of life existed side by side and that the concept of human limits or limitations was alien to the primitive vision. The forces of the universe were felt so strongly by each individual that it was impossible to talk in terms of an external physical environment: the individual was seen to be so bound to the cosmos that he/she was somehow the center of magnetic forces. Also, all these cosmological systems of thought believed that the individual could be altered or changed by the powers that they themselves or someone else possessed. Thus the transforming energy of the cosmos inhered in each individual life. This way of understanding the world is possibly evident in the Mary Poppins books, especially when we meet those strange characters engaged in "abnormal" activities (e.g., one makes a wish that immediately becomes true; another laughs so much that he begins to float into the air) or when the Banks children come face to face with the most incredible experiences. On the surface, these appear to signal a complete break with any kind of logic, and yet this is not the case. These experiences take place beyond the logic and laws governing everyday "normal" or social life, but on a very profound level are seen to be in harmony with the cosmos as a whole and its own "logic." They really are only apparently gratuitous and casual; they belong to the greater life and breath of the universe, taking place, as they do, always at very particular moments (solstices, equinoxes, full moons, midsummer, midnight), following specific astral movements, and being linked by a series of coincidences that creates a sense of harmony and reaches out to the idea of the eternal.

The primitive vision of life and the world found no clear distinction between person and object, and relationships between people were expressed on a symbolic level—through gestures, rites, and gifts. Again, we find something very similar in the Mary Poppins books:

"Am I not—?" he paused and looked around him.

"The lord of the jungle," hissed all the snakes in unison, as if the question and the answer were part of a well-known ceremony.

The Hamadryad nodded. "So," he said, "what seems good to me will seem so to you. It is a small enough gift, dear Mary, but it may serve for a belt or a pair of shoes, even a hatband—these things all come in useful you know."

And with that he began to sway gently from side to side, and it seemed to Jane and Michael as they watched that little waves were running up his body from the tail to the head. Suddenly he gave a long, twisting, corkscrew leap and his olden outer skin lay on the floor, and in its place he was wearing a new coat of shining silver.

"Wait!" said the Hamadryad as Mary Poppins bent to pick up the skin. "I will write a Greeting upon it." And he ran his tail very quickly along his thrown skin, deftly bent the golden sheath into a circle, and diving his head through this as though it were a crown, offered it graciously to Mary Poppins. She took it, bowing. (I, pp. 140–141)

And again:

Mary Poppins bowed toward the Hamadryad very ceremoniously, and without a backwards glance at the children went running towards the huge green square in the centre of the zoo.

"You may leave us," said the Hamadryad to the Brown Bear who, after bowing humbly, ran off with his cap in his hand to where the other animals were congregating around Mary Poppins. (I, p. 142)

In another equally unusual scene, Maia, one of the Pleiades stars, descends to the earth in the form of a bright, vivacious little girl. This time it is Mary Poppins who presents the gift sanctioning the contact between the two different dimensions. As long as it is performed ritually, these scenes all seem to say, the contact is both possible and not dangerous.

[Mary Poppins] whipped off her new gloves and thrust one on to each of Maia's hands.

"There!" she said gruffly. "It's cold today. You'll be glad of them."

Maia looked at the gloves, hanging very large and almost empty upon her hands. She said nothing, but moving very close to Mary Poppins, she reached up her spare arm and put it round Mary Poppins' neck and kissed her. A long look passed between them, and they smiled as people smile who understand each other. Maia turned then, and with her hand lightly touched the cheeks of Jane and Michael. And for a moment they all stood in a ring at the windy corner gazing at each other as though they were enchanted. (I, p. 157)

Anthropologists underline, in fact, how these exchanges and ritual gestures in primitive visions of the world—like the one brought about by Mary Poppins—could take place either between humans or between humans and cosmic entities. Primitive thought saw the world almost as a thinking, intelligent entity that functioned according to a set of decipherable symbols and signs. The world, seen from this perspective, is a supreme interlocutor; it is something that, being so intertwined with man, cannot be seen as "other," nor can it be left "outside the door."

Mary Poppins (and all that she does) is surrounded and encompassed at all times by a sense of necessity, which presents itself as a force that must be followed (evidenced, for example, by the wind that carries her toward the Banks household or out of it again). This necessity that she embraces and brings with her pushes the "normal" people she comes across to act in ways that correspond no longer to their conscious will but, quite surprisingly, to what their deepest needs might be; these needs running so deep, in fact, that they were previously unexpressed and were not even recognized. This very often causes great pleasure, especially to the children who know how to let themselves go and who feel suddenly full of new possibilities; yet, at the same time, their adventures are never merely entertaining: whatever happens is profoundly sacred and inexorably powerful. What moves everything is a highly dramatic force that must be approached with utmost respect and that requires total commitment—indeed, it seems to demand that we give ourselves up to it entirely, or that someone does so on our behalf. Such a figure would then embody the essence and power of this necessity (in much the same way that the Bacchante embody the essence of Dionysus) and would allow us to participate in the "sphere of necessity" (seen paradoxically as liberated possibility) without the danger of our losing the ability to live among our fellow men in a more ordered, limited environment, which is, however, familiar, reassuring, and as necessary for us.

It is interesting to note, in this respect, that in her writing, Travers is careful never to alienate or distance her readers too much from their "real" world. Each potentially solemn or moving scene that renders the figure of Mary Poppins overly serious or profound is tempered by some comic or laughable detail that mitigates the tension of the moment and allows the child-reader to experience once again a sensation of familiarity and intimacy. Travers employs precisely this technique in the above-mentioned scene depicting the wonderful, breathtaking adventure in the sky on the back of peppermint walking sticks: the children are brought back home with characteristic punctuality and are put to bed, only to awaken during the night to find that the candy sticks left in the corner of their room magically take flight once more. They drift out of the window and head towards a full, blue-colored moon. The significance of this becomes clear if we remember that before the adventure had taken place, Mr. Banks had answered his children's pleas to go horseback riding by saying that he would buy them a horse the day the moon turned blue. As he spoke these words, the Banks children noted how Mary Poppins had smiled mysteriously:

> They turned together from the window and the moon's blue light streamed into the room. It lay like water upon the floor. It crept across the children's cots till it reached the bed in the corner. Then, full and clear and bold and blue, it shone upon Mary Poppins. She did not wake. But she smiled a secret, satisfied smile as though, even in her deepest dreams, she was thoroughly pleased with herself. They stood beside her hardly breathing as they watched that curious smile. Then they looked at each other and nodded wisely.
>
> "She knows," said Michael, in a whisper. And Jane breathed an answering "Yes."
>
> For a moment they smiled at her sleeping figure. Then they tiptoed back to their beds.
>
> The blue moonlight lay over their pillows. It lapped them round as they closed their eyes. It gleamed upon Mary Poppins' nose as she lay in her old camp bed. And presently, as though blue moons were nothing to her, she turned her face away. She pulled the sheet up over her head and huddled down deeper under the blankets. And soon the only sound in the Nursery was Mary Poppins' snoring. (III, pp. 125–126)

Although Travers is careful to render Mary Poppins as familiar as possible to the reader by means of a funny and laughable physical description that makes her somehow more "human" or more like us, she never actually reduces the sense we have of her being something quite powerful. The reader gains security and a sense of possible proximity from descriptions of the governess snoring, or of her inordinately large feet and scarecrow-like gait. And yet her halo of "otherness" is never lost: it is her defining characteristic and that which makes her so significant as the figure whose task it is to convey to the bourgeois family that alternative ways of life exist. Although Travers assigns her governess a whole series of comic habits and amusing moods, we never lose the sense of her being very special. Her competence, elegance and total self-sufficiency lend her an air of dignity and nobility that distance her from all potential compromise or small-mindedness: it is clear from her behavior that she never works towards personal ends, nor just mechanically (like so many of the "ordinary" people seem to do) but in keeping with the principle of absolute necessity.

Mary Poppins's difference from all other characters populating the everyday world and her distance from any truly recognizable role (her role as governess quickly reveals itself to be a mask, or rather, an expedient enabling her to draw others into her pursuit of necessity) make her irresistibly fascinating to the children of the Banks household who are captivated by her integrity, confidence, style, seriousness, silence, and inner solitude, and who are still young enough to believe in the same absolutes that underpin Mary Poppins's existence as something that is not "beyond" but can and must be experienced in everyday life. No other "normal" adult points to this, all of whom being simply and blindly at the service of their specific social order or position. In her refusal to conform to the premises and interests of the everyday social world, Mary Poppins reaches the status of hero—a hero not only of her own time but, intimately connected as she is to everything, a timeless and mythical hero.

A CHILDLIKE VISION OF THE WORLD:
THE PRE-OEDIPAL PHASE

From a psychoanalytic rather than anthropological point of view, which more specifically refers not to whole cultures but to the individual's inner world, we find that the above-described ideas regarding the cosmos and our place in it or relationship to the external world also characterize the pre-oedipal phase of a child's development. Freud defined the sensations governing this phase as "oceanic."[38] Psychoanalytical theory posits that a child at the mother's breast distinguishes no boundary between the mother and itself, and the mother's body is perceived as a continuous extension of its own body. Thus, it would be quite reasonable to suggest that the adult's sense of self is a restricted residue of a more inclusive relationship uniting the self with the rest of the external world. The adult's sense of self is clearly delimited by the boundary of the body that is separated from an external world perceived as "other" to the self. This, however, does not preclude the possibility of our experiencing a latent, more primitive, and obscure sense of continuity between the self and the external world and the notion of a fluid unity existing prior to the emergence of difference inheres in the memory.

The notion of wholeness, founded on correspondence and identity rather than on differentiation, underpins the episodes involving the youngest of the Banks children—the twins, John and Barbara, in the first book, and the newborn baby, Annabella, in the second. These scenes signal the fact that unlike adults and older children, young children experience an intimate, immediate bond with the natural world whose language is by no means alien to them. In "John and Barbara's Story" the twins, who are lying in their cots whilst Mary Poppins busies herself with her own affairs, suddenly begin conversing with the natural world. They speak to the sun, to the wind, to the shadows of the trees, and, finally, to a starling who tells them that soon they will lose this "natural language" just as Jane and Michael already have.

Why, only last Monday I heard Jane remark that she wished she knew what language the Wind spoke.

"I know," said Barbara. "It's astonishing. And Michael always insists—haven't you heard him? That the starling says "Wee-Twe-ee-ee!" He seems not to know that the starling says nothing of the kind, but speaks exactly the same language as we do. [...]"

"They did once," said Mary Poppins, folding one of Jane's nightgowns.

"What?" said John and Barbara together in a very surprised voice.

"Really? You mean they understood the starling and the Wind and—"

"And what the trees say and the language of the sunlight and stars—of course they did! *Once,*—" said Mary Poppins.

"But how is it that they have forgotten it all?" said John, wrinkling up his forehead and trying to understand. [...]

"Because they've grown older," explained Mary Poppins. "Barbara, put on your socks at once, please".

"That's a silly reason," said John, looking sternly at her.

"It's the true one, then," said Mary Poppins. [...]

"Well, [...] I know *I* shan't forget when *I* get older."

"Nor I," said Barbara. [...]

"Yes, you will," said Mary Poppins firmly.

"Huh!" said the starling contemptuously. [...] "Of course you'll forget—same as Jane and Michael." [...] "It isn't your fault of course," he added more kindly. "You'll forget because you just can't help it. There never was a human being that remembered after the age of one—at the very latest—except, of course, Her." And he jerked his head over his shoulder at Mary Poppins. [...]

It was not very long afterwards that the teeth, after much trouble, came through as all teeth must and the Twins had their first birthday.

The day after the birthday party the starling, who had been on holiday at Bournemouth, came back to Number Seventeen, Cherry Tree Lane. [...]

"Well, Barbarina," he began in his soft, wheedling voice, "anything for the old fellow today?"

"Be-lah-belah-belah!" said Barbara, crooning gently as she continued to eat her arrowroot biscuit.

The starling, with a start of surprise, hopped a little nearer.

"I said," he repeated more distinctly, "is there anything for the old fellow today, Barby dear?"

"Ba-loo-ba-loo-ba-loo!" murmured Barbara. [...]

The starling stared at her.

"Ha!" he said suddenly, and turned and looked enquiringly at Mary Poppins. Her quiet glance met his in a long look. [...]

"So it's happened!" he said quietly to Mary Poppins.

She nodded. (I, pp. 117—123)

In *Mary Poppins Comes Back* a similar scene takes place in which the newborn baby, Annabella, begins talking to a starling. Once again, the child who has not yet entered the realm of language and reason is seen to be in close contact with the four elements of the cosmos; Annabella repeats that she comes from the sea, from the sun and stars, from the earth's forests and wild animals, and that she traveled to where she is now in a dream from which she has only just awoken. Such a scene is reminiscent of Wordsworth's famous "Ode to Immortality":

Our birth is but a sleep and a forgetting:
　　The soul that rises with us, our life's star,
　　Hath had elsewhere its setting,
　　And cometh form afar:
　　Not in entire forgetfulness,
　　And not in entire nakedness,
　　But trailing clouds of glory do we come
　　From God who is our Home:
　　Heaven lies about us in our infancy![39]

The notion that what we lose with our conscious mind remains in our dreams is also a familiar theme running through the Aboriginal mythology and cosmogony of Australia, Travers's country of birth. Both Travers and Wordsworth seem to be saying that newborn infants exist within this original cosmic unity but that, as the child grows, this sense of unity and wholeness quickly transforms itself into a fading memory.

In a book that applies psychoanalytical readings to the works of female authors, the feminist critic Jean Wyatt[40] suggests that the self has a double identity (notwithstanding the loss of memory); whilst the more evident of these identities is socially constructed, the deeper identity is formed from the play of a different set of desires and cognitive possibilities, which makes it impossible for the self to be entirely coherent and consistent. Thus, the self cannot be entirely subject to the influences of culture and society because it contains that primordial form of energy capable of undermining and transgressing social formation. According to Wyatt, the fluidity of self-identity and the oscillation between symbiosis and differentiation, between being separate and being together, that characterizes the pre-oedipal structure (that is, the way in which very young children perceive themselves), threatens the very basis of the Western patriarchal system. Wyatt describes this system as being exemplified by the distinct self-contained and unitary individual, who is positioned at the heart of syntax (as the subject "I"), at the center of democratic bourgeois ideology (as the citizen) and at the top of the hierarchical scale of development as forwarded by post-Freudian orthodoxy (as the separate and self-contained self).[41]

Wyatt's study deals with the liberating and transformative potential of the pre-oedipal perspective in the novels of certain women writers. In her book, she examines the breaks introduced into the narrative discourse—and thus into the reader's mind—by pre-oedipal contradictions or impertinences, and explores the various ways in which a recovery of the indeterminacy between the self and what is other-than-the-self can liberate creativity.

Wyatt's text makes it clear that it is not only women who can enter into this more genuine and prejudice-free relationship with the world, and points out that the ecstatic return to this all-encompassing relationship with the maternal world also lies at the heart of the poetic vision of Keats and Wordsworth (whom Travers counted among her favorite poets, together with Blake) and many writers belonging to the romantic movement. Wyatt's attention however centers on contemporary female writers whose fiction is characterized by a high degree of fluidity on the level of plot, characterization, style, etc. The concept of language is fundamental to Wyatt's argument, and certain of the observations she puts forward form direct parallels with Mary Poppins's professed opinions on language or attitude toward it (the less you use it, the better, is what we learn from her). Wyatt claims that in using language, the individual subjects him/herself to logical forms that are the same forms that lie at the base of authority and control. To use language, then, means to find oneself inexorably caught up in the structures and demands of a patriarchal discourse whose categories and divisions feign neutrality but subtly organize the individual's thought according to predetermined, hierarchical constructs. In this respect, if we return to our discussion of the pre-oedipal twins of the Mary Poppins books, it is interesting to note that these young children are no longer able to understand and communicate with the voice of nature (and feel for the first time separate and other from it) at precisely the point at which they begin to learn the logically grammatical language of their parents—that is, when they begin to speak their very first words. The pre-oedipal phase coincides with the infant's first few months of life and is thus a preverbal phase, located outside social discourse that uses logic to make itself understood. If this is true:

> The idea that the pre-oedipal could introduce change seems preposterous, then, since it can only turn people inward, towards unnameable delights, leaving untouched the political sphere of shared language, responsibility, community and political agency, the domain where transformation is effected.[42]

Wyatt however is not in agreement, since to her:

> Pre-oedipal drive energies *can* get into language, and when they do they throw the fixed positions of language and the fixed categories of traditional epistemology into question. [...] Texts that incorporate a pre-oedipal perspective undermine the cognitive foundations of western epistemology.[43]

The grammar and syntax of our Western languages shape our understanding of the world and, in particular, the use of the first person pronoun indicates a distinct and separate subject, distanced from all that is not "I." Yet, for a text to be considered pre-oedipal in nature, its grammar and syntax do not necessarily have to be illogical. A text can be considered pre-oedipal, for example, if it chooses to omit the usual spatial and temporal specifications used to locate the reader in a concretely physical world; or again, if the narrator plays with the categories of being and nonbeing, subverting those most fundamentally logical and ontological concepts underpinning western philosophy.

Julia Kristeva[44] has shown how pre-oedipal energy and impulses participate in the production of language. Man produces meaning through a series of semiotic processes originating in the preverbal phase that are dialectically related to a series of symbolic processes brought into play by the speaking subject inscribed in a sociolinguistic system. Entry into the symbolic order, in which sign systems are used to create a specific meaning, automatically implies the division of the child into speaking subject and unconscious self. Kristeva points out that the speaking subject is the product of language structures and the ideology determining these structures, whilst the desires and impulses that cannot be subsumed into the sociolinguistic system make up the unconscious, which Kristeva considers to be a receptacle for the flux of primitive energy. Originating outside the symbolic order and its ideology, these pre-oedipal impulses circulate beneath language but are a continuous, potential source of input and threat for its logical structure and for our logical mind. Semiotic energy is essentially counter-cultural. Indeed, the main task of the pre-oedipal is to regain the lost unity of the self, and as such it undermines the demands of the symbolic order that stipulate that in order to comment on and interact with the object world, the speaking subject must be cut off from that world. Pre-oedipal energy inevitably enters the symbolic order (founded on the repression of this energy), and when it does so, it upsets and subverts that order; nowhere is this more evident than in literature. The semiotic processes evident in a literary work are not simply destructive: they are highly versatile and mutable, meaning that any subversion of standard ideology that takes place leads to the forging of a new literary form and of a whole new world—the ideological universe of the writer.

Pre-oedipal energy manifests itself in literary texts in various different ways. Syntactical laws might be undermined in an attempt to bring to the fore the rhythmic quality of language; traditional word order might be transgressed in order to create the effect of alliteration; or grammatical structures might be subverted in the creation of assonance, repetition, etc. Travers's writing is by no means alien to this form of linguistic subversion. In one particular scene, the Banks children emerge disorientated from another adventure, and when questioned by their father (who refuses to accept or understand any form of difference), they react in the following way:

> But Jane and Michael could not answer. [...] They writhed and rolled and rocked on the floor and gulped and gurgled with laughter. (II, p. 178)

In this description Travers undermines traditional rules governing punctuation by omitting the commas that would usually separate the verbs. This heightens the rhythmic effect of the section which, when read aloud, is reminiscent of a nursery rhyme; moreover, the repetition of "liquid" consonants ("r" and "l" in this case) creates a sense of fluidity that might be said to symbolize the flux of energy running between and linking self and things. We find the same technique being used in other episodes, for example, when the children visit the fairground, or when the ring of dancing animals is described, or again when the children come face to face with symbols of cosmic unity; here we find phrases such as "turning and turning and round and round" or "Bird and beast and stone and star—we all one, all one", constructions that have a liberating effect on readers, encouraging them to let go, and enabling them to step outside the rigid confines of self-control.

Kristeva defines this type of language use as poetic and emphasizes its subversive effect on the reader. Discourse that privileges rhythm and sound quality over content releases the reader's pre-oedipal energy whose roots can be traced back to infancy when language was experienced as sound and rhythm rather than as a carrier of meaning. When the sound quality of language is emphasized, syntax and word order are often compromised, which in turn implies the compromising of the sociolinguistically constructed self; this supposedly unitary self which is fixed and entirely present unto itself begins to dissolve and is replaced by a flux of pre-oedipal energy that reacts far more strongly to the material qualities of language than to the logic and meaning of the words.

> The unity of the speaking subject breaks down; this is a revolutionary moment, for the reader has to recognize his/her own heterogeneity and hence the inadequacy of the social construct of his or her own identity as singular and coherent. Thrown into a flux of drive energies, the reading subject becomes a questionable subject-in-process no longer fixed but in transit towards a new construction of identity. Hence, he/she is open to new possibilities. [45]

Answering the claim that the pre-oedipal flux of energy is socially useless because it exists beyond the socially constructed language system, Kristeva points out that only the subject-in-process can take part in social change, and that it is only when this fluid identity is allowed to emerge (in and through language) that change can be provoked or accelerated.

Pre-oedipal energy, of course, speaks many languages. It is a language of the senses and transports us back to that time when contact with the world was filtered exclusively through the senses. The reader's pre-oedipal, sensual character is thus stimulated not just by the sound of "poetic" language, but also by the penetrating description of smells, by the evocation of light and shade and color, and by scenes of bodies coming into contact. Fiction that makes recourse to a wide range of inputs capable of recalling or immediately reconnecting us to the pre-oedipal, then, works simultaneously on two different levels. On one level, these sensuous descriptions stir in the reader an unconscious response, whilst the narrative content appeals to the conscious mind and its need to process information logically. Thus the reader absorbs a sort of subtext—images strike the senses and allow him/her to enter into a relationship with the "real," which differs greatly from the "realistic" relationship encouraged by content-based elements such as traditional plotlines, specific spatio-temporal definitions, or the realistic description of officially recognizable characters.

Wyatt suggests that the self is divided into separate parts that react in different ways to language. She then goes on to explain how reading a text that taps into the pre-oedipal energy of the reader can upset and modify the reader's socially constructed identity. If the reader's conscious, rational self were not underscored by his/her pre-oedipal self, "subversive" textual moments would go unnoticed, and it is the "subversive" language of touch, song, smells, of hot and cold, of heaviness and lightness, and more generally of the senses that allows us to experience a nonlogical connection with the world.

The Mary Poppins books lend themselves well to a reading of this sort; the story can be read simultaneously on two different levels, each corresponding to two different ways of approaching and understanding the world. The conscious reading of the text involves an appreciation of the surface narrative, whilst the subconscious reading sidesteps the urge to rationalize and responds to the uncontrollable immediacy of sensitive stimuli. Wyatt calls this a challenge to the socially indoctrinated, conscious subject.[46] At a first glance, the Mary Poppins books appear to be written in a very traditional narrative style. Tradition—and the notion of "sticking to the rules"—is also conveyed in the content by means of the repeated advice, admonitions, and warnings of the parents, park keepers, and bourgeois adults and in the continual references to "good manners" and "common sense" as things to be respected, learned, and acted upon. This language of abstract, though familiar signs, speaks to the conscious mind of the reader and appeals to that set of commonsensical values and "proper" behavioral strategies learned during childhood and which, as a form of cultural ideology, constitute a scale of judgment into which all possible action is fed. And yet at the same time, the reader is presented with a string of concretely subversive scenes and images showing people acting in ways or doing things that undermine not merely because social, legal, or moral rules are being broken, but because, on a deeper level, what is described would be deemed utterly impossible (but obviously maybe it isn't) by the ordered world.

This idea is conveyed for example in the chapter "The Laughing Gas" where the protagonists cannot stop laughing and start to float, or in Robertson Ay's ode to idling away as the best means to attain wisdom, or again when objects come to life and move out of their usual context in order to interact with the other characters and the reader, or when the characters take flight, and walk on clouds or along rainbows, or set foot on the moon. It also clearly underpins all those occasions on which Mary Poppins's "Beyond places" are described as being populated by images of chaos and circularity, two motifs that challenge and undermine social structures and their attendant mentalities (orderly and linear). The circles of dancing bodies we often find in the books challenge the patriarchal structure and its need to define social relations according to a strict hierarchy, because the circle expresses the continuity of the pre-oedipal phase, a unity without beginning or end and without limits that precedes the patriarchal exigencies of differentiation and distinction.

One of the reasons why these books (and their main character) have been so successful might be precisely because they succeed in speaking to both sides of the reader. On the one hand, they appeal to the familiar and generalized ideas of "right" and "good"; and yet, on the other hand, they also speak independently to the repressed and forgotten impulses directed toward autonomy and possibility that live alongside our surrendered, conformist identities.

Books like the Mary Poppins series make use of immediately recognizable figures and emblems (rather than rational discourse) to expose the ideological contradictions inherent in our social lives. The novelty of these narrative moments and their alienation from the usual, more official, or ideological representations of social living serve to trip the reader, and the resulting reading experience is significantly complex because the reader is called upon to entertain two opposing existential and cognitive perspectives at the same time. Ultimately, this potentially destabilizing process is to be seen as constructive, not in any traditional "educational" or strictly "civilizing" sense, of course, but for the fact that its novelty reinvigorates and rejuvenates and points to different possibilities.

Freud's description of an "oceanic sensation"—the sensation of a limitless connection to the world—as existing side by side with the separated self (and his theory that previous phases of development can be drawn upon throughout life) split the academic community. On the one hand, it was thought that seeking refuge in a primitive vision of the world was a form of regression and implied immaturity; on the other, this move was considered ultimately creative because it allowed the individual to seek innovatively to integrate previous modes of thought with present modes. Any impulse that challenges the socially constructed self leads toward change and possibility. If this is true, then qualities that have been considered "immature" by orthodox Freudians can be given a new value or meaning. Literature embodies this challenge to the maturity of the socially constructed civil self by presenting a series

of alternatives that, far from being synonymous with failure or immaturity, quite simply privilege the quality of difference. The original and
more intimate, more involving levels of integration between self and
world can indeed be found intact in the adult as the dynamic sources of
a different and no less valid way of thinking as well as a higher sense of
(otherwise impossible) creativity.

Psychologists and theorists in the field of art agree that new
ideas are the fruit of a strategic "withdrawal" from the dominant,
socially acceptable modes of thinking; if these common structures
are not rejected or abandoned, the conscious self will apply the rigid
frames organizing officially accepted perspectives on the world
to the vagueness and imprecision of subconscious intuitions, thus
diminishing their value. Indeed, it might just be that in order to go
forward, one must first go back. Going backwards is a way of not
standing still, for if we stand still we refuse to enter the flux of life,
we refuse to live life as autonomously and fully as possible. And ultimately this refusal implies acceptance of the discontent produced
by habitual ways of thinking and espouses a mechanical, automated
and predetermined approach to life. All hope of finding a way to
really live and participate in life, something that implies risk and
audacity and that necessitates a continual throwing into question of
the structures governing life, would be lost. Only with the rejection
of habitual modes of thought can the individual establish an innovatively meaningful and continually significant (and thus creative)
relationship with the external world and live each new moment as if
for the first time.[47]

Giving meaning to, or finding the meaning of, things is a "transitional" experience ("trans," as in the case of shamans, of flight, of
dance, of any going beyond is, again, a key word) linking the internal
world to the external world, in which the subject's ontological status
equates with its being both a part of the self and a part of the independent external world. In this transitional phase, the otherwise opposing
subject and object act on each other, forming a reciprocal relationship
founded on the negotiation of meaning (expressing itself not merely
as cognitive meaning but rather vital meaning), something that creates itself in quite an unpredictable manner, only in the moment in
which it actually takes place, and always with the complete involvement of both players. Paul Klee has called this transitional moment—
or dimension—he always longed to enter, an "intermediary world."[48]
In this, the consciousness of the subject has evolved to such an extent
that it can penetrate the surface reality of natural phenomenon and
see (and, hopefully, be able to represent) all that actually belongs to

nature as its potential and possible act. For Paul Klee, it was art that allowed access to this world—a natural (not an invented) world that, in order to be properly seen, required a very special way of looking, one that

> belongs to children, to madmen, and to primitives. What I am talking about is the kingdom of the unborn and the dead, the kingdom of that which might yet come or which wants to come, but which must not come: this is the intermediary world.[49]

Klee called this the intermediary world because it existed somewhere between the perceived worlds. He was able to grasp it at a deep level and succeeded in finding its equivalent (i.e., representable) form. Such an approach—essential to an effective and provocative art—opposes both positivist realism and pure fantasy; it gives access to a space in which habit dies and in which the revolutionary suddenly becomes possible (the possible being something latent in the very reality and needing someone to perceive and represent it). When symbolized, the structure of this world and the action represented become a system of signs in which each element is called into play, less as an art form than a form of life. Each represented element frees itself from the chains of determinism and quite simply expresses its own essence. All that counts in such a dimension is that things become, and take on the shape of, themselves (beyond the official and limiting definitions they were previously framed in).

Rosetta Infelise Fronza links this intermediary state to the spontaneous wisdom characterizing a child's perception:

> Representation deconstructs and reconstructs historical experience, transforming this into something new and quite beyond any banal reception. Intermediary images unfold rather than explain the world.[50]

Fronza thinks, like Travers, that the intermediary world expresses itself through dreams and myth and implies a potential loss of the self. And Paul Klee, again, illustrates the point: "I am but an apprentice with whom the great sorcerer plays his game of hide-and-seek. I lose myself in the intermediary world."[51] In saying this, Klee shows just how important it would be to have a figure like Mary Poppins to act as guide through this obscure world where there are no final words to define and clarify. It is a world not completely "other" because it is made up of those mute, unrecognized, and unperceived signs existing in the everyday reality. It is a world, though, where boundaries are abolished and all that "should" remain separate, ordered, and static becomes animated, somehow upset. Through the vision of what simply is (or, rather, becomes) something for which there are no words, the relationship between subject and thing is liberated of all moral judgment and tendency toward instrumentalization; such a relationship is suddenly denuded and, as we have seen in the Mary Poppins books, gains force and power. What in effect takes place is a liberation of the forces previously contained in myth which in turn breaks the spell of stasis that stultifies existence. The intermediary world reinstates that childlike wisdom that sees everything as being on the point of becoming, open to the future. Such wisdom is expressed as a universal and original dimension, not in the sense that it precedes history, but rather that it exists inside history, as a possible and unpredictably subverting force. And in this intermediary world, the socially constructed adult can regain that state in which, to borrow Musil's description of what happened in childhood, "objects came flying to us."[52]

In moments such as this, the subject's contact with, and understanding of, the world is a creative act where that which previously seemed not to exist is suddenly visible and where difference (from the self, from the known world) is encountered and somehow "understood." The term "understand" preoccupied Travers:

> To understand: for years I pondered on that word and tried to define its effect on myself. At last I came to the conclusion that what it means is the opposite of what it says; to understand is to stand under. Later I discovered that this was, in very fact, its meaning in Middle English. So, in order to understand, I come to something with my unknowing—my nakedness if you like: I stand under it and let it teach me, rain down its trust on me. That is, I think, what children do; they let it make room in them for a sense of justice, for the wicked fairy as well as the Sleeping Beauty, for dragons as well as princes. This grasping of the whole stick is an essential feature of the hero.[53]

One's mind (and identity) must remain open, in a state of "becoming," coming into being only at that moment in which it enters into contact with what will eventually define it. The mind must harmonize with the inherently flexible nature of internal and external boundaries; it must learn to change and move beyond its present structures. And this is something that must happen each time it comes into contact with what will become, in the absence of prejudice and fear, vividly singular, new, and, above all, worthy of attention:

The issue of "changing one's mind" [...] then takes the form: how can one give up one's habitual orientation to reality, one's reliance on distinct categories of thought, to slide back into a less differentiated way of thinking? An adult used to defending the line between inner and outer worlds, between self and other, may need some special solvent to diffuse the habitual containments of mental and emotional life.[54]

This "special solvent" could well be a figure like Mary Poppins who throws open all the doors and knocks down all the walls separating our different realities. Mary Poppins also comes to mind when Wyatt discusses the pre-oedipal (as opposed to oedipal) representations of the family. For Wyatt, the typical patriarchal family (as represented by the bourgeois Edwardian Banks family) is a prime example of a structure that encourages a bipolar binary thought process in which the world is structured according to the mutually exclusive (and excluding) notions of thesis and antithesis. This structuring, of course, stands in the way of the play of opposites that triggers creativity (that Travers champions) and that lies at the heart of the ability to mentally embrace two or more contradictory ideas, to conceive simultaneously of two or more opposing concepts.

The dichotomy separating paternal authority from maternal care, distinguishing the power and autonomy associated with the father from the dependence and subordination associated with the mother, leads the child at a certain point in its development to begin to view the world from a polarizing perspective. Two choices exist: either the child will become like its mother, the care provider, caught up in a system of symbiotic, natural relationships whose realm is the home and whose prime concern is to increase the well-being of others; or the child will become like the father, moving self-sufficiently through the external world, acquiring the security and the freedom of he who, in physical terms, is beholden to no one, and obtaining a position of power and respect.

Before he has learned these (in no way natural, but socially imposed) distinctions, the child's pre-oedipal vision of family relationships offers important structural alternatives that go beyond the power imbalances of the oedipal family unit that is inclined, as we have seen, to respect and obey the word of the father or father figure. In its total dependence on her, the pre-oedipal child sees the mother as the sole source of comfort, happiness, or deprival, and invests her with complete power.

Wyatt shows how "domestic" fiction such as *Little Women* or *The Color Purple* creates family structures that not only celebrate the good that comes from the mother (something that traditional representations also do) but also seek to give value to the mother's work. Such books convey a sense of respect for the mother's actual activities, and even when these are centered around the traditional task of running the household, they are imbued with a sense of stimulating richness, fascination, and even magic. We have already discussed the fact that what seems to characterize Mary Poppins more than anything else on an initial reading is the—at the same time amazing and "normal"—character's activities in the nursery (a place of tidied harmony and warm security, filled with wonderful smells and tastes, thanks to Mary Poppins). It is her domestic competence, before her magic, even, that provokes the admiration, trust, and respect of the children, and makes her infinitely more interesting than any other person they know.

Yet despite being totally dedicated to the care of the children, Mary Poppins is in no way bound by obligation to that single context: she comes and goes, enters and exits, she moves about in the private and public worlds, and although she allows herself to correspond to the stereotypical female role, she nevertheless remains true only to herself. Wyatt argues that it is only when the traditionally irreconcilable and contradictory roles of care provider (i.e., she who brings comfort and order to the domestic space and all who inhabit it) and authority (i.e., he who is autonomous and retains ultimate power within and beyond the domestic space) are seen to be shared between both parents that the growing individual can develop a capacity for continuous, creative, and stimulating thought. If these roles coincide within the same person, as is the case with Mary Poppins, the stimulus received by the child is even greater. Indeed, the Banks children find that Mary Poppins (who continually transgresses and undermines all predetermined criteria) unites the oppositions inherent in the traditionally distinct maternal and paternal roles, and as a result they learn to accommodate all the contradictions and ambiguity that such schemes embody and begin to conceive of life itself as "continuity." They begin to see points of contact between all those different elements that culture seeks to maintain as distinct and separate. This is not to say that they find similarities or sameness between these elements; quite to the contrary, they learn to appreciate the difference in the world and the way in which such difference can exist as a form of marvelously provocative unity. Fiction of this sort, says Wyatt, broadens the mind and enables us to imagine and desire something new.

THE PATH OF DESIRE

This notion of desiring something new is not quite as simple as it may seem. Desire is linked to the pleasure principle whose powerful drives influence the behavior of the individual. These drives often necessarily run counter to the sort of behavior determined by the reality principle that seeks to adapt such behavior to the exigencies of the social. Desire in this case is not just a deliberate and selfish wanting something, but rather a deeper, inalienable human impulse that reaches out towards something external to the self and that establishes a recognizably true and emotional relationship between the self and the not-self. This desire has the power to attract, impassion, and provoke the subject, endowing life with a sense of vitality (because the subject and all its senses are ultimately challenged), yet at the same time it can provoke a loss of stability that strikes the subject's sense of self as a self-conscious, self-controlling entity. Desire is always, ultimately, toward something "other" that is, as such, mysterious and unknown.

From a literary and etymological perspective, the term "desire" can be equated with our notion of flight, understood as a transcending of the fixed, closed quotidian reality in which we live. The Latin root of the verb "to desire" (*desiderare*) encompasses the word for "star" (*sidus, sideris*). It is perhaps toward the stars, then, that desire is directed in a voyage that leaves behind all that appears important only to the waking world of quotidian reality. It goes without saying, of course, that to any ordered reality bound up in the need to continually justify and maintain the supremacy of its laws and defining criteria (designed to uphold that order, faith in which is seen as vital for its raison d'être and survival), looking for, seeing, and, even more importantly, allowing the self to feel attraction towards, and fascination for, something different prove to be highly threatening.

The strength and persuasive legitimizing power of any institution, system or order rests on its ability to convince its subjects that its ways and needs are inherently "normal" and that only if the subject learns to reproduce these ways and needs can he/she be considered "normal" and will be granted a place, name and rights within that order. The strategy adopted (possibly unconsciously, but always collectively) by all conventional institutions is to try and make its citizens look inwards and to reject, and make them reject, all that is external or in any way different and unrecognizable; it is a strategy that drives and convinces its subjects to act according to its own ends, distributing power, responsibility, and trust to individuals only insofar as they respect its exigencies and definitions.

This is not to say that systems of this sort do not recognize intuitively that something different and "other" to their own official order (only official up to a certain point) exists and has always existed. Running parallel to this recognition is the realization that such difference can only gain power if and when it is allowed to manifest itself and demand attention. It is for this reason, then, that in order to remove the threat of difference (difference having the power to undermine the absolute value of its structures), the order refuses to acknowledge or account for that difference potentially and dangerously attracting towards itself by subsuming, redefining, and redirecting people's desire toward innocuous ends.

When left unchecked, desire is a force driving toward who knows where and its inherent openness (as opposed to fixity and closure) toward the Other threatens the self with a sense of loss. The subject forgets itself and its social commitment in its curiosity for the "other," and it is for this reason that with the rise of the bourgeoisie (whose system's stability required a set of subjects as solid and socialized as possible), desire was exposed to significant re-invention or re-definition. The redefinition of desire was achieved by restricting its inherent uncontrollability. Desire, when released, spontaneously reaches out towards the infinite: it is a continuously renewed and renewing search for judgment-free contact with the "other." This experience appears too dangerous and undermining for its given social order, and the bourgeoisie in the course of its civilizing process suggested or imposed precise models of desirability that not only prohibited the exploration of difference, but also, more radically, inhibited the desire to explore that difference.

Complete self-possession, a lucid mind, and undisturbed consciousness: these were the qualities man decided he—as subject—could and had to make his own for a presumably complete control over the world (seen as a passive object). At a certain point in time, man realized that in order to maintain and reinforce his own dominance he had to present and think of himself as being the only active, meaningful, and possibly creative being. Usurping all claims to spirituality and action, he felt he had the right to decide and regulate all relationships—no longer spontaneous and inevitable, but personally chosen and controlled by him—with the external world. This can be traced back in some measure to ancient Greek philosophy, then to the Christian tradition, was reinforced by Descartes in the seventeenth century, and has found a new and convincing expression in nineteenth-century idealism, which gave epistemological credence to such an attitude.

Literature, and fiction in particular, is where the beliefs of a given culture can be questioned and its eventual demystification staged.

Where literature and its systems of representation transgress the structures governing the self and its relationship with the external world—structures that have, of course, been established by the social order and that have gained legitimacy through consensus—that which would otherwise have amounted to the control of cultural meaning is challenged. The result is that ideology is replaced by a set of new, transgressive perspectives that undermine the power of the social order. Yet this form of subversion, challenge, or conflict need not necessarily be openly declared; even a small difference (with respect to normality), incongruence (with respect to expectations) and a discreet introduction of disruption, intrusion, and incoherence into the plot of everyday life and its distinctive and otherwise valid order shake the foundations of that order and release a powerfully strong voice that is significant even in the indefinability of its message.

The mere "strangeness" of Mary Poppins, as a subject in her own right and as a female subject, is enough to throw into question all the absolute truths governing the possibilities and modes of being and behavior constructed by the social order. And it is enough to throw into question the very nature and essence of desire—a desire that brings the subject out of itself toward what is other and that always exists, but that society bans the individual from recognizing, knowing, and even feeling in its true form. And in the presence of Mary Poppins, that which is "other" and attracts us, lying at the other end of the chain of desire, becomes a very vivid and lively reality and hence gains in power. In fact, it is this force, and not conscious will, that drives all that takes place in the Mary Poppins books, and to admit this is already to transgress the idea that nothing beyond the self can present itself as having a life or initiative of its own because all that stands outside the self is consigned to the role of "object," and as such is a passive entity awaiting action by the subject. At the same time, this "beyond-the-self," which in Travers's books draws the subject towards itself, would remain uncontrollable, phantasmagoric, and ultimately unexplored were it not for the presence of a Dionysian mediator like Mary Poppins.

And even though the experiences lived with, enjoyed, and recognized as desirable through Mary Poppins remain inexplicable, they are no less powerful, attractive, real, or impossible to resist. The children have no choice but to go along with the adventures that inevitably must take place, and Mary Poppins (who opens doors and gives the children the gift of flight) must be considered nothing short of revolutionary. What these books stage in an ultimately effective manner is the object's seduction of the subject. The object (that is, all that is other to the self and to what it already knows) is invested with the power of action and is released from the inertia into which a certain social, philosophical, and psychological order has cast it; in a world invigorated by the presence of Mary Poppins, the beyond-the-self refuses stasis and order, it refuses to stand still passively while the subject seeks to grasp, categorize, analyze it, and keep it at bay.

Given that Mary Poppins is the cause of this reinvigoration of the life of things, we should talk of the governess not in terms of her being some sort of "educator" but more precisely an "animator." After all, what she does is to provoke and activate the inevitable, uncontrollable, and unexpected relationship between the consciousness or interior life of the children and all that exists in the external world. That is, under her influence, the previously separate entities of self and not-self can no longer be considered mutually exclusive, static or distinct, but are catapulted into a dimension of reciprocal attraction ultimately favoring the creation of authentic meaning and giving value to life.

The world existing beyond the door, to which the children always want to return, is obviously excluded from the social order and remains "other" to the common definitions governing "official" reality. It amounts to an antisocial desire because it remains unmotivated by any obvious or material considerations and refuses all rational explanation. And yet, such is its power and force that it makes itself felt, even if only on the surface, by upsetting and throwing into crisis social experience.

Travers depicts the yearning and attraction felt by the Banks children as a form of desire that exists way beyond the confines of "culture" (understood as that which is learned, explained, justifiable and regulated) and as such succeeds in designing a blueprint for the self in "nature"— indeed, we might say that Travers's achievement lies in the fact that she sets down the foundations for a new form of human nature.

Representation in the Mary Poppins books can be described as an explosion of life; it is not only the newly curious and stimulated children who come to life, but the whole of the object world that surrounds them, and this continues to astound the children. What results is chaos, as we suddenly come face to face with the unnaturalness of the conventions and common sense that up to this point man has used to qualify experience. This confusion cannot help but redefine the boundaries of individual identity, which is reconstructed (along with the whole of the external world) in a way that no longer respects the exigencies of social and genealogical determinism because, now liberated, the individual's destiny and development are strictly linked to his/her desire and the attraction he/she feels for the Other, for openness, and for encounters, all of which are now experienced as possibilities. As a result, the possibilities and prerogatives of subjectivity are immensely increased. What this amounts to is an important operation that literature brings to fruition: the meaning-giving process becomes a prerogative of the subject, but only insofar as it values and recognizes, rather than negates and diminishes, the unpredictable power inherent in, and belonging to, the object world (or what is other-than-the self).

It is perhaps not by chance that in the Mary Poppins books the desiring subjects (whose dreams become reality and who find themselves conversing with what can no longer be considered passive things) are children; subjects, that is, who are without any form of socially recognizable power. They are, as such, quite different from those subjects whose duty, responsibility, office, or role implies having to control, dominate, and represent reality in such a way as to keep that reality at bay—approaching it only with the utmost caution and insofar as that reality can be made to fulfill certain specific ends.

In the Mary Poppins books, desire undoubtedly becomes a reality in itself, equivalent to (and often in conflict with) the reality principle. Each element pertaining to the narrative (a narrative that presents itself as a reorganization of the recognizably real material world) signals desire, that is, this willingness to be open instead of closed and to transcend one's self and so give way to a spatio-temporal dimension of its own in which each "thing" is transfigured in its own meaning and value, this being no longer one of "use" but simply one of existence and of possibility to stimulate forms of unbiased relationship. In this way, the narrative principle that reorganizes the living world, giving it a unitary (though dynamic and multiplicitous) form, becomes an original causal principle, and gains some sort of universal meaning awaiting discovery.

Instances of divergence from what was considered socially and culturally acceptable can, of course, be found in the official or "high" English literary tradition as well as in those marginal "children's books" that, given their supposed audience, were not taken very seriously and thus could contain, in the disguised form of simple entertainment, subversive messages. Such divergence announced itself also in certain books that, for example, encouraged the formation of an alternative consciousness or created figures that embodied a thoroughly "modern" desire that threw into question the political identity (i.e., actual power) and self-knowledge of the individual.

The domestic novel, of particular interest to the present argument, started life as a "respectable" art form—Richardson's *Pamela* is a case in point and heralded the inception of this genre. This form of writing effectively erased all (conscious) suggestions of erotic desire, understood in its most general sense as that which responds either to the pleasure principle or to a creative, natural fusion. It was Emily Brönte who changed the course of traditional narrative with *Wuthering Heights*. With this novel, though respecting the norms of the domestic genre, began a battle in defense of the need to socially recognize the desires and impulses that lie at the base of the individual's true identity and his/her possibility for full development.

Domestic fiction dominated the nineteenth-century Victorian literary scene. This tells us something particularly important about the theory of power seen—in a very subtle sense—as the set of possibilities and rights given to the few to determine the meaning, significance and worldview of and for the many. It reveals, for example, how power rested not so much in the legal or economic systems, but rather, on cultural hegemony—in the notion of family, in the norms of behavior governing the relationship between the sexes, in what was considered to be a correct and appropriately "civilized" way of dressing, as well as in how people should spend their free time, and so on.

Much writing gained respectability and indeed literary status by providing, where deemed socially necessary, the means to discipline the mind of the individual. What was considered virtuous, for example, was rewarded, whilst subversive and fascinatingly ambiguous characters were often depicted as monstrous, abhorrent or in some way horrific. What gained thematic importance, in fact, and indeed what was officially appreciated, was a literature that provided the means to limit the individual's perception of his/her own relationship to the political, that is, to his/her rights to have some kind of power to determine his/her own destiny, to the truth of his/her own possibilities.

Emily Brönte was one of the first writers to oppose this tradition. Brönte lived on the margins of society, and this peripheral, almost isolated position as well as the fact that she was an autodidact whose learning and reading extended well beyond the books labeled "high literature" remind us of Travers's own social and cultural background. The tradition of domestic fiction up until Brönte's works was lacking in one important area: in no sense did it adequately give expression to that deepest and most genuine part of the individual—that is, the tensions, the emotions, the hopes and the inexpressible or illegitimate powers that underscored the life of the subject.

The literary aesthetics underpinning officially recognized and socially acceptable narratives were preoccupied with the mores of social behavior and the definition of what was considered good (and bad) manners. This was what governed the individual's relationship with others and with the outside world. Nowhere did these aesthetics seek to embrace the more complex and intimate worlds of the human spirit, mind, or instinct. Emily Brönte's achievement, therefore, lies partly in the fact that she effectively remapped the territory of the self by delving beyond the codes governing civil behavior to touch upon the inexpressibly powerful, inherently creative, and socially dangerous theme of human desire. In her representation of the tensions, passions, and needs of the individual (which her fellow writers had shied away from), Brönte made use of a set of characters who either could not be considered entirely socially acceptable or which hailed (ultimately) from the supernatural world, from a world, that is, where dreams and deep needs and imagination could be given expression. Through these characters and the situations in which they find themselves, Brönte traced the course of a very real, if invisible (ghostly), emotional force. In order to actually represent desire, that is, Brönte had to push back the boundaries of semiotic space and in so doing exposed a dimension that until then had not even been envisaged by officially approved literature.

Wuthering Heights depicts this "other" dimension that distinguishes itself so drastically from socially recognizable or "realistic" representation. And yet Brönte's description of this new universe is conscientiously open-ended; it refuses closure in terms of clear-cut conclusions and thus liberates and keeps alive that incredible ambiguity between the possible and the impossible. Like the Mary Poppins books that stage a similar form of powerful alterity and interpretative open-endedness, *Wuthering Heights* is a profoundly provocative text because it manages to insert itself into a system at the very moment in which it proclaims the meaninglessness of that system, offering its own, different representation. The text releases an explosion of centrifugal energy which paradoxically gains force precisely because its meaning remains unclear, ungraspable, or unresolved. These are the features that make Brönte's novel (and Travers's books, which have a similar structure) irresistibly fascinating and subversively powerful; its enigmatic fleetingness escapes our need to achieve closure through the application of clear-cut conclusions, and as such, the novel's power and fascination remain intact.

MARY POPPINS AND HUSSERL:
INTENTIONAL CONSCIOUSNESS

From a philosophical perspective, the subject's "openness" toward the world and toward possibility is what Edmund Husserl (1859–1938) terms the most basic characteristic of the subjective consciousness. For Husserl, the subject is, in fact, constitutively "open to" whilst the object is such only in as much as it is "revealing to." Intentionality is the name he gives to the way in which consciousness uses intuition to transform a naturalistic approach to the world (in which it is understood as "other," objective, material, and passive in relation to the subject; or, more simply, as that which, given and still, remains beyond our arbitrary door) into true knowledge.

Intentionality forms the basis of an essential relationship that expresses itself as a form of openness and "movement toward," on our part, and as the power to attract, to give themselves over to us, on the part of objects. This operation, or rather disposition, actually forms consciousness. What often happens, however, is that this is not always recognized as being the most authentic part of the self—its being a self "in relation" (which sidesteps notions of separation in favor of a deeper form of union). Indeed, that more essential part of the self that is the only part of us capable of bringing about an authentic relationship with the world is very often left forgotten or rejected.

This, of course, greatly reduces the possible, to which we can only gain access by living to the full the nature of our intentionality as intentional beings. We *are* (authentically) only if we manage to transcend the fact of our being highly specific individuals belonging to the world of facts, and open ourselves up to an exchange with all that is outside, without our being able to predefine or know what this might be. For Husserl, an openness toward possibility is the most authentic of human attitudes and guards against all forms of dogmatism as well as mitigating the risk of determinism.

To not recognize the intentionality of the self (the self's most genuine being-in-relation with all that is not self; the part of the self that is open to the future and thus open to adventure) is to passively accept and adopt all political, social, and cultural conditioning, which in effect amounts to the renunciation of one's personal freedom. Given these philosophical premises, we cannot help but see the figure of Mary Poppins as a solution or remedy to this existential problem. She encourages the children to live to the full their very own but previously-unstimulated intentionality by revealing the fascination inherent in the possible. She enables that spontaneous openness toward things that characterizes the deepest part of our selves and that is curbed or forgotten, growing up within a certain context. This would explain, therefore, the importance that this governess gives to developing in the children a taste for adventure, for uncertainty, for the new, and for visions and glimpses of distant (possible) horizons. Given that the children are continually called upon to do, go, try and experience things firsthand, this form of education cannot be considered anything but "active," and mirrors Husserl's affirmation that man must actively look for meaning and must actively live an authentic life.

If we understand authenticity as being "open to the possible," we must then accept that this is not something that can be stipulated "for all," as it were, but must be recreated continuously in the concrete life of each individual subject. For Husserl, the only really authentic experience is an entirely *lived* experience. And the only "real" world is that which offers itself to perception. This is where the endless integration of the subject and the object can take place—endless because the task of bringing to light the essence of reality, and thus understanding the possible more fully, is a never-ending undertaking.

Truth for Husserl, as well as for the dandy and certainly for Mary Poppins, is something that reveals itself a side at a time, never revealing the whole of itself at any one moment. Like truth, reality cannot be considered a given. It is for this reason that Husserl encourages modern man to seek a more authentic self and warns of the deception inherent in "factual science" because this professes to reveal truths but, in fact, does nothing more than cloud the mind with idol-like preconceptions. This same idea is repeatedly conveyed in the Mary Poppins books, in which we find many examples of the ways in which blind rationality drives the members of the everyday world, who when faced with something inexplicable that escapes definition, simply refuse to believe their eyes.

Husserl realizes that human beings must be freed from these prejudices and false idols if they are to find once more the capacity to construct their own truth (valid only for the moment, not an absolute). Mary Poppins seems to be driven by this same, and only, aim. We see this, for example, when others try to express to her their gratitude, and she very simply replies:

> "You owe me nothing" [...] "Except of course," she added severely, "not to be so foolish in the future." (IV, p. 199)

Husserl's criticism is not only aimed at superficial prejudice, but also throws into question man's most fundamental assumptions about the nature of the world in which he lives. In giving access to the "Beyond places" and introducing the children to figures from imagination, from mythology, from fairy tales, and from the animal kingdom as creatures that now become a living part of their own reality, Mary Poppins poses the same questions and adopts a similar radical philosophical position.

Husserl also warns us not to take the world for granted and presume that our approach to that world counts for nothing. Only if we are open to, attentive, and projected towards that world will it gain meaning—and only then will we be able to live our own meaning authentically and to the full.

Husserl's term *epoché* describes the process by which the individual can free him/herself from the naturalistic conditioning that forces him/her to see the world as a distinct and separate "other." This process involves bracketing the "given" nature of the world so as to pretend (or maybe even believe) that it can be started over again, from scratch as it were, and that it is we who will give that world a new impetus by establishing between it and ourselves a truly creative, genuine, and meaningful relationship.

Such a process is vital because it allows us to reach the authentic nucleus of life, or *Erlebnis*, as Husserl calls it. Only if we transcend all that is not "alive life," i.e., abstraction and analysis, and only if we cease to see the world as a distant "other," something to use for our own ends, will we be able to gain access to this authentic nucleus. This is not to say that we should entirely reject the idea that the world is indeed "out there," and that it is in many ways a "given" (the idea that justifies all material, quotidian, and ends-motivated action)—it simply means that this idea is not absolute. Indeed, it is a characteristic of the above-mentioned process that consciousness can choose to repossess all that it previously bracketed (and left on this side of the door while consciousness itself took flight) though, of course, with a different general understanding, which will give to the reality usually deemed given a whole new meaning.

To apply this notion of *epoché* to reality means no longer to consider reality as ready-made or external, but as an involving and involved dimension that we help to constitute. It also means that we turn our back on, or suspend, all biased or unfair interests as well as the mechanisms that society uses to render somehow sacred these self-serving interests. Husserl's fears regarding the objectivized external world are clearly shared by the figure of Mary Poppins; both are involved in the struggle against the reduction of the individual to a technical function and both seek to return the individual to a state of wholeness and authenticity.

The notion of *epoché* also frees the self from all governing theories of the "I" and from all practices that seek to make a subject very specific. What emerges is the true self of self, that irreducible nucleus that is an act of life. Individual subjective identity, which is what this amounts to, is also of prime importance in Mary Poppins's universe. Subjective identity is a powerful, obscure, and irrational reality in this universe, and the fact that this identity reveals itself in the most extraordinary and exceptional circumstances shows that it is often harder to "be one's true self" when one is inserted into the ordinary reality, which requires that people are their socially acceptable selves. The importance of the individual subject and subjectivity is represented in the Mary Poppins books, for example, by the fact that strange things often happen on the children's birthdays. Gravity is suddenly defied, or dreams suddenly come true, or creatures and things are liberated during strange rituals precisely on that occasion. Or by the fact that people float up into the air clutching balloons with their names etched across the front—their first names, as opposed to the definition of their social roles (policeman, park keeper, waitress), which is how the narrator refers to them in "normal" circumstances.

Husserl reminds us however that even when liberated with *epoché*, the self is not merely a current of life but rather an identical self that acts in more or less the same way most of the time. Even when transformed by *epoché*, the self retains its constant characteristics (a concept we find staged especially in the way in which Mary Poppins manages to keep her impeccable appearance intact, even when she ventures out toward the "places Beyond"). Above all, this self retains its very concrete nature—we need just consider the way in which the subject's body and senses are significantly present each time a "Beyond place" is visited in the Mary Poppins books. In fact, in relating to the outside world, the body is presented as the zero point, as the center point at which all things converge, including the self itself that is so closely bound to the body as to form a single, unique reality. In the sphere of our authenticity, we experience the body as an immediate, animated, and fully lived reality. The individual is thus an irreducible psycho-physical unit, and, for example, if his/her soul is light enough, the laws of nature dictate that sooner or later the individual will certainly take flight.

Another important aspect of Husserl's philosophy that elucidates the present argument regarding the authenticity of the self is the notion of *motivation*, which Husserl identifies as being far more important to "action" than any notion of "cause." The world motivates—but this world is not that of the empirical sciences, but one that is personally constructed and perceived. According to the laws of motivation, we neither analyze, explain, nor utilize the objects of the world; we simply comprehend them or understand their *meaning*—their meaning *for us*, which is no less important—indeed, it is all that really counts. Reborn as they are into this new consciousness, objects and the whole of reality can subsequently be inserted into the world of the spirit, just as man is, and because they are inextricably related to him.

In the final analysis, Husserl calls on man to be *in* the world but not *of* the world. Husserl's proposal echoes the Kierkegaardian dialectic in which the individual who *leaps* toward the world of meaning, otherwise known as the Infinite (an act of distance-taking from the everyday world because any contact with the absolute implies a movement beyond a purely human dimension), succeeds in reconquering the Finite and in giving this latter significance and value.

This assigning value (implying that reality must be rendered subjective) is clearly highly important: the subject and its relationship with the object world are qualitatively connoted by this value-giving operation. Husserl's whole philosophical undertaking is aimed at liberating the individual, and he shows that in order to reach authenticity, the individual must understand that what stands between man and objectivity (that burdensome "given") is man himself with his *possibilities*. Such an affirmation cannot be divorced from his urging us to be ready, vigilant, and to avoid passivity at all times—and, as such, to be full of life. It is, in the final analysis, a state of affairs to which Mary Poppins has already alerted us.

4

THE GOVERNESS AT THE DOOR

The governess was a figure familiar to Victorian society and is equally well-known to readers of nineteenth-century English fiction. The governess began life before the rise of Victorian society, but it was during these years that she reached a high point in terms of importance, power, and familiarity, though her heyday was equally characterized by problems, contradictions, and crises.

It was the population explosion of the eighteenth century that led to an increased demand for servants and domestic help, which, in turn, doubtlessly intensified what was to become, especially in the following century, an increasingly rigid relationship between the individual and society. The dominant vision of the world in that context was essentially platonic and saw the individual's social position as having been assigned directly by God. This social position was immediately identifiable and translated itself into a particular function that was, above all, permanent. It was generally supposed that if each person kept to their respective positions, society would run smoothly and harmoniously. The task of domestic servants within this highly ordered social structure was to look after the day-to-day lives of wealthy, upper-class families; the children of the latter, in particular, were entrusted to governesses, the demand for whom was so great that the figure was almost an institution in its own right.

The Industrial Revolution and subsequent urbanization provided the backdrop to the sudden rise in births, and it was felt that this growing population needed to be regulated, controlled, and structured according to strict and rigid categories of role and function. At the same time, there was a significant rise in disposable and accumulated wealth that was concentrated in the hands of the few. Both these factors influenced the increase in demand for the governess, who was quickly considered indispensable by the society in which she operated.

It was seen as only fitting that the rich minority should surround itself with an increasingly large number of servants (a testimony that these families were rich and important enough to be able to afford them), and servants of all kinds were very easy to find as a great part of the population was in desperate need of money. The newly rich members of this privileged group who had made their money with the increased opportunities offered by industrialization and who could not boast an upper-class or aristocratic heritage sought to prove their membership in this elite group by hiring a conspicuously large number of servants and above all by entrusting their children to a governess who would teach them the manners, discipline, and ethos of the upper class. A survey of the "classifieds" section of English newspapers, especially *The Times*, proves that governesses were not solely the prerogative of the upper class; indeed, from the mid-nineteenth century onwards demand grew significantly within the middle classes, and by the end of the century so vital was this figure to the social status of the middle-class family that if it were not able to boast the existence in its home of at least one governess, it risked losing its social standing.

Along with the servants and other paraphernalia of gentility, the governess began to symbolize the economic power of the middle-class father and indicated the extent to which his wife could be considered a "lady of leisure."[1] Traditionally speaking, the mother's role in the family was that of running the household (or organizing the servants to do so) and overseeing the education of the children. In previous centuries, the governess was employed to teach good manners to the daughters of the family in order to prepare them for the marriage market, whilst the sons were entrusted to tutors and then sent off to school. Over time, the role of the governess altered in line with an increasingly busy and modern society, so that by the end of the nineteenth century she was overseeing the upbringing of both the daughters and the sons of these middle- and upper-class families and was instrumental in distancing the wives and mothers from all domestic preoccupations until they could be considered purely ornamental. In fact, the "ideal woman" of the nineteenth century was expected to dedicate herself to leisure and entertainment and to what today we would call "public relations." The idea of employment outside the home was not only inappropriate, but to use the words of one social commentator, it was considered "a deplorable dereliction."[2] This image of the lady of luxury surrounded by her intimate circle of family and friends and financially supported by her husband or father was reinforced, of course, by what in effect amounted to a ban on paid employment. So influential, in fact, was this ban that women writing for publication often used pseudonyms or signed their work with the words "by a lady" to avoid being identified.

This led to a somewhat paradoxical situation however. Several of the families of this upper section of society who had met with financial crises (increasingly common in this new economic context) could no longer afford to keep all their daughters in this way. It was therefore considered acceptable for these well brought up women, who had been born into the privileged classes, to seek employment. The rising demand on the part of wealthy middle- and upper-class families for help in educating and bringing up their children coupled with the need of these gentlewomen to find (a contradiction in terms) some form of paid employment meant that the role of the governess quickly began to be seen as the only socially acceptable form of employment for a middle- or upper-class woman. The governess was not, therefore, thought to be on the same level as the other servants in the household and was kept separate from them by a strict hierarchical structure that the wealthy Victorians imposed on their domestic help; this took the form of a rigid code of discipline, duties, and powers that prevented any form of disorder from entering the ranks of servants and that, in many cases, was almost military in nature. In *Mary Poppins,* for example, we find the following:

> So it was settled, and that was how the Banks family came to live at Number Seventeen, with Mrs Brill to cook for them, and Ellen to lay the tables, and Robertson Ay to cut the lawn and clean the knives and polish the shoes and, as Mr Banks always said, "to waste his time and my money." (I, p. 10)

Or again, elsewhere, we find a further example:

> Miss Lark lived Next Door.
>
> But before we go any further, I must tell you what Next Door looked like. It was a very grand house, by far the grandest in Cherry Tree Lane. Even Admiral Boom had been known to envy Miss Lark her wonderful house [...] And the reason for Admiral Boom's jealously was that Miss Lark had two gates.
>
> One was for Miss Lark's friends and relations, and the other for the Butcher and the Baker and the Milkman.
>
> Once the Baker had made a mistake and had come in through the gate reserved for friends and relations, and Miss Lark was so angry that she said she wouldn't have any more bread ever. (I, p. 45)

THE GOVERNESS AS INSTITUTION

It was against this backdrop that the role of the governess became increasingly consolidated, and during the period 1850–1890 her position in the household, her powers, duties, and even dress code were formalized. The growth and increasing specification of the profession was accompanied by a move to establish some sort of uniform for these women, and so between 1870 and 1880 certain distinctive features began to characterize the governess's dress. These included the distinctive cap or hat (her head was never exposed), the familiar long grey skirt, the wide belt, the all-important collars, and the boots. This basic uniform naturally allowed for variation, and the governess followed the gradual shifts in fashion like any other woman of her class. Yet, by the end of the nineteenth century, it was unusual to find a governess who did not wear a uniform of this sort, and any woman who chose not to certainly exposed herself to comment or criticism. Thus the governess was as easily recognizable by her uniform as was a soldier, for example, or any other uniformed functionary of the Victorian period. Mary Poppins follows this dress code and as such her role is immediately recognizable to all those around her. Yet, although her clothes can be described as typical, so much so that she is always considered not merely *a* governess, but *the* governess, it is nevertheless the peculiarities of her dress that draw attention, details such as her gloves or the buckles of her shoes, her handkerchief or scarf, which she wears so proudly and which in the end signal the evident uniqueness of her character.

In the middle of the nineteenth century a new invention was introduced that revolutionized the daily life of the governess. The pram increased the mobility of the governess who could now venture beyond the four walls of the home, invariably in the direction of the park, which now became for the children in her charge a sort of antithesis to the home and as such was invested with all those stimulating connotations that always characterize external or unfamiliar places. The home-park opposition repeated in many ways the traditional archetypal opposition between nature and culture, a configuration that gains poetic relevance in the adventures of Mary Poppins. The invention of the pram and the governess's increased freedom also led to what was to become a very familiar sight—the large gatherings of governesses and children who met every day in the park. These meetings became very fashionable during the 1920s in particular, and are described by Jonathan Gathorne-Hardy in his study of the rise and fall of the governess:

The centre of the Nanny community in London was the park. Hyde Park! How an old Nanny, as Englishmen did once for Agincourt, thrills still to the mention of that name. For many, the richest moments of their lives were passed there. Nannies were going to it before the first World War, but it was during the 1920s and '30s that it seems it have reached the zenith of its popularity (a development no doubt facilitated by the technical improvements of the pram.) The morning might be spent in numerous Square Gardens, but in the afternoon Nanny and the children set out for the park. Many walked literally miles to reach it, ignoring nearer, greener, less fashionable recreation grounds.[3]

Gathorne-Hardy's book contains extracts from the memoirs of Bridgett Tisdall, which evoke the atmosphere of these meetings in the park so familiar to the readers of Mary Poppins:

> My sister and I had a double pram for a short period. [...] I would be wheeled daily into Hyde Park up Sloane Street... past Gooch, now Harvey Nichols, across Knightsbridge, past the French Embassy and the stages on Albert Gate. Here sat the Balloon woman with her bunch of balloons and red and yellow windmills on sticks which the Nannies bought their charges. We would then cross Rotten Row, pass the little sylvan, fenced-in enclosure with its rabbits, moorhens, lake and waterfall, and turn right into The Daisy Walk where upper crust Nannies with crested prams sat knitting, complaining, and generally comparing each other's situations. It was rather dull in The Daisy Walk. We toddled about, picked daisies and were called to attention with monotonous regularity by Nanny. If a little boy pinched a little girl their respective nannies were at each other's throats. [...] If you were naughty you had to sit beside Nanny and rock the pram. Odd it may seem, but children obeyed.[4]

The theme of the park with its fascinating geography and typical, almost fairy-tale-like characters (such as the balloon seller who, in the Mary Poppins books, is given a chapter of her own), is taken up by Travers in her books and rendered magically tangible by the back cover illustration of *Mary Poppins in the Park*. This miniature medieval-style map of the park suggests that the reader will be in for one of those gloriously classic adventures down the park's winding paths and around its various obstacles, identifying with characters who will surely be some sort of treasure-seeking heroes.

Special schools were very quickly introduced (the first was established in 1848) with the aim of training young women to enter the profession of governess. These schools aimed to offer what the Norland

School, one of the most advanced educational establishments of the 1890s, called: "a new career to gentlewomen of birth and upbringing" and "to well brought up and well mannered young women." Gathorne-Hardy visited the school while researching his book and reports how a period of work experience was considered vital to the training of the young women in that it offered them the opportunity to master the various requirements of their future career. Areas of instruction included embroidery, sewing, household management skills, history, geography, blackboard drawing, singing, and reading. But above all, these schools sought to instill in their students the qualities of precision, punctuality, personal cleanliness, tact, and a sense of measure. When the Norland School's curriculum was expanded in 1930, it stated that in order to pass the final exam allowing the student to officially enter the profession, what was needed was the apparently vague but paradoxically precise requirement of "general tone."[5] The expression tells us something fundamental about what was expected; the profession of "governess" was more than a mere job—it was a complete way of life, a distinct way of being and appearing to others.[6]

THE ADVENT OF THE GOVERNESS
The Law of Order (The Unspoiled Children)

One of the most interesting and recognizable features characterizing the governess was her faultless and smooth-running competence. In researching his book, Gathorne-Hardy interviewed a great number of current and ex-governesses as well as a whole range of people who had come into contact with governesses at some point in their lives, and he studied a wide array of their letters and diary entries. What he found was that almost all governesses established a rigidly regulated and highly disciplined routine. This routine was apparently simple in that its requirements were very clear, yet at the same time it was characterized by a high degree of complexity, evident for example in the various rules that had to be respected and that gave life to a whole series of strange routines, such as the wrapping up before going out and other such every day activities like getting washed or sitting down to table—all of which were done in a very precise and definite manner. The day was organized around a whole series of these rigid habits which very rarely, if ever, could be dropped. Thus the arrival of the governess meant that the rules governing the behavior of the children—what they were supposed to do and when they were supposed to do it—took on a concrete form. This undoubtedly frustrated the unarticulated wants and needs of the children whose world was regulated by this set of limitations that made their lives seem tough, though at the same time safe and even comfortable. This fact is highlighted by the accounts of people who, when children, were entrusted to the care of a governess; if she was sometimes considered to be a sort of tyrannical enemy, she was also and always remembered for the sense of security she brought to the lives of the children. What is certain is that the children of the privileged English classes during this period did not receive this sense of security from those who should have communicated it more naturally, that is, their own parents. Yet it might be true to say that the mother (and indeed no one other than the governess herself) could never have surrounded her children with exactly this same sense of safety. There is something very particularly English about the sense of safety and the other peculiar emotions that were conveyed by a governess and by her steady presence. The child's relationship with her was inevitably intimate—even when conflictual—and whilst being highly contradictory, it was also more stimulating, enriching, and unpredictable than a simpler or more "natural" parent-child relationship.

One of the main reasons for the intimate relationship was, needless to say, the fact that the governess was entirely (and only) concentrated on her charges—she had no other duty to speak of, at least not during the period in question. The emergence of the governess as a powerful, intimate, and yet contradictory figure within the family (and at the center of a kingdom with precise confines and unmistakably familiar characteristics) was also influenced by a seemingly banal though highly concrete factor: the development of that new architectural space, the nursery. The nursery was, in fact, essential to the way in which a whole generation of children was brought up—a generation that would grow up to fill the highest and most influential positions in Victorian and Edwardian England. This room was far more complex than we might at first imagine and was certainly typical of a very English upbringing. It was an austere place filled with furniture and objects that could not be used anywhere else in the house. It was usually set off from the rest of the house, either located in the attics or in a separate wing of the house. It had its own stairs and outside entrance and the door leading to the rest of the house was often covered with a thick green curtain that muffled the noise of the children. The parents and servants hardly ever entered the nursery and knew very little about what went on inside as it was the place where the children were brought up, as if they didn't belong to the reality and the world adults were actually involved and interested in.

By the end of the nineteenth century the employment of domestic servants was on the decline. This was partly due to the increased job opportunities in other areas of the employment market, but it was also influenced by a more flexible outlook regarding relationships between individuals, one that began to demand that each individual be considered as a person rather than as belonging to a particular class, a development that undermined the strict social hierarchy and that made it not so easy for the upper classes to treat their employees as inferiors. Yet, despite this, the governess was more than ever in demand. So, whilst servants were becoming increasingly bothersome to their employers, having gained an awareness of themselves and their rights, together with their duties, the governess was considered by the privileged classes to be absolutely vital to the efficient and successful upbringing of their children. Moreover, the governess having been present through generations, the mothers of some households were so used to relying on the governess that they would not have known how to raise their own children; never before had a group of women been less capable or so distressed by the idea of raising their offspring. The governess's day off was therefore somewhat dreaded by the parents, especially if there were no other servants available to take care of the children. For the children, however, this could turn into a stimulating opportunity, as we learn from the Mary Poppins books:

> "We are hurrying," said Mary Poppins with awful distinctness, "because this is the Second Thursday and I am going out."
>
> "Oh!" groaned Michael, who had quite forgotten. "That means an evening with Ellen! I can't bear Ellen!" Michael grumbled. [...]
>
> "If there weren't any Thursdays," he said to Jane, "Mary Poppins would never go out!"
>
> But unfortunately, every week had a Thursday and once Mary Poppins was out of the house it was no good calling her back. There she went now, tripping down the Lane. She wore her black straw hat with the daisies and her best blue coat with the silver buttons. The children leaned from the nursery window and watched her retreating back. (III, pp. 128–129)

Then, after the servant Ellen has put the children to bed (with much difficulty), she leaves the room:

> "Thank Goodness!" said Michael. "Now let's do something!"
>
> If Mary Poppins had been on duty they would never have dared to do anything. But nobody took any notice of Ellen. She simply didn't count. (III, p.129)

That even a temporary absence of the governess was experienced as such an uncomfortable and extraordinary event is demonstrated, in

Mary Poppins, by the fact that an entire chapter is devoted to the subject and is entitled quite simply, "The Day Out."

On all other days, the mother of the house may have appeared in the nursery at about 10:00 a.m., and the children would go down to the drawing room for afternoon tea—impeccably dressed and even more impeccably mannered. There was little more contact between the children and their parents than this. The presence of their governess totally filled the children's lives.

Up until the beginning of World War II, which was what finally put an end to her supremacy, the governess's power grew steadily within the household. It was the governess who chose the children's clothes, food, books, presents, friends, and activities; and it was she who regulated the organization of the day and took care of even the tiniest details with her uncompromising tone and manner, which remained unchanged until the world itself changed and the governess suddenly disappeared altogether. So up until the years preceding World War II, the governess was a constant in the lives of her charges. Her watchful presence and the fact that she came from a place "other" than the family proved highly stimulating to the children who found in her all the imaginative engagement and interest that books, television, comics, and friends might now provide. Of course, her authority could border, at times, on the tyrannical (as we find in various novels representing this period). Yet this authority, together with her reigning over the nursery and her control of the lives of the children were the features characterizing the profession of the governess.

The Threat of Disorder (The Stolen Children)

More than any other quality, the nursery was characterized by its *separateness*. And this notion of separateness was also reflected in the governess herself who was seen as distinct and distanced from the rest of the adult world. The governess occupied a strange space, that between the children's mother or parents and the rest of the household staff; she was half parent and half servant; half familiar and half stranger.

This separateness was desired and seen as necessary if upper- and middle-class parents wanted to keep their children away from their own everyday lives. However, this became a somehow disquieting and disturbing condition, giving rise to fears and suspicions regarding what the governess might do (or even who she might really be) given that she was for the most part out of sight.

This idea of the governess's separateness and of the potential mysteries associated with such a separateness is expressed over and over again in the literature of the time. We find it, for example, in the melodramatic novel of Mrs. Wood, entitled *East Lynne*. Written in the mid-nineteenth century, the book was categorized as "low" literature because of its exaggerated tone, unconvincing plot line, and overly pompous style. The book is difficult to find today, so little was it considered worthy of attention, but it is mentioned in Katherine West's study of representations of the governess in British fiction.[7] Despite being unworthy of classification amongst the ranks of "high" literature, West identifies in this book "a morbid fascination" and "contagious influence."[8] The book recounts the life of Lady Isabel Vane from her childhood through to her adult age. She gets married, becomes a mother, and is subsequently alienated from society until the day when she finally becomes a governess. Lady Isabel leaves her husband and children at a certain point for a brief affair with an odious baron, but she and the baron are involved in an accident that leaves him dead and her horribly disfigured. Her family and friends all believe her to have been killed, and, while she convalesces in a remote cottage, her husband remarries. Too ashamed of what has happened and of her horribly mutilated face, she is reluctant to let her husband and family know that she has survived. And so she decides that in order to earn a living she must become a governess. Taking the French name Madame de Vine and concealing her face behind a series of veils (signaling the mystery and alterity characteristic of the part-strange, part-familiar governess), she begins looking for a family. Hearing that the new Mrs. Carlysle of East Lynne (her husband's new wife) is looking for a governess, Isabel cannot turn down the chance to see her children again, convinced as she is that no one will recognize her—indeed the veils and her strange accent succeed in concealing her true identity even from her husband and offspring.

What we find highlighted in this situation is the absurd ease with which English parents of that particular era were ready to hand over their children to complete strangers they hired via newspaper ads. In giving up their children to this mysterious (literally veiled) woman, the Carlysles take this irresponsibility to the extreme (or probably show it for what it was, fiction using metaphors to express concepts in a striking way). And so, with characteristic English phlegm, the children silently accept this mystery in much the same way that the Pied Piper's children accept and follow the mysterious figure, and end up falling for the enigmatic Madame de Vine. The new Mrs. Carlysle is kind and sensitive but adheres to the then fashionable theory that mothers should not be involved in the trivialities of their children's day-to-day lives, but should be seen as someone special and quite distant to whom the children could turn for guidance in matters such as, for example, religion. This, of course, gave the governess carte blanche in all other matters.

Lady Isabel is very nearly unable to contain her emotions before her children, especially when having to nurse her youngest son, William, through what will turn out to be a fatal illness. When William dies, she too falls ill, and struck by her devotion, the family decides to do all they can to save her, but their efforts come too late and Isabel dies. The case of Lady Isabel Vane is interesting as an example sui generis. Despite the fact that this book and its protagonist cast light on the upper middle-class milieu, Lady Isabel cannot really be considered a "normal" governess, her own position being in fact quite false. Yet her fictional situation reveals many of the real contradictions that were connected to the position of the governess within the middle-class household at that time. What the plot of this book seems to suggest is that a mother could easily abandon her children, as the protagonist does by escaping with her lover, only to rediscover a strong bond with them the moment she comes back in the form of a stranger. It suggests that children are more likely to form a successful, stimulating, and authentic relationship with unknown, unfamiliar, and strange figures, than with someone who biologically belongs to their family circle. English children's "classics" of the late nineteenth and early twentieth centuries (starting a tradition that continues today)—from *Peter Pan* to *The Jungle Books*, from *Kim* to *The Secret Garden*, from *Treasure Island* to the Mary Poppins books and so on—in one form or another all seem to express this very idea that children do not need their "real" parents to take care of them, in order to grow up (in what becomes then a very stimulating, possibly dangerous, but in the end fulfilling way). The widespread presence of the governess in so many households must have brought this idea to the fore. When the governess was an institution in Great Britain, childhood was invested with a wonderful paradox: it was apparently kept under a very strict control, thanks to the governess who had been invented precisely for this purpose; and yet children did in fact find themselves in a somehow liberating position, because this control was exerted by a figure who herself escaped all forms of control and whose strange position exposed the very arbitrary nature of official adult norms, schemes, and values.

The governess represents a form of "Beyond" for the family, to whom she has no "natural" relationship. This sense of "Beyond" is transmitted as much by her obscure origins as by her status, her character, her body, and the unique independence that she is awarded in a household where all others have (familiar) links. And yet despite this sense of otherness and the risk that always accompanies discourses of the Other, she was totally trusted, and she was entrusted with the care of the children. And the children, accordingly, find refuge in her, follow no one but her, and with her depart and distance themselves from the house, in both a literal and metaphorical way. They are contaminated by her alterity and extraneousness, so much so that they run the risk of becoming alien, ungraspable, or Other for their own parents.

In his novel *The Turn of The Screw*, Henry James presents an ingenious reading of just such a situation, needing, like Emily Brönte, to turn to ghosts in order to express otherwise inexpressible intuitions and anxieties. The plot includes a ghostly governess who returns to haunt and seek revenge over her former charges now in the care of a new governess. This latter finds herself having to battle against the horrors of the former governess, Miss Jessel, to save the souls of the children. The battle is between good and evil, having as its pawns children who are threatened and defended, offended and rescued throughout the story not by figures naturally familiar to them but by two governesses who here become characters capable of condensing and embodying a whole range of mythically potent symbols. At the center of this game or struggle is the dichotomy inherent in the figure of the governess herself—her figure and presence evoked both conscious ideas and unconscious fears meaning that she was perceived as straddling quite primordial binaries; the bourgeois family's view of the governess was not based exclusively on how well she performed her duties, but was the fruit of much deeper contradictory considerations, resulting in her appearing either entirely salvific or explicitly diabolic, either the incarnation of total bliss or of terrifying doom. Even when occupying a peripheral position with respect to the main plot, Henry James's governesses are never simple and unambiguous characters. The figure of the governess is also of prime importance to another James novel, *What Maisie Knew*. The forces of good and evil battle it out around the sensitive young girl, Maisie, whose two governesses are represented as protective goddess and evil witch, respectively. A linear analysis of the plot cannot do justice to this syntactically complex work, but what is of interest to the present argument is the way in which James sets Maisie at the center of a web of disequilibrium and pain caused by the divorce of her parents. In a move reminiscent of many traditional fairy tales, James has the girl's father marry the governess, who becomes for Maisie a stepmother. After the death of her natural mother, Maisie finally decides to liberate herself from all natural (and, in this context, inherently painful) bonds by choosing to live with her second governess, the kindly, sensitive and reassuring Mrs. Wix.

Oscar Wilde also portrays the complex ambiguity of the supposedly untrustworthy and contradictory governess in his play *The Importance of Being Earnest,* in which Lady Bracknell accuses the latter of being "a female of repellent aspect" and, more important to the present argument, as it seems to be a literary topos concerning governesses, of having kidnapped a baby. The north European and especially the Celtic fairy-tale tradition is full of representations of this sort, where the alien and mysterious figures are described as some kind of fearfully sinister fairies intent on kidnapping the children and leaving a changeling in their place, and yet in certain audacious twists of the plot, this is seen to greatly benefit the supposed victim of these violent acts.

This idea of the governess as psychological or physical "kidnapper" of the children relates back to the fact that the governess was entirely "other" to the children and the world of their parents and was accentuated by the way in which, after having taken over the lives of the children, and after having almost contaminated their whole existence with her presence, she was destined to leave them. She came and stayed during the crucial years of the children's lives, and then she left and was gone forever. A child's attachment to his or her governess was far from simple and at times was violently strong on an emotional level. Indeed this attachment could also be physical, giving rise to feelings of jealousy, passion, desire, adoration and, at certain times, a sense of intimate peace.

In Pamela Travers's books we find rare but very much longed for moments of physical intimacy between the children and Mary Poppins. These occasional moments in which we find the governess allowing the children to approach her in this way are depicted as a way of satisfying some primordial need in these children who have in effect been orphaned, as a result of her presence, from any other source of emotional and physical warmth.

> He watched her go into the next room, and presently she returned and put something warm into his hands.
>
> Michael sipped it, tasting every drop several times with his tongue, making it last as long as possible so that Mary Poppins should stay beside him.
>
> She stood there without saying a word, watching the milk slowly disappear. He could smell her crackling white apron and the faint flavour of toast that hung about her so deliciously. (I, pp. 87–88)
>
> "Mary Poppins! Mary Poppins! Mary Poppins!" Half laughing, half crying they flung themselves upon her.

"You've c-come b-back, at last!" stammered Michael excitedly, as he clutched her neatly shod foot. It was warm and bony and quite real and smelt of Black-Boot polish. (III, p. 19)

Up and down the nursery went Mary Poppins, tucking them all in. They could smell her old familiar smell, a mixture of toast and starchy aprons. They could feel her old familiar shape, solid and real beneath her clothes. They watched her in adoring silence, drinking her in. (III, pp. 25–26)

"Well, here we are again!" shrieked Miss Corry, as she grinned at the staring children. "H'm! Growing up fast, aren't they, Mary Poppins? I can see they won't need you much longer!" Mary Poppins gave a nod of agreement as Michael, with a cry of protest, rushed to her side.

"We'll always need her—always!" he cried, hugging Mary Poppins' waist so tightly that he felt her strong hard bones. (III, p. 186)

In cases where the governess had been a source of relief and regeneration for the children of the household, her eventual departure was experienced as a terrible feeling of loss. In much of the literature that depicts the figure of the governess, as well as in the various accounts present in Gathorne-Hardy's study, this sudden loss is frequently described as being incomprehensible and brutal. Indeed, Gathorne-Hardy reports how the Norland Nursery Training College sought to prepare its aspiring governesses for the fact that they would be destined one day to leave their charges and how this was experienced as a sort of shadow hanging over the whole time these women spent in any one household. The Norland School's training program first taught its students how to manage a nursery, it then sent them to a hospital where, for three months, they gained nursing experience and then spent the next nine months learning how to look after children up to seven years of age. This last period of training was practically oriented, and "real" children were used whose parents were either away on holiday, or were professionals working full-time; occasionally the children came from problematic backgrounds or were the sons and daughters of foreign diplomats working in the country. Most of these children stayed at the school for a matter of weeks, though some stayed for several months and a few others remained for a matter of years. Each student was given the responsibility of looking after one individual child for a period of thirty days. During that time, the student spent all her time with that child, washing, feeding, and even sleeping with him. At the end of the thirty days, the child was taken away from her and replaced with another. The fact that Mary Poppins comes and goes with the wind, giving no indication

as to whether she will ever return, and that after being such a fundamental part of the children's lives for so long she can simply disappear,
is therefore not only a deeply existential reminder to the Banks children
(and we readers) that nothing lasts forever—it also reflects the reality of
this very English tradition of prestigious governesses whose training
sought to give them the tools necessary to disengage themselves physically and emotionally from their charges.

THE GOVERNESS AND THE MOTHER:
SEXUALITY IN VICTORIAN TIMES

As we find in the Mary Poppins books, the children's natural mother
is incapable of substituting for the governess. Indeed, the child-mother
relationship was entirely different from the child-governess relationship on a qualitative level.

Other than preside over the running of their households, upper-class
English women had nothing with which to occupy themselves other
than the rites and rituals of their social lives. It is hardly surprising,
therefore, that these women often experienced a sense of futility that, in
turn, expressed itself in depression and psychological problems that had
them confined to the sofa or their bedrooms for years on end. The figure of the sick mother can be found in many novels and autobiographical accounts having a governess as an important character, the most
memorable of which is perhaps Edward Sackville-West's *Simpson*.[9]

The fact that these sick mothers were such a common occurrence in
Victorian and Edwardian literature, and especially in children's literature, certainly suggests more than a reality: it must be a literary device
connected to the figure of the governess as such. These mothers were
often so debilitated and alienated by the emotional and educational
relationship that the all-important governess had with the children that
it may have seemed more fitting to represent them as being confined
to their sick beds, rather than being involved in a whole other world of
experiences. The almost stereotypical representation of the privileged
mother's fragile beauty, her pallor, and her passivity contrasted greatly
with, and doubtlessly influenced, the early twentieth-century representations, in the cartoons of satirical magazines such as *Punch*, of the
aberrant, masculine, and strong-minded suffragettes and early feminists. This pitting of the fragile evanescence of the respectable mother
(whose refinement, education and good manners made her the only
sort of woman considered legitimately desirable and charming) against
the active and certainly disturbing vitality of the New Woman, can be

associated with the "problem" of sexuality that characterized the rise of the Victorian upper middle classes.[10]

Victorian society conceived of female sexuality according to a binary structure that saw the model upper-class women as being totally lacking in sexual appetite, whilst their "vulgar" lower-class counterparts were allowed to express their sexuality as openly and freely as their fellow men. And it was not just the moralistic novel that represented female sexuality in this way; nineteenth-century scientific works were equally interested in forwarding this Victorian take on sexual instinct. In William Acton's *The Functions and Disorders of Reproductive Organs in Childhood, Youth, Adult Age and Advanced Life Considered in Their Psychological, Social and Moral Relations* we find the following:

> Having taken pains to obtain and compare abundant evidence on this subject I should say that the majority of women (happily for them) are not very much troubled by sexual feelings of any kind. What men are habitually, women are only exceptionally … there can be no doubt that sexual feeling in the female is in the majority of cases in abeyance… and even if roused (which in many instances it can never be) is very moderate compared with that of the male. Many men, and particularly young men, form their ideas of women's feelings from what they notice early in life from loose, or at least low and vulgar women… Any susceptible boy is easily led to believe, whether he is altogether overcome by the siren or not, that she, and therefore all women, must have at least as strong passions as himself. Such women however give a very false idea of the condition of human feeling in general… As a general rule, a modest woman seldom desires any sexual gratification for herself. She submits to her husband, but only to please him; and but for the desire for maternity, would far rather be relieved of his attentions.[11]

This point of view is corroborated by many other sources and is almost a commonplace in nineteenth-century British society that sought to categorize sexuality in the same way that it sought to categorize its citizens into the rigid three-tier class structure.

> It is a delusion under which many a previously incontinent man suffers to suppose that in newly married life he will be required to treat his wife as he used to treat his mistress. It is not so in the case of any modest English woman. He need not fear that his wife will require the excitement, or in any respect imitate the ways of a courtesan.[12]

It was almost taken for granted that a middle-class man would take several lovers from the lower classes (courtesans were always of the lower class), and one of the most interesting aspects to emerge from contemporary research into the Victorian period is that the respectable face of Victorian society in fact concealed a whole underworld of sexual activity. Behind the measured, reasonable, prudent, and sexually inhibited "official" existence of Victorian society that purportedly valued self-discipline also and especially as a form of marital fidelity (the bourgeois family being considered in itself the example of all that was desirable, right and perfect in its internal balance of functions and roles), lay a whole other world of unimaginable sexuality that played itself out behind the closed doors of squalid urban quarters.

Here, the rules of engagement were such that the poor, hungry daughters of working-class families would give themselves up to rich upper-class men, often (though not always) for payment. This phenomenon, ironically, was partly the result of that same situation that led to the rise of the governess, that is, the sudden population explosion and the unfair distribution of wealth. If this economic and demographic development had forced certain women to seek employment, it also allowed upper middle-class men to elaborate the theory that their own ladies—their wives and governesses—were to remain pure, asexual creatures. They could, of course, permit themselves this distinction and the "luxury" of officially associating only with ideal women, given the hoards of lower-class women who were prepared to assuage their desires in hidden and unofficial contexts; these women were in fact visited and kept at a distance in their own "Beyond" places and were seen as something "other" to the respectable everyday lives of the men who so readily took advantage of them.

Prostitution was made illegal in 1885, and subsequently the number of brothels decreased, but not necessarily the number of prostitutes. Demand for working-class girls seems to have remained high until World War II, and Hyde Park acted as a stage for these nighttime encounters between these heavily made-up, perfumed girls and their wealthier counterparts. Paradoxically, the same park acted as backdrop to the equally energetic daytime gatherings of the governesses and their charges.

Gathorne-Hardy's study of the rise and fall of the governess during the period 1850–1939 shows how the latter corresponded to the rise and fall of the upper-class vision of the ideal woman as sexually and emotionally pure. It is noteworthy in this respect that the wealthy classes selected their supposed morally impeccable governesses (women of whom they knew nothing, whom they had never met before, and who were recruited through newspaper ads) from among the upper strata of society, as if this were sufficient guarantee of their conforming to the ideal. Governesses were obviously strictly linked, like prostitutes though in the opposite sense, to the official British Victorian attitude towards sex and because of this negative identification they nevertheless ended up being inevitably sex-related.

Gathorne-Hardy's study of the memories and letters of governesses reveals that a strong sexual atmosphere surrounded this figure, an atmosphere that gained in force the more it was denied and repressed. We can relate this argument back to the figure of Mary Poppins, of course, whose attitude toward physical contact is always of a very particular (and particularly frustrating) sort:

> "I'll thank you to let go of my shoes!" she snapped. "I am not an object in a Bargain Basement." She shook them off and stepped down [...] as John and Barbara, mewing like kittens, rushed over the grass towards her.
>
> "Hyenas!" she said with an angry glare, as she loosened their clutching fingers. (III, p. 21)
>
> With a sniff, she turned away from them. (III, p. 26)
>
> She glared at him like an angry panther.
>
> "Kindly do not crush me Michael! I am not a sardine in a tin!" she said wrathfully as she gave him a little push. (III, p. 186)

Gathorne-Hardy also highlights the extent to which the governess feared nudity and in an amusing passage reports how she mastered the art of getting undressed without ever showing a patch of bare skin.[13] We find something very similar in *Mary Poppins Opens the Door*:

> [Mary Poppins] unfolded a flannel nightgown.
>
> Jane and Michael [...] watched her comical scarecrow movements as she undressed beneath the nightgown. Clip, clip—the buttons flew apart. Off went her petticoat—swish, swish, swish! A peaceful feeling cocooned the children. And they knew that it came from Mary Poppins. (III, p. 26)

But the governess's avoidance of anything related to sexuality often took a more concrete form and expressed itself in a total refusal to acknowledge and allow expression to even the most innocent of primary impulses in the youngest of her charges, something that certainly fed into the desire for privacy of the upper echelons of English society when growing up. Pleasure was seen as something that should be sought, discovered, and ultimately experienced alone and out of others' sight. And that classic English stereotype of the upper-class man hidden behind the protective façade of his newspaper in his gentlemen's club or in the carriages of a first-class train compartment may have had more to do with the gentleman's rooted need to escape the watchful eye of the governess than anything else.

This situation, together with the bourgeois vision of the ideal woman as distanced from the masculine world of work and ambition, must have played an important part in the genesis and eventual success of that exclusively masculine world of schools, clubs, and sport that occupied the minds of Victorian and Edwardian men, and in the very austere task that they so willingly took upon themselves of constructing and maintaining the supremacy—far away from home—of the British Empire.

MANNERS

The governesses' attitudes toward nudity and sexuality fed into their more general opinion that in order for children not to be spoiled they must not be allowed to experience any form of gratuitous pleasure. This revulsion toward spoiled children found its roots in the Puritanical tradition that demanded that children be treated with the utmost severity, but was absorbed into that peculiar mixture of hypocrisy, self-satisfaction, severity, and almost violent conformism that was Victorian morality. This incredible need to conform, which grew as the century advanced, could in many ways be seen as a veiled form of defense. As the social and economic situation in England began to change, and as new intellectual and cultural ideas began to attack the ideals on which Victorian society was founded, so too did the class structure change, which, in turn, led to the increased fragility of the upper classes. In any case, the governesses' severe treatment of their charges was motivated by what was seen as an unquestionable necessity to avoid spoiling children, spoiling both in terms of their becoming used to getting what they wanted, but also in the sense of ruining them, of allowing them to depart from the ideal model of behavior (implying, especially in times of crisis, the necessity of an even more absolute self-control).

Lady Christabel Aberconway highlights the absurdity of this attitude in her autobiography, *A Wiser Woman?*:

> I like to think, indeed I do believe, that the first friend I made, and made entirely by myself, was Oscar Wilde. Surely I do remember that bulky form bending over my pram, and a glove being removed and I myself clasping a soft white finger and grabbing a sparkling ring? And I can still hear my Nanny saying to another Nanny, and later to my mother, 'That dreadful Mr. Wilde stopped me *again* today and talked to Baby—and she *smiled* at him!'[14]

This wonderful excerpt displays to the full the governess's instinctive disapproval of any form or slightest sign of pleasure, the most innocent smile being of course an example of this. A similar example can be found in the writings of Lady Anethill, when she recalls her childhood with a governess:

> Being 'over-excited' (laughing too much and being 'silly') was a great pleasure that was much frowned upon. If ever I was particularly enjoying myself, my every movement would be followed by Nanny's eyes as she knitted, with a chilling, sour, disapproving look on her face. 'It'll end in a cry', she said... and it usually did. [15]

In the chapter entitled "Laughing Gas" in *Mary Poppins* the governess displays a similar sense of disapproval for her uncle who, unable to control himself despite his fear and embarrassment before his niece, laughs so much that he rises up to the ceiling and remains suspended there. Her stern expression and indifference to the enthusiasm, euphoria, and enjoyment of the other characters show just how much Mary Poppins reflects the attitudes and embodies the values of nineteenth-century governesses, and of that specific category of women who, despite finding a place in the very heart of society, did not really belong there, or not in any simple way. As we shall see later, this ambiguous relationship to their surroundings was the source of a great many contradictions that underpinned the life of the governess. For the moment it suffices to say that behind the severe disapproval of the governess, behind the rigid order of the nurseries, and underneath all those intransigent routines and incalculable restrictions that permeated the lives of the children, lay the desire to combat all forms of pleasure.

The ways in which pleasure was guarded against were manifold and included the necessity for silence during mealtimes, silence in bed, no playing on Sundays, gloves designed to stop children sucking their fingers, the banning of books (especially when full of wonderful illustrations), the endless washing and preening of bodies, the walking or indeed marching in single file at particular times of the day as well as the vital importance of remembering to say one's *pleases* and *thank-yous*. These manners, however, were often so incomprehensibly elaborate and eccentric that they seemed less designed to pursue what was considered "good" behavior and to be more of a histrionic invention of a very strange race of people.

This discussion of manners obviously calls to mind the figure of the dandy. In Peter de Polnay's 1939 book *Children, My Children*[16] analyzed by Katherine West, manners are for the governess, Miss Davies, far more than something that ought to be learned; manners for de Polnay's governess amount to nothing less than a philosophy of life. Miss Davies repeatedly stops reading or interrupts the war bulletins on the radio to correct the children's table manners:

How do you hold your fork, Edith? [17]

Or:

Ivor, where's your hand? [18]

Miss Davies is a decisive, severe and confident governess, obsessed with etiquette. When Molly asks her what a snob is, she answers:

Common people call good-mannered people snobs. It is all jealousy. The one thing in life is perfect manners, especially perfect table manners. [...] Manners are everything.[19]

And as we have seen, Oscar Wilde expressed these very same views in his works.

What today may seem an overly rigid approach to the upbringing of children did not necessarily imply cruelty, unkindness, or severity on the part of the governess, however. As is shown time and again by Mary Poppins, this approach could be turned into a sort of game, almost a meta-language. All it took was a little imagination for these rigid rules to be transfigured into something ultimately pleasureful and creative. More often than not, of course, these rigid regimes expressed the frustration and neurotic irritability of the governess who occasionally resented the difficult and in many ways conflictual position that she occupied. Indeed, it is this negative side that, although mainly absent from the representation of Mary Poppins, fueled those stereotypical images of the suffocatingly cruel and frightening governess found in so much fiction of the time—images that succeeded in likening the governess to the archetypical monster.

TERATOLOGY AND THE GOVERNESS

This familiar image of the cruel governess is not absent from the pages of the Mary Poppins books. Miss Andrew—Mr. Banks's old governess—is Mary Poppins's antithesis, and from time to time she crops up in the adventures of the latter who openly fights against the anxiety caused by these typically oppressive and irrationally "militaresque" governesses whose oppressive nihilism haunts the lives of their charges way beyond the end of childhood.

Mr. Banks paused for a moment. "Euphemia Andrew."
Mrs. Banks gave a little shriek [...]

> Mr. Banks sat down on a chair and put his head in his hands. Miss Andrew had been his governess when he was a little boy [...] a lady so strict, so stern, so forbidding that everyone knew her as the Holy Terror. And now she, of all people, was coming to live next door to him... (V, pp. 2–23)

This theme was popular in nineteenth-century literature, although often treated with a more dramatic and serious tone, and Sheridan le Fanu's 1864 novel *Uncle Silas* is a case in point. Sheridan le Fanu was a master of atmosphere and is well known for his creation of monstrous characters. *Uncle Silas* is a thriller, and what immediately strikes the reader is the atmosphere of calm and regulated serenity that surrounds the typical Victorian routines described and that offset the increasingly mysterious plot that develops. The introduction of the governess into this atmosphere is a moment of tension where a sense of strangeness, fear and anguish collide. Maud, the young protagonist, is sitting calmly in the drawing room when suddenly she sees a horrific-looking woman on the terrace. Her fear turns to desperation when she realizes that this horrendous woman is to be her new governess.

> Every girl of my age knows how much is involved in such an advent. Was it really the arrival of a governess? Was that appari-tion that had impressed me so unpleasantly to take the command of me—to sit alone with me and haunt me perpetually with her sinister look and shrill gabble?[20]

What is noteworthy in this excerpt is the fact that we find one of the rare examples of a pupil expressing her opinions about her governess, a governess who incarnates her deepest fears. Madame de Rougierre's physical appearance is enough to frighten the wits out of the poor Maud, and it gradually transpires that this woman of French origin has been sent to the house by Maud's cruel uncle, Silas, who has his mind set on robbing the possessions of Maud's father and marrying Maud off to his own son. And what the book doesn't state explicitly, but can be imag-ined, is that the evil Madame de Rougierre will have come highly rec-ommended and with the highest credentials, as is always the case with the most evil of governesses. Maud continues in her hatred of the gov-erness without even knowing why, while the latter works away in secret at her odious plan. The governess is depicted as a grotesque figure, her bony frame concealed in outmoded clothes, with her monstrous wig and atrocious accent, and yet this does not detract from the horror con-veyed. For the poor Maud who cannot escape the (legitimately) watchful eye of Madame, the governess is, from the moment she first sets eyes on her to when she finally breaks her neck, the incarnation of evil.

Indeed, because of the role afforded her, the governess is unimaginably pernicious and when Maud exclaims to her cousin that the governess could teach her vulgar turns of speech and vulgar manners "and God knows what else," she is voicing her acknowledgement (and the anthropologically provable theory) that accepting a stranger into one's intimate sphere means to run the risk of contaminating that sphere with the stranger's otherness. Maud describes her governess in another passage as being very deep, audacious, and without scruples, qualities that clearly undermine the upper-middle class ethos of the Victorian era, which valued form, the absence of audacity, and an incredibly scrupulous approach to all situations imaginable. The governess is the absolute Other in this case, and yet is able to obtain a position (that of governess) that any enemy would envy and that gives her far more access to the house's secrets, information, and power than any other servant.

If we extend our analysis of representations of the governess to take in other literary genres, we find that this figure is often in some way mixed up with the sinister underworld of criminals and their crimes. A brief look at detective stories, for example, immediately yields results: Conan Doyle's celebrated Sherlock Holmes series includes a reference to the governess in the form of Dr. Watson's first wife, who met her husband and Sherlock Holmes whilst still in service and involved in a complicated crime case.[21]

Joseph Conrad's *Chance* is another example of the literary treatment of the governess depicted as monstrous by a bourgeois sentiment that celebrated this figure whilst at the same time fearing her. Published in 1914, the novel's psychologically profound plot tells of human pity and horror and takes place at the end of the nineteenth century. It revolves around the figure of Flora de Barral, whose young life has been upturned by a series of unfortunate events. Her father, mother, friends, and even husband all prove to be incredibly negative influences on the poor girl, but more than anyone else, it is her childhood governess who delivers the coup de grace to her innocence and devastates her faith in herself. The governess is never named, and this anonymity and insistence on the impersonal intensifies the sinister aspect of this figure who evades specificity to become the universal agent of evil. Once again, Conrad underlines in his depiction of this governess the ambiguity of a figure who can adopt the rigidly conventional manners of a perfect lady in order to conceal the heart of a shameless brigand. Given the fact that the girl's mother is dead and her father shows no interest in Flora, the governess's sinister plotting, which she cleverly conceals behind an intriguing nature, goes unrecognized. This sinister plot depends on convincing the innocent Flora to marry a young rogue with whom the governess herself is infatuated. So blind is her passion that she hopes to be able to buy this boy with Flora's own money. Once sure of her power over the Barral family and household, the unnamed governess no longer bothers to hide her plans. Having erected a façade of impeccable respectability, the governess is almost untouchable. The family and neighbors have grown used to this "rigorously practical—terribly practical" black-clad, bony figure moving about the house, but underneath her admirable manners and unsuspecting appearance, Conrad's governess conceals ungovernable passions that are doubtlessly heightened by the absurd, inhuman repression to which they are subjected and which was necessary if the individual wanted to be accepted as "normal". The governess desperately clings to her infatuation and when the Barrals find themselves in financial difficulties (thus thwarting her plans to win over the object of her desires with their money) she dreams up a vendetta and determines that no "decent" feeling should stand in the way of her enjoying one last emotional orgy. Her plan is to destroy the innocent and unsuspecting Flora's faith in her own father, in human nature, and ultimately in herself. And the monster's plan is realized with terrible precision. Though in order to understand Flora's final reaction to her governess, we must remember that, as Conrad states quite clearly, the two had been bound up in the most intimate of relationships, though one that was totally devoid of affection.[22]

There was never any love lost between Flora and her governess, and yet the latter had been for so long an integral and irreducible part of her everyday existence. Even when her mother was still alive, the governess provided the impetus in the household, and always represented the spirit of order and safety. She became for Flora the sole measure of value, the sole interpreter of life. It is no wonder, then, that the girl should be frozen with fear when the governess suddenly exits her role as the cool and distant protective goddess and comes exploding into Flora's room while she herself is quietly painting, dragging her lover behind her, having suddenly and unexpectedly become the harbinger of an irrational and shameless vendetta.

From this moment on in the scene, Flora's paralysis, immobility, and the repeated demands that she keep silent gain a significance that reaches beyond the simple fear of the girl. When the governess asks her, with an as yet unseen violence (and perhaps speaking not only to Flora, but to the whole of the British middle class) "whether she imagined that there was anything in her, apart from her money, to induce any intelligent person to take any sort of interest in her existence,"[23] Flora is unable to respond, and what we find therefore is a situation in which the epistemological subject (the economically secure and culturally influential nineteenth-century upper-middle class self), that which had been the dominant subject (that constructed itself in contradistinction to the supposedly passive, weakened Other), faced with this unexpected turn of events, loses its voice. And with the loss of its voice, it also loses power—a power that rested on the definition of self as "the only self" and the Other as object, deprived of an autonomous life of its own and therefore controllable in all its forms and manifestations, which had so rigidly been regulated.

When "she was viciously assured that she was in heart, mind, manner and appearance an utterly common and insipid creature,"[24] Flora is too afraid even to be angry. The words of this Other (the governess, though in a contradictory way, belongs to the class of dominated others) who suddenly becomes powerfully autonomous and is the only speaking self, penetrate deep into Flora's subconscious: "she stood, a frail and passive vessel into which the other went on pouring all the accumulated dislike for all her pupils, her scorn of all her employers, the accumulated resentment, the infinite hatred of all those unrelieved years."[25] It is not hard to imagine the governess's sense of wasted energy and lost opportunities that underpinned all those years spent pretending polite kindness. She continues with her cruel invective while Flora remains silent until she is called "the child of a cheat and swindler."[26] If we extend the analysis that sees Flora as representative of a whole middle class found guilty of having created a tailor-made though false reality that could be defined and dominated at will, this phrase is deeply shocking: the self-defined signifying subject suddenly learns from the supposedly voiceless Other she herself is not in fact the product of natural and necessary causes, but is the product of deceit, of trickery, and of make-believe. And it is interesting that Flora manages to get a grip on herself only when she hears this final accusation, though it is not to defend herself that she speaks, but in order to safeguard the unquestionability of certain fundamental definitions (which alone could give life to the reality desired). "You mustn't *speak* like this of Papa."[27]

After the governess leaves the house, Flora seeks refuge with her neighbor Mrs. Fyne, who puts her to bed and tries to comfort her. Flora pleads with her, "Oh, Mrs. Fyne, don't tell me that she wasn't mad."[28] But her well-intentioned friend, who elsewhere has proved herself to be a theorizer and scrupulous upholder of truth, realizes that her values will be compromised if she grants Flora this reassurance, the only thing that will heal and save her. She therefore replies that "she is a vile woman"[29] not really allowing for the hoped-for possibility that the governess might be mad. And so Flora alone must carry the burden passed on to her by the cruel governess, the most desolating effects of which are the anguished doubt and sense of disorientation that the governess's words have provoked: i.e., from then on, an "ineradicable suspicion of herself and others."[30] In other words, she becomes unable not to believe the inconceivable truth that has been revealed (inconceivable, because if true, all that she has so far believed and taken for granted must be false). This same throwing into question—but by light and entertaining means, through adventure and myth—is present at every turn in the Mary Poppins books.

THE GOVERNESS AS BULWARK OF BOURGEOIS VALUES

Whatever her real motives, and especially the fictional ones, the governess was inherently linked to the ethos of the dominant class, and ultimately it was to her that they turned to instruct and teach their children. As we shall see later, the upper-middle class families had their own reasons for fearing that they might not be recognized as belonging to the only class that mattered. The governess was useful and indeed valuable to the creation and maintaining of certain fundamental aspects of English society in the late nineteenth and early twentieth centuries. It would be an exaggeration to suggest that she was entirely responsible for that powerful sense of discipline that characterized the English state during those years, and yet we should not overlook the fact that the governess was nevertheless a dominant figure in the lives of most of the men and women who brought that society into being.

In the film version of Mary Poppins, Mr. Banks describes the ideal governess:

> The British Nanny must be a general
> > The British Empire lies within her grasp
> > Tradition, discipline and rule
> > Must be the school
> > Without them disorder, anarchy […]
> > In short a ghastly mess.[31]

For a governess to be chosen by these middle-class parents, she had to be unequivocally typical, both as a discipliner and as a woman. These two quite specifically defined roles were held to be norms, and if a governess wanted to be considered "normal," she had to conform to them faithfully. Yet, given the irreconcilable contradictions inherent in her position, this was no easy task and led to what was called the "governess problem," which made itself felt well beyond the pages of literary fiction.

This problem was already being posed in novels written during the 1830s, and by the 1840s it had caught the attention of journals and magazines. In part, this increased attention was fuelled by the yearly reports of the Governess Benevolent Institution (GBI), a charity founded in 1841 with the aim of offering private and discreet financial help and assistance to "ladies" who found themselves temporarily in difficulty.[32] The GBI's activities were an answer to the notion that the governess problem was one that ought to preoccupy the whole of the middle class. And the Victorians' interest in this figure, which manifested itself through the many novels in which she appears and the various sociological studies which focused on the governess as a woman at work, was far-reaching and stretched beyond the fields of literature and sociology.

Historical studies of English society reveal that after 1830 the governess began to experience increasing hardship. The economic crisis of the 1830s suddenly, and for the first time, left many upper-middle-class families with serious financial problems. The educated daughters of these families who could once have looked forward to a life of leisure, now realized that with the fall of their fathers' empires, they themselves could no longer expect to be kept and would have to go out to work. This new situation, together with the fact that there was a great discrepancy between the number of men and women of marriageable age and the fact that men tended to marry later in life, meant that a high number of spinsters, widows, and daughters of crisis-ridden middle-class families eventually began seeking employment.

As the economic conditions pushed women to seek jobs, the range of activities considered socially acceptable for women of the "respectable" classes actually diminished. Whilst in previous centuries and up until the beginning of the nineteenth century, middle-class wives and daughters certainly contributed to the accumulation of family wealth, working as dressmakers, shop assistants and such like, the prospects for female employment were greatly reduced in the 1840s and 1850s. Among those jobs seen as acceptable, that of the governess was widely considered to be the noblest. The job of governess was in many ways a "non-job" and was therefore closely in keeping with the middle-class vision of women, i.e., the ideal woman as full-time, domestic woman and "naturally" a wife and mother.

These conditions led to a saturation of the profession (which allowed women the opportunity to earn a living without losing their respectability), and this saturation, in turn, led to a drastic drop in pay and an equally drastic rise in competition. At the same time, those families employing a governess could and did demand a wider and increasingly bizarre range of services. In a very popular novel written in 1839, *The*

Governess by Lady Blessington (who also wrote articles and theoretical essays on the subject), we are presented with a newspaper ad that signals the beginning of the heroine's adventures:

> Wanted in a highly distinguished family a person as governess to undertake the education of three young ladies of nine, seven and five. She must be of prepossessing appearance, of refined manners, and a perfect musician. She is required to instruct her pupils in French, Italian and English; Geography and the use of globes, drawing and dancing in all of which branches of education she is expected to be proficient. Equanimity of temper and cheerfulness of disposition, joined to uninterrupted health are indispensable requisites. She must understand cutting out and making the children's dresses. Salary 25 guineas a year. [33]

In the words of the girl's aunt, who reads the ad with her, these requirements are altogether unreasonable: all these qualities, she says, together with physical and moral perfection, "have never fallen to the lot of one human being."[34] This problem of the job advertisement certainly raised tensions within the profession. Apart from when the governess came personally recommended, she was for the most part hired "blind" via newspapers and turned up at the house on her first day of work not really knowing what to expect. Letters were thought to be too formal and arduous train journeys made personal interviews improbable. It was a risky question of "take it or leave it." And with every new ad, the situation replicated that which we find so successfully described in *Mary Poppins*:

> Mrs Banks went into the drawing room and sat there all day long writing letters to the papers and begging them to send some nannies to her at once as she was waiting, and upstairs in the nursery, Jane and Michael watched at the window and wondered who would come. (I, p. 10)

This same situation is reported by Gathorne-Hardy in his citing of memoirs written during the 1920s and 1930s:

> I had eleven nannies in eleven years and added each to my prayers [...] yet, with two exceptions, I never again heard from or met any of them when they left [...] In continuing to pray for these lost nannies some of whom I had hated, I must have been praying for and trying to preserve my own past. During the depression a queue of would-be nannies stretched right round our block and up to our doorstep in response to an advertisement [...]. The queue was

directly outside our nursery windows, we peeped at the women with a real sense of humility: how could so many women want to look after us? We also knew […] that they would have to sleep in the day nursery, without even a dressing table of their own.[35]

THE GOVERNESS AS THRESHOLD FIGURE

Historians claim that given the relatively low number of women having to put up with the problems associated with the governess's profession, the attention that this figure received from the mid-nineteenth century onwards was in fact disproportionate to the actual problem. The 1851 census for example lists 25,000 governesses working in England. The figure seems high until we compare it to the 750,000 women employed as domestic servants during that same year. The working conditions and pay of the latter were lower than that of the governess but clearly seemed more acceptable. This increased attention and the fact that the governess's situation was a source of tension is highly significant. Mary Poovey[36] suggests that the social tension suffered by the governess was at least in part due to the economic and political crises of the so-called "Hungry Years." These years of hardship had driven the members of the middle class (who had witnessed the crumbling of their personal empires and the fall of a system that had until that point seemed perfect) to ask for protection against the erosion of the suppositions and values of their class, suppositions and values that had not foreseen the failure of their economic system despite having in part caused it. Given the position that women, and especially governesses, occupied in middle-class ideology, these (whose explicit task was to educate—or, rather, to socialize—the youngsters) were called upon to act as bulwarks (with all the conflict, ambiguity, and contradiction that this might imply) against any further erosion.

The cornerstone of Victorian society (and what more than anything else allowed that society to function in the way it did) was the family. As previously mentioned, the role of the lady within this family was to preside over the continuity of the family's values and behavior, and the governess was hired (and paid) to do the same. The above-mentioned suppositions regarding the perfect, ideal woman implied that she be totally economically dependent on the male because the sphere over which she presided, the family and its home, had to be seen as distinct and separate from the world of work, money, interests, competition, and movement. That said, and given the conditions and pressures that characterized or were imposed on the governess, this latter suddenly began to find herself caught up in a web of irreconcilable contradictions.

The job of governess was the only one fit for a lady, as it allowed her to remain in the home, far from the public sphere seen as masculine and somewhat vulgar, yet this governess was neither wife nor mother; she was not even really "at home" in the home. The fact that she worked and was subsequently paid meant that she retained her independence. So becoming a governess was the only role fit for a lady, but this paradoxically meant that the woman who filled this role could never really be a true lady.

She was thus a real threshold figure, and her ambiguity (meaning that she would always be considered slightly dangerous) was founded on the fact that she straddled the two most important Victorian representations of the female: the incarnation of the domestic ideal (teaching and maintaining the modes of behavior and positions necessitated by the strict categorization of society, preserving the sense of safety resulting from this, and creating a sense of closure and privacy with respect to the outside world) on the one hand, and the threat to this ideal (coming from the outside, being a stranger to the family, closing the gap between the domestic and professional spheres, and thus shaking the very foundations of middle-class society) on the other.

The type of work entrusted to the governess likened her, of course, to the middle-class mother whom she effectively replaced in the home, and yet, at the same time, the fact that she earned her own living meant that she was also in a similar position to working-class women who also earned their own living or indeed her middle-class male counterparts who enjoyed a similar level of independence from the family as that of the governess. As such the governess exasperated all attempts to neatly categorize and define, occupying as she did that space between male and female, between rich and poor, between inside and outside, between the Here and the Beyond the Door, and this, of course, calls to mind our own governess, Mary Poppins, whose author chose for her third book the metaphorical title *Mary Poppins Opens the Door*.

One of the ways in which the governess's contemporaries dealt with their fears or misgivings that she might not in the end be willing or able to act as a bulwark against immorality, was to associate the latter with the erosion of the class system and to believe that she was the route through which the terrible habits of the working class could infiltrate the morally respectable world of the middle classes. The belief that the ranks of governesses were being invaded by the daughters of salesmen (or even humbler categories) began to spread and as such provoked what Poovey calls the degeneration of a body of women that was in fact

vital to the moral interests of society.[37] In order to combat this degeneration, middle-class commentators proposed a series of defensive
measures that aimed at bolstering the wall that not only divided the
classes but also kept morality separate from its negative other. Even the
Governesses' Benevolent Fund began distinguishing between what it
called ladies "with character" and all the other women and maintained
separate funds and accommodation for the former.[38]

In the narrative of this period, those governesses who turned out to
be evil or immoral were almost always of humble origin. For example,
Thackeray's Becky Sharp was the daughter of a poor artist and a French
singer; the evil Miss Gullit found in the pages of Wilkie Collins's *Arma-
dale* had been abandoned and brought up by adoptive parents of limited means.

A continual source of anxiety present in all reflections on and dis-
cussions of the governess derived from the intuition that the difficulties experienced by a woman filling this role were neither physical nor
economic, but more specifically were emotional in nature, and as such
threatened the self-control of the governess—and it was precisely this
self-control that she had been hired to teach. Lady Elizabeth Eastlake
defended governesses in an 1848 article, in which she writes:

> There is no other class which so cruelly requires its members to
> be, in birth, mind and manner, above their station in order to fit
> them in their station.[39]

And yet even more dangerous than the governess's potential loss of
self-control was the problem of her sexual neutrality. This problem was
given much space in those novels of the time that examined the role
of the governess as seducer or seduced; *Jane Eyre* and *Becky Sharp* are
representatives from the genre of "high" literature, but popular fiction
also contained reflections of this sort. In the 1857 novel *John Halifax,
Gentleman*, the book's author, Dina Maria Mulock Craik, has the lady
of an exemplary middle-class house complain that her two noble sons
have been sullied by the influence of the governess. "Would that she had
never crossed my door" she exclaims, when she finds out that her two
sons have fallen in love with this governess of French Jacobin descent
whose perseverance is in the end rewarded when she finally ends up
marrying one of the brothers.

The governess's sexual susceptibility is discussed in more indirect
terms within the pages of contemporary periodicals and essays, and this
indirectness helps to shed light on the complex system of associations
in which the governess was caught up. Within the home, the governess
was treated like a lady, and as such she was like the other, "real" lady of

the house; and yet at the same time this gave rise to a problematic contradiction because, if one lady was hired and presided over by another, a certain difference had to be implicit. As Eastlake suggests, the problem was that this difference was not necessarily natural:

> [the problem] is not one which will take care of itself, as in the case of a servant. If she [the governess] sits at the table she does not shock you—if she opens her mouth she does not distress you—her appearance and manners are likely to be as good as your own—her education rather better; there is nothing upon the face of the thing to stamp her as having been called to a different state of life from that in which it has pleased God to place you, and therefore the distinction has to be kept up by a furious barrier which presses with cruel weight upon the mental strength or constitutional vanity of a woman.[40]

Lady Eastlake's final remarks call to mind another interesting aspect that ought to be taken into consideration, that of the governess frequently being likened to another figure whose sexuality was equally dangerous, and whose sexual repression was equally important, i.e., the madwoman. The link that contemporaries found between the governess and the lunatic or madwoman was initially coincidental. According to the author of "Hints on the Modern Governess System,"[41] and according to Lady Eastlake,[42] governesses constituted the widest category of women found in mental asylums. Lady Eastlake accounts for this by suggesting that it was the governess's constantly wounded pride that was the source of her mental imbalance, yet the author of "Hints on the Modern Governess System" claims that any imbalance on the part of the governess was motivated by sexual repression. Any girl having trained as a governess and possessing as a consequence "refined and elegant manners," once hired, could look forward to a life in which any "desire for pleasure" would necessarily be suffocated and denied.

> She must live daily amidst the trials of a home without its blessings; she must bear about on her heart the sins she witnesses and the responsibilities that crush her; without any consent of her will she is made the confidante of many family secrets; she must live in a familial circle as if her eyes did not perceive the tokens of bitterness; she must appear not to hear sharp sayings and mal-a-propos speeches; kindly words of courtesy must always be on her lips; she must be ever on her guard; let her relax her self-restraint for

one moment, and who shall say what mischief and misery might ensue to all from one heedless expression of hers?[43]

Commentators of the time frequently associated the governess with the madwoman, both of whom were thought to possess a dangerous vitality that needed to be repressed. The madwoman's vitality was dangerous because it was pathologically uncontrollable, whilst the governess's vitality was simply potentially dangerous: the very idea was upsetting. And even when such a vitality wasn't exhibited or excessive, middle-class people could not help but suspect that, even though she was hired to carefully direct and express "naturalness" only in the most acceptable and specific of manners, this was somehow a very hard or even impossible task, and projected onto her their fear of demanding too much of themselves. This repressed naturalness (another symbol of which was Mr. Hyde, a character created in those same years) would somehow explode. This potential uncontrollability and the abnormality, danger and lack of self-control associated with the governess's feared surplus of vitality bring to mind another figure whose abnormality is not so much pathological but moral: the prostitute. The introduction of a woman into the middle-class home, a woman whose ambiguous position could produce allusions to a dangerous vitality and perverse sexuality, could certainly be read as a sort of incitement to revolution, especially during this period when outside tensions, aggressions, and pressures were very real and threatened change and upheaval, and there were groups such as the "strong-minded women" capable of organizing themselves with the precise aim of achieving moral reform. Indeed, those commentators who linked the figure of the governess to the first feminists and their calls for emancipation were not being merely provocative.

The Queen's College was founded in London in 1848 to train governesses. The school aimed to increase the competency and professionalism with which its students approached this traditional female role, and whilst the college originally catered to the training of governesses, it ended up admitting future wives and mothers. It was the first school to admit women, and its teachers came from various boys' schools. The "Lectures to Ladies" were extremely successful and even if the teachers' aims to impart a "female knowledge"[44] were modest and somewhat vague, for the women who followed the course, and who were even ignorant of the rules of grammar and arithmetic, this was by no means a serious problem and already a great achievement. Even if the women who were finally to improve the position and credibility of the school were not themselves governesses, it would nevertheless be true to say that it was the education of governesses that laid the real foundations for the future education of women in general.

Very quickly, the school's students began to divide themselves according to two distinct categories; there were those whose aim it was to become and remain governesses, whilst others took a more entrepreneurial perspective, forming in 1858 the "Association for the Promotion and Employment of Women," whose energies were directed toward finding situations and positions suitable for unemployed governesses, but they also sought to persuade these women to seek or at least consider other forms of employment. Here, however, a certain residual and contradictory pride characteristic of the governess stood in the way of new ideas. These women, in fact, felt that it did not matter how underpaid, repressed or even maltreated they were, as governesses they would at least be considered ladies; if they were to lower themselves to take on any other form of employment, it might seem as if they had been forced to do so because they had found themselves in cruel circumstances. In this way, those often cruel circumstances in which the governess found herself were condoned and confirmed.

INEVITABLE CONTRADICTIONS

A careful observer of Victorian life made the following affirmation about the governess's situation:

> The real discomfort of a governess's position in a private family arises from the fact that it is undefined. She is not a relation, she is not a guest, not a mistress, not a servant—but something made up of all. No-one knows exactly how to treat her.[45]

This accurate observation defines the governess's problem as being one related to social status and role. The uneasiness surrounding the figure of the governess was the result of a set of contradictory definitions of her position, or the impossibility of finding a harmonious definition that would sit well with the way in which the rest of society was organized. An individual's social position is closely linked to the way in which others behave toward him or her and to what is expected of him or her—this is the way roles are created. Any conflict in the organization of one's social characteristics or an incongruous social position will inevitably lead to ambiguous behavior both on the part of the individual in question and those around him. It is therefore hardly surprising that:

According to general reports, the position of an upper servant in England (they manage these things better abroad) is infinitely preferable to that of a governess.[46]

The humbler servants and members of the domestic staff could boast an unambiguous position and could draw much comfort from knowing exactly what their position was.

Apart from being seen as potentially dangerous, the governess also often experienced tense relationships with both the men and women of the household:

She is a bore to almost any gentleman, as a tabooed woman, to whom he is interdicted from granting the usual privileges of the sex, and yet who is perpetually crossing his path. She is a bore to most ladies by the same rule, and a reproach too—for her dull, fagging bread-and-water life is perpetually putting their pampered listlessness to shame.[47]

Of particular interest here is the conflict between the way in which the gentlemen behaved toward the ladies and their treatment of the governess. There was no room for any simple kindness, attraction, or game of seduction between the latter because the two were not of equal social standing. Nor, however, could the gentleman treat the governess in the same way that he might treat any of his female servants because she could not be classed as his inferior.

As if the problems the governess experienced with both the children and the parents were not enough, she also had to deal with the household's servants who reacted against the incongruence of having an "employed lady" in the house. Lady Eastlake observes that:

The servants invariably detest her, for she is a dependent like themselves and yet, for all that, as much their superior in other respects as the family they both serve.[48]

The governess was only relatively more important than the rest of the servants in the household, and yet it was expected that they serve her. And the servants resented the fact that she acted like a lady, though they would have criticized her for any other form of behavior. This is reminiscent of the end of *Mary Poppins* when, after the governess leaves we find the servant commenting on her:

"Well, if I ever did! Her going away and leaving you poor dear children in the lurch like that", said Mrs Brill, a moment later, bustling in and setting to work on them, "A heart of stone, that's what that girl had [...] Always keeping herself to herself, too, and

not even a lace handkerchief or a hatpin to remember her by."
[...] "How we stood her so long, I don't know—with her airs and
graces and all." (I, p. 167)

Born and bred into the same set of values as those of the people who
subsequently employed her, the governess was the first to realize the
incongruence of her own social position. She tended to measure herself against traditional norms, yet these of course left her wondering
how she should behave. In general, two different types of reaction took
shape. The first was self-pity, and it was extremely common to find this
quality in books about governesses, especially in popular books that
were all very similar and ended up creating types, such as the type of
the oppressed and derelict governess. The tone of these books and their
characters was invariably pathetic—a fact that feeds into the discussion
of the governess as threshold figure and as an entity that seems not to
belong anywhere, not conforming to notions of normality. The self-pity
of the pathetic genre results from a character's recognition of his or her
marginalization, possibly misfortune, and difference from a center that
has for some reason rejected him or her. Such recognition does not,
in this case, point to a specific change, but certainly to a confirmation
of the suffering it causes. The pathetic is interesting because whilst it
is not inherently constructive, it does, however, rest on the negation
of the self's ability to conform to the norms of homogenization that
have the power to accept or reject, praise or condemn, and even violently mistreat someone. As such, it was used to provoke and implicitly
blame those who had decided that certain "others" should be excluded
precisely by exaggerating the suffering and irreconcilable difference of
those excluded.

The second form of reaction to the governess's deplorable situation
was somehow the opposite, and as often represented in Victorian fiction. In these cases, the governess was seen to be excessively proud and
snobbish, attitudes that compensated for her fear of not being respected
in the way she ought to be. Both reactions made the governess an irk-
some presence in the middle-class household.

The fact that governesses accounted for a majority in mental asylums is corroborated by the social commentator Harriett Martineau.[49]
This, of course, is hardly surprising if we consider the inconsistent
and fluctuating attitude that others showed her; it must have thrown
her self-esteem into confusion. Nor did the melodramatic fiction of
the Victorian period do the situation justice when it tended simply to
repackage the problem as a series of insignificant, normal, and, thus,
understandable work-related problems. In reality, these problems were

the product of a conflict that pervaded the whole of the highly complex social structure that was Victorian society.

We should not jump to the conclusion that the governess's problematic situation, depicted in the fiction of the time, was the reality of the time. We can assert, however, that the frequency of articles and essays discussing the treatment of a governess and urging parents to uphold her authority (possibly seeking to combat her feelings of marginalization) suggests that the domestic dramas of the Victorian era did indeed have solid foundations in the reality of English social life.[50]

The governess found herself at the center of those problematic roles and the ambiguously constructed social definitions with their categorizations of "normal" and "abnormal." One way of fleeing what was, in fact, the most obvious contradiction in terms, that of being "an employed gentlewoman" was to deny or at least to minimize the notion of "employment." Newspaper ads of the time often emphasized the fact that what was being offered by the family was a home, rather than conditions for employment; a home in which the governess could feel "one of the family,"[51] describing the position in terms of its reflecting some sort of traditional relationship rather than any new and overly sterile business rapport. But traditional relations, even traditional working relations, were not sterile and implied obligations, responsibilities, and, above all, a deep and total commitment; if this resolved the ambiguous problem of giving paid employment to a lady, it certainly created others—not least those resulting from the governess finding herself exposed to and implicated in a whole series of risky emotional relationships with which by rights she should have had nothing to do.

The denial of the governess's femininity and sexuality (by means of her required clothing and codes of behavior) was seen as a way of reducing this conflict. We find an interesting passage in *Governess Life*, which shows the highly explosive nature of this pretext that only too often revealed itself to be just that, i.e., a pretext:

> Frightful instances have been discovered in which she, to whom the care of the young has been entrusted, instead of guarding their minds in innocence and purity, has become their corrupter—she has been the first to lead and to initiate into sin, to suggest and carry on intrigues, and finally to be the instrument of destroying the peace of families [...] These are the grosser forms of sin which have generally been concealed from public notice [...] but none of the cases are imaginary ones, and they are but too well known in the circle amongst which they occurred. In some instances again, the love and admiration has led the

governess to try and make herself necessary to the comfort of the father of the family in which she resides, and by delicate and unnoticed flattery gradually to gain her point, to the disparagement of the mother, and the destruction of mutual happiness. When the latter was homely, or occupied with domestic cares, opportunity was found to bring forward attractive accomplishments, or by sedulous attention to supply her lack of them; or the sons were in some instances objects of notice and flirtation, or when occasion offered, visitors at the house. This kind of conduct has led to the inquiry which is frequently made before engaging an instructress, "Is she handsome or attractive?" If so, it is conclusively against her.[52]

This is how the stereotypical image of the governess—as often portrayed, for example, in *Punch*—came to be the one of a highly unseductive, plain, strict, and totally unfeminine woman.

FORTUNATE CONTRADICTIONS

The trustworthy Mrs. Garth in the novel entitled *No Name* by Wilkie Collins published in 1862[53] has a deeply lined face, a thin, bony body, and is known for her "masculine readiness and decision of movement." Represented in such a way, she can hardly seem threatening, and as such is entrusted with the task of taking care of the whole house:

> The self-possession of her progress down the stairs and the air of habitual authority with which she looked above her, spoke well for her position in Mr Wanstone's family.[54]

The author continues:

> This was evidently not one of the forlorn, persecuted pitiably dependent order of governesses. Here was a woman who lived on ascertained and honorable terms with her employers—a woman who looked capable of sending any parents in England to the right-about if they failed to rate her at her proper value.[55]

Mary Poppins is described in a similar way when she first appears in the Banks household:

> Mary Poppins regarded them steadily, looking from one to the other as though she were making up her mind whether she liked them or not.
> "Will we do?" asked Michael. [...]

Mary Poppins continued to regard the four children search-ingly. Then, with a long, loud sniff that seemed to indicate that she had made up her mind, she said:

"I'll take the position."

"For all the world," as Mrs Banks said to her husband later, "as though she were doing us a signal honour." (I, p. 15)

Similar cases offering ways of avoiding conflicts of this sort are pres-ent throughout much of the fiction concerning governesses. We find one such solution in Ivy Compton-Burnett's 1944 novel *Elders and Bet-ters*.[56] The novel contains many hints that the story is set in the past with respect to the publication date. Several allusions and the total absence of others (explicitly referring to the contemporary way of life) seem to claim that the story is set at some point during the nineteenth century, and yet it would be more appropriate to suggest that, like the Mary Poppins books, to decide that this book is set in the Edwardian or, even earlier, in the Victorian period simply because it contains no precise references, for example, to technology of some sort, would be arbitrary, because what the text seems to convey is the sense that its story could belong to any time.

The governess, Miss Lucy, has a predilection, or rather a real passion for umbrellas. She is kind and above all quite peculiar and the chil-dren and adults alike gradually become used to her rather theatrical manners. We find a similar situation being described at the end of the opening chapter to *Mary Poppins*:

And that is how Mary Poppins came to live at Number Seventeen, Cherry Tree Lane. And although they sometimes found them-selves wishing for the quieter, more ordinary days when Katie Nanna ruled the household, everybody, on the whole, was glad of Mary Poppins' arrival. (I, p. 19)

Miss Lucy's philosophy regarding the farces and tragedies of the family is to "live and let live." And of Mary Poppins we read that:

But nobody ever knew what Mary Poppins felt about it, for Mary Poppins never told anybody anything. (I, p. 20)

One of her most oft-repeated expressions is:

Never trouble Trouble till Trouble troubles you. (III, p. 152)

Miss Lucy resists the desire to influence the lives of anyone but her charges and seems ultimately focused only on herself. What is most striking about this governess, however, is the fact that she is always perfectly aware of her role—indeed, she is proud of this role; she sees it as a form of vocation or mission. She is convinced that as *the* governess, she is beyond judgment and cannot be compared to any of the other characters who are defined by bonds and criteria that cannot be applied to her; as such she can feel totally sure of herself. She holds her position and vocation in high esteem and throws herself into fulfilling her role with complete conviction and no little self-satisfaction, which cannot but raise other people's opinions of her. She completely identifies with her "calling" (almost as if it were something sacred), carries out all the attendant tasks to perfection, and never knows even a moment of embarrassment or uneasiness. Because she is the first to hold her position in high regard, Miss Lucy cannot entertain the idea that others may not hold her and her position in a similar high regard. And all the other characters do, indeed, hold her in high regard, and it could be argued that this high level of esteem in which the governess is held comes to take center stage in Compton-Burnett's novel.

This novel was published in 1944, when the first three books in the Mary Poppins series had already been published. *Mary Poppins* and *Mary Poppins Comes Back* had appeared ten years earlier, then, after many years (which as far as the story and its protagonist are concerned, seemed no time at all, or rather, served to render more incisive both protagonist and story), in 1943 to be precise, and to both public and critical acclaim, the third book in the series, *Mary Poppins Opens the Door*, appeared.

It is very likely that Ivy Compton-Burnett herself kept a copy on her bedside table.

NOTES

CHAPTER 1

1. The six books in the Mary Poppins series are as follows: *Mary Poppins* (London: Collins, 1934); *Mary Poppins Comes Back* (London: Collins, 1935); *Mary Poppins Opens the Door* (London: Collins, 1943); *Mary Poppins in the Park* (London: Collins, 1952); *Mary Poppins in Cherry Tree Lane* (London: Collins, 1982); *Mary Poppins and the House Next Door* (London: Collins, 1989).
2. All the page references in the text will refer to the above books. *Mary Poppins* is designated by roman numeral I, *Mary Poppins Comes Back* by II, *Mary Poppins Opens the Door* by III, *Mary Poppins in the Park* by IV, *Mary Poppins in Cherry Tree Lane* by V, and *Mary Poppins and the House Next Door* by VI.
3. Caitlin Flanagan, "Becoming Mary Poppins. P. L. Travers, Walt Disney and the Making of a Myth," *The New Yorker* (December 19, 2005): 40–46.
4. Paul Thompson, *The Edwardians* (London: Weidenfeld and Nicolson, 1975), 43.
5. Carlo Ginzburg, *I Benandanti* (Turin: Einaudi, 1966). In this study the historian Carlo Ginzburg traces different kinds of documents that describe the nocturnal "flights" of people, mostly from the lower classes, who, from medieval times onwards, have been thought or found able to lift and move against the laws of gravity, in ecstatic experiences during which all forms of physical suffering and deprivation were soothed and healed.
6. I will deal with this concept in more detail in the section "A Childlike Vision of the World: the Pre-Oedipal Phase," in chapter 3.
7. Novalis, *Werke und Briefe*, ed. Alfred Kelletat. (Munich: Winkler, 1962), 351. My translation.
8. Emanuella Scarano, "I modi dell'autenticazione," in *La Narrazione Fantastica* (Pisa: Nistri-Lischi, 1983), 355–398.

CHAPTER 2

1. Pamela Lyndon Travers, *What the Bee Knows: Reflections on Myth, Symbol and Story* (Wellingborough: The Aquarian Press, 1989), 295.
2. Ibid., 285–303.
3. Ibid., 170.
4. Ibid., 170–171.
5. Ibid., 208.
6. Ibid., 287.
7. Ibid., 287.
8. Ibid., 287–288.
9. Ibid., 288–289.

10. Ibid., 237–238.
11. Ibid., 239–240.
12. Ibid., 240.
13. Cited in *The Junior Book of Authors*, eds. Kunitz and Haycraft (2nd rev. ed.) (New York: Wilson, 1951), 288.
14. Ibid., 288.
15. P.L. Travers, *What the Bee Knows: Reflections on Myth, Symbol and Story* (Wellingborough: The Aquarian Press, 1989), 290.
16. Ibid., 293.
17. Ibid., 293.
18. Ibid., 293–297.
19. Ibid., 302.
20. Ibid., 301–302.
21. Ibid., 301.

CHAPTER 3

1. See Mary Douglas, *Purity and Danger: An Analysis of Concepts of Pollution and Taboo* (New York: Routledge, 1984).
2. Mircea Eliade, *Shamanism: Archaic Techniques of Ecstasy* (Princeton, NJ: Princeton University Press, 1972).
3. Arthur O. Lovejoy, *The Great Chain of Being. A Study of the History of an Idea* (Cambridge, MA: Harvard University Press, 1936).
4. Georges Bachelard, *L'Air et le Songes. Essay sur l'Imagination du Mouvement* (Paris: J. Corti, 1943). See also Gilbert Durand, *Les structures anthropologiques de l'imaginaire* (Paris: Bordas, 1969).
5. Mircea Eliade, *Shamanism: Archaic Techniques of Ecstasy*, 511.
6. For a discussion of the concept of "aestethic adventure" see Vladimir Jankélévitch, *L'Aventure, l'Ennui, le Serieux* (Paris: 1963).
7. Charles Baudelaire, *L'Art Romantique* (Geneva: Ed. d'Art, 1945), 88. My translation.
8. Cowper J. Powys, "Wilde as a Symbolic Figure," in *Oscar Wilde. The Critical Heritage*, edited by K. Beckson (London: Routledge, 1970), 358.
9. Oscar Wilde, *Complete Works* (London: Collins, 1966), 488.
10. Ibid., 1084.
11. Staffan Bergsten, *Mary Poppins and Myth* (Stockholm: Almqvist and Wiskell International, 1978), 71.
12. Ibid., 71.
13. The concept is expressed throughout Wilde's works. See Oscar Wilde, *Complete Works*.
14. Ibid., 474.
15. Ibid., 459.
16. Giovanna Franci, *Il sistema del Dandy* (Bologna: Patron, 1987), 140.
17. Roland Barthes, *Le Dandysme et la Mode*, in Emilien Carassus, *Le Mythe du Dandy,* (Paris: Colin, 1971), 314.
18. Pamela Lyndon Travers, *Friend Monkey* (London, Collins, 1972).
19. Cited in P.L. Travers, *What the Bee Knows. Reflections on Myth, Symbol and Story,* 4.
20. For a fascinating analysis of this idea see Carlo Ginzburg, *Storia Notturna. Una decifrazione del Sabba* (Turin: Einaudi, 1989).
21. Ferruccio Masini, "Il Segno di Dioniso," in *Lo Scriba del Caos. Interpretazioni di Nietzsche* (Bologna: Il Mulino, 1978), 238. My translation.
22. Ibid., p. 444. My translation.

23. Italo Calvino, *Six Memos for the Next Millenium* (Cambridge, MA: Harvard University Press, 1988).
24. Ibid. My translation.
25. Ibid. My translation
26. Ibid. My translation.
27. Ibid. My translation.
28. Ibid. My translation.
29. Ibid. My translation.
30. Ibid. My translation.
31. Ibid. My translation.
32. Ibid. My translation.
33. Ibid. My translation.
34. Johann Jakob Bachofen, *Myth, Religion and Mother Right*, (Princeton, NJ: Princeton University Press, 1967).
35. A point made by psychologist Corinna Cristiani in the collective volume edited by Fulvio Scaparro, *Volere la Luna. La crescita attraverso l'Avventura* (Milano: Unicopli, 1987).
36. See Johann Jakob Bachofen, *Myth, Religion and Mother Right*, 97.
37. Mary Douglas, *Purity and Danger: An Analysis of Concepts of Pollution and Taboo*.
38. See Jean Wyatt, *Reconstructing Desire. The Role of the Unconscious in Women's Reading and Writing* (Chapel Hill: The University of North Carolina Press, 1990).
39. William Wordsworth, *Ode to Immortality,* cited in Thomas Hutchinson, and Ernest De Selincourt, *Poetical Works of Wordsworth* (Oxford: Oxford University Press, 1960), 588.
40. Jean Wyatt, *Reconstructing Desire. The Role of the Unconscious in Women's Reading and Writing*, 2.
41. Ibid., 2.
42. Ibid., 4.
43. Ibid., 4.
44. Julia Kristeva, *Revolution in Poetic Language* (New York, Columbia University Press, 1984).
45. Ibid., 79.
46. Jean Wyatt, *Reconstructing Desire. The Role of the Unconscious in Women's Reading and Writing*, 10.
47. For a very illuminating discussion of this concept see Adam Phillips, *The Beast in the Nursery* (New York: Pantheon, 1998).
48. Felix Klee, *Vita e Opere di Paul Klee* (Turin: Einaudi, 1960), 161.
49. Ibid. My translation.
50. Rosetta Infelise Fronza, "La saggezza dell'infanzia e il mondo intermedio," in *Aut Aut* (September-December 1982): 160–61. My translation.
51. Felix Klee, *Vita e Opere di Paul Klee*, 162. My translation.
52. Robert Musil, *The Man without Qualities* (London: Picador, 1954, vol. II), 874.
53. Pamela Lyndon Travers, *What the Bee Knows. Reflections on Myth, Symbol and Story*, 15.
54. Jean Wyatt, *Reconstructing Desire. The Role of the Unconscious in Women's Reading and Writing*, 17.

CHAPTER 4

1. See Martha Vicinus, *Suffer and Be Still. Women in the Victorian Age* (Bloomington: Indiana University Press, 1973).

2. See Frances Power Cobbe, *Life of Frances Power Cobbe*, vol. I, (London: Richard Bentley & Son, 1894), 164.

3. Jonathan Gathorne-Hardy, *The Rise and Fall of the British Nanny* (London: Weidenfeld & Nicolson, 1993), 197.

4. Ibid., 198.

5. Ibid., 60.

6. For a wider discussion of the process leading to the characterization of specific categories of society, and especially of the notion of *habitus*, see Pierre Bourdieu, *Distinction*, (New York: Routledge & Kegan Paul, 1984).

7. Katharine West, *Chapter of Governesses. A Study of the Governess in English Fiction. 1800–1949* (London: Cohen & West, 1949).

8. Ibid., 101.

9. Edward Sackville-West, *Simpson. A life* (New York: Knopf, 1931).

10. This problem continued to preoccupy British society well into the 1930s and 1940s, as is evidenced by those beautifully fragile and untouchable heroines appearing in the novels of Ryder Haggard, John Buchan, and Conan Doyle; J. M. Barry's female characters also often fit this mould, as do the female characters of many musicals and plays written in the years leading up to World War II.

11. Cited in Gathorne-Hardy, *The Rise and Fall of the British Nanny*, 93.

12. Ibid., 94.

13. Ibid., 97.

14. Ibid., 86.

15. Ibid., 88.

16. Peter de Polnay, *Children, My Children* (London, Hutchinson, 1939).

17. Ibid., p. 68.

18. Ibid., p. 69.

19. Gathorne-Hardy notes how this attitude, which was particularly surprising because set against the backdrop of the war, was common to many of the governesses he studied. There are many cases in which the governess emerges as an incredibly courageous figure, capable of maintaining her stiff upper lip at all times. She is totally nursery-centric in this regard and is entirely committed to the care of her children to the extent that she manages to protect them from all external events, such as the war and wartime bombings. Gathorne-Hardy reports how Mrs. Priscilla Napier told of how in 1940 a daytime bombing had just commenced and her young brother had asked their governess what the noise was. "Bombs, dear. Elbows off the table" was her response.

20. J. Sheridan Le Fanu, *Uncle Silas*, Harmondsworth, (England: Penguin 2001; 1st ed. 1864), 112.

21. A. Conan Doyle, *The Sign of Four* (London: Spencer Blockett, 1890).

22. J. Conrad, *Chance* (London: Methuen, 1914).

23. Ibid.

24. Ibid.

25. Ibid.

26. Ibid.

27. Ibid.

28. Ibid.

29. Ibid.

30. Ibid.

31. Wonderland Music Company Inc., © Walt Disney's *Mary Poppins* original motion picture soundtrack, 1963.

32. Patricia Thomson, "That Noble Body of Governesses," in *The Victorian Heroine, A Changing Ideal*, (London: Oxford University Press, 1956), 38.

33. Cited in Katharine West, *Chapter of Governesses. A Study of the Governess in English Fiction.* 51.
34. Ibid.
35. Jonathan Gathorne-Hardy, *The Rise and Fall of the British Nanny*, 98.
36. Mary Poovey, "The Anathematized Race: The Governess and Jane Eyre," in *The Proper Lady and the Woman Writer* (Chicago: Chicago University Press, 1985), 127.
37. Ibid., 129.
38. Martha Vicinus, *Suffer and Be Still. Women in the Victorian Age*, 17.
39. Elizabeth Eastlake, "Vanity Fair, Jane Eyre, and The Governesses' Benevolent Institution," *Quarterly Review*, 84 (December 1848): 177.
40. Ibid., 177.
41. "Hints on the Modern Governess System," in *Fraser's Magazine* (April 1844): 571–583.
42. Eastlake's 1847 commentary on the annual report of the GBI, cited in Poovey, 1984, 129.
43. Cited in Poovey, 1984, 130.
44. Patricia Thomson, "That Noble Body of Governesses," in *The Victorian Heroine, A changing Idea*, 38.
45. Elizabeth Sewell, *Principles of Education, Drawn From Nature and Revelation and Applied to Female Education in the Upper Classes*, vol. II, (New York, Appleton and Company, 1866), 240.
46. Ibid., 237.
47. E. Eastlake, 1848, 177.
48. Ibid., 177.
49. Harriet Martineau, "Female Industry," *Edinburgh Review*, 109 (April 1859), cited in M. Vicinus, *Suffer and Be Still. Women in the Victorian Age*, 13.
50. See Elizabeth Sewell, *Principles of Education, Drawn From Nature and Revelation and Applied to Female Education in the Upper Classes; Governess Life: Its Trials, Duties, and Encouragements*, vol. II, London, 1849; *Hints to Governesses By One of Themselves* (London, 1856).
51. Elizabeth Sewell, *Principles of Education, Drawn From Nature and Revelation and Applied to Female Education in the Upper Classes*, vol. II, 211, 250, 258.
52. Elizabeth Sewell, *Governess Life: Its Trials, Duties, and Encouragements* (London, 1849), 127.
53. Wilkie Collins, *No Name* (London: Sampson Low, 1862).
54. Ibid.
55. Ibid.
56. Ivy Compton-Burnett, *Elders and Betters* (London: Victor Gollancz, 1944).

BIBLIOGRAPHY

Adburgham, Alison. *A Punch History of Manners and Modes.* 1841–1940. London: Hutchinson, 1961.

Ariès, Philip, and Duby, Georges. *A History of Private Life.* Vol. IV. Cambridge, MA: Harvard University Press, 1987.

Armstrong, Nancy. *Desire and Domestic Fiction. A Political History of the Novel.* New York: Oxford University Press, 1987.

Bachelard, Georges. *L'Air et les Songes. Essay sur l'Imagination du Mouvement.* Paris: José Corti, 1943.

Bachofen, Johann Jakob. *Myth, Religion and Mother Right.* Princeton, NJ: Princeton University Press, 1967.

Baudelaire Charles. *L'Art Romantique.* Geneva: Ed. d'Art, 1945.

Becchi, Egle. *Storia dell'Educazione.* Florence: La Nuova Italia, 1987.

Beckson, Karl, ed. *Oscar Wilde. The Critical Heritage.* London: Routledge & Kegan Paul, 1970.

Bergsten, Staffan. *Mary Poppins and Myth.* Stockholm: Almqvist and Wiskell International, 1978.

Bertolini, Piero. *Pedagogia al limite.* Florence: La Nuova Italia, 1988.

_____. *L'Esistere Pedagogico.* Florence: La Nuova Italia, 1990.

Borghi, Liana, and Cristiano Camporesi. *L'Etica Sociale nell'Età Vittoriana.* Turin: Loescher, 1978.

Bourdieu, Pierre. *Distinction.* London: Routledge & Kegan Paul, 1984.

Boyd, William. *History of Western Education.* New York: Barnes & Noble Books, 1980.

Branca, Patricia. *Silent Sisterhood. Middle-class Women in the Victorian Home.* London: Croom Helm, 1975.

Brendon, Piers. *Eminent Edwardians.* London: Secker & Warburg, 1979.

Brönte, Charlotte. *Jane Eyre.* London: Smith, Elder, and Co., 1847.

Brönte, Emily. *Wuthering Heights.* London: Thomas Cautley Newby, 1847.

Buckler, Willam E. *The Victorian Imagination.* New York: The Harvester Press, 1980.

Calvino, Italo. *Six Memos for the Next Millenium.* Cambridge, MA: Harvard University Press, 1988.

Carassus, Emilien. *Le Mythe du Dandy.* Paris: Colin, 1971.

Chatwin, Bruce. *Songlines.* New York: Viking Press, 1987.

Cobbe, Frances Power. *Life of Frances Power Cobbe.* London: Richard Bentley & Son, 1894.

Collins, Wilkie. *No Name.* London: Sampson Low, 1862.

Compton-Burnett, Ivy. *Elders and Betters.* London: Victor Gollancz, 1944.

Conan Doyle, Arthur. *The Sign of Four.* London: Spencer Blockett, 1890.

Conrad, Joseph. *Chance.* London: Methuen, 1914.

Cook, Elizabeth. *The Ordinary and the Fabulous. An Introduction to Myths, Legends and Fairy Tales.* Cambridge: Cambridge University Press, 1976.

Craik, Dina, Maria, Murdock. *John Halifax, Gentleman*. London: Georges Newnes Limited, 1898.

Darton, Harvey FJ. *Children's Books in England: Five Centuries of Social Life*. Cambridge: Cambridge University Press, 1958.

De Polnay, Peter. *Children, My Children*. London: Hutchinson, 1939.

Douglas, Mary. *Purity and Danger: An Analysis of Concepts of Pollution and Taboo*. New York: Routledge, 1984.

Doyle, Brian. *English and Englishness*. London: Routledge, 1989.

Duby, Georges, and Perrot, Michelle. *A History of Women in the West*. Cambridge, MA: Harvard University Press, 1994.

Durand, Gilbert. *Les structures anthropologiques de l'imaginaire*. Paris: Bordas, 1969.

Eastlake, Elizabeth. "Vanity Fair, Jane Eyre, and The Governesses' Benevolent Institution." *Quarterly Review* 84, (December, 1848).

Eliade, Mircea. *Shamanism: Archaic Techniques of Ecstasy*. Princeton, NJ: Princeton University Press, 1972.

Euripides, *Bacchae*. New York: Viking Press, 1954.

Faeti, Antonio. *Letteratura per l'Infanzia*. Florence: La Nuova Italia, 1977.

Flanagan, Caitlin. "Becoming Mary Poppins. P.L. Travers, Walt Disney and the Making of a Myth." *The New Yorker* (December 19, 2005): 40–46.

Franci, Giovanna. *Il sistema del Dandy*. Bologna: Patron, 1987.

Freud, Sigmund. *Uncanny*. London: Penguin, 1960.

Fronza, Rosetta Infelise. "La saggezza dell'infanzia e il mondo intermedio." *Aut Aut* (September-December, 1982): 159–166.

Frye, Northrop. *Anatomy of Criticism*. Princeton, NJ: Princeton University Press, 1957.

Gathorne-Hardy, Jonathan. *The Rise and Fall of the British Nanny*. London: Weidenfeld & Nicolson, 1993.

Gilbert, Sandra, and Gubar, Susan. *The Madwoman in the Attic: The Woman Writer and the Nineteenth-Century Literary Imagination*. New Haven, CT: Yale University Press, 1979.

Gillis, John R. *Youth and History: Tradition and Change in European Age Relations. 1770 to the Present*. New York: Academic Press, 1974.

Ginzburg, Carlo. *I Benandanti*. Turin: Einaudi, 1966;

_____. "Spie. Radici di un paradigma indiziario." In *Crisi della Ragione*. Ed. A. Gargani. Turin: Einaudi, 1979.

_____. *Storia Notturna. Una decifrazione del Sabba*. Turin: Einaudi, 1989.

Gordon, Peter and John White. *Philosophers as Educational Reformers. The Influence of Idealism on British Educational Thought and Practice*. London: Routledge & Kegan Paul, 1979.

Gourvish, Terry R., and Alan O'Day. *Later Victorian Britain. 1867–1900*. London: Macmillan, 1988.

Grisewood, Harman. *Ideas and Beliefs of the Victorians*. London: Sylvan Press, 1949.

Hecht, Jean J. *The Domestic Servant Class in Eighteenth-century England*. London: Routledge & Kegan Paul, 1956.

Hobsbawm, Eric, J. *The Age of Capital. 1845–1875*. London: Weidenfeld & Nicolson, 1975.

Houghton, Walter. *The Victorian Frame of Mind*. New Haven, CT: Yale University Press, 1957.

Hughes, Stuart H. *Consciousness and Society. The Reorientation of European Social Thought. 1890–1930*. New York: Vintage, 1961.

Husserl, Edmund. *La crisi delle scienze europee e la fenomenologia trascendentale*. Milan: Il Saggiatore, 1975.

_____. *L'obiettivismo moderno*. Milan: Il Saggiatore, 1976.

_____. *Fenomenologia e teoria della conoscenza*. Milan: Bompiani 2004.

Hutchinson, Thomas, and Ernest De Selincourt. *Poetical Works of Wordsworth*. Oxford: Oxford University Press, 1960.

Hyde, Lewis. *Trickster Makes This World. Mischief, Myth and Art*. New York: Farrar, Strauss & Giroux, 1998.

Inglis, Fred. *The Promise of Happiness. Value and Meaning in Children's Fiction*. Cambridge: Cambridge University Press, 1981.

Jalland, Patricia. *Women, Marriage, and Politics*. Oxford: Oxford University Press, 1988.

Jankélévitch, Vladimir. *L'Aventure, l'Ennui, le Serieux*. Paris, 1963.

James, Henry. *What Maisie Knew*. London: W. Heinemann, 1897.

_____. *The Turn of the Screw*, London: W. Heinemann, 1898.

Jung, Carl Gustav. *Man and His Symbols*. New York: Dell, 1984.

Kanner, Barbara. *The Women of England*. London: Mausell, 1980.

Klee, Felix. *Vita e Opere di Paul Klee*. Turin: Einaudi, 1960.

Kristeva, Julia. *Revolution in Poetic Language*. New York, Columbia University Press, 1984.

Kunitz, Stanley, and Howard Haycraft. *The Junior Book of Authors*. 2nd rev. ed. New York: Wilson, 1951.

Laslett, Peter. *The World We Have Lost*. London: Methuen, 1965.

Lawson, John and Harold Silver. *A Social History of Education in England*. London: Methuen, 1973.

Le Fanu, John Seridan. *Uncle Silas*. Harmondsworth, England: Penguin, 2001. First edition published 1964.

Levi-Strauss, Charles. *Anthropologie Structurale*. Paris: Plon, 1960.

Lovejoy, Arthur Oncken. *The Great Chain of Being. A Study of the History of an Idea*. Cambridge, MA: Harvard University Press, 1936.

Masini, Ferruccio. "Il Segno di Dioniso." In *Lo Scriba del Caos. Interpretazioni di Nietzsche*. Bologna: Il Mulino, 1978

Massa, Riccardo. *Linee di Fuga. L'Avventura nella Formazione Umana*. Florence: La Nuova Italia, 1989.

Musil, Robert. *The Man without Qualities*. London: Picador, 1954.

Nicolson, Harold. *Good Behaviour*. London: Constable 1955.

Novalis, *Werke und Briefe*. Edited by Alfred Kelletat. Munich: Winkler, 1962.

Paci, Enzo. *La Filosofia Contemporanea*. Milan: Garzanti, 1974.

Paxman, Jeremy. *The English. A Portrait of a People*. London: Penguin, 1999.

Phillips, Adam. *The Beast in the Nursery: On Curiosity and Other Appetites*. New York: Pantheon, 1998.

Pollock, Linda A. *Forgotten Children. Parent-child Relations from 1500 to 1900*. Cambridge: Cambridge University Press, 1983.

Poovey, Mary. "The Anathematized Race: The Governess and Jane Eyre," In *The Proper Lady and the Woman Writer*. Chicago: Chicago University Press, 1985

Read, Donald. *England 1868–1914*. London: Longman, 1979.

Rockwell, Joan. *Fact in Fiction. The Use of Literature in the Systematic Study of Society*. London: Routledge & Kegan Paul, 1974.

Roebuck, Janet. *The Making of Modern English Society From 1850*. London: Routledge & Kegan Paul, 1973.

Rubinstein, William D. *Capitalism, Culture and Decline in Britain*. London and New York: Routledge, 1994.

Sackville-West, Edward. *Simpson. A life*. New York: Knopf, 1931.

Scarano, Emanuella. "I modi dell'autenticazione." In *La Narrazione Fantastica*, 355–398. Pisa: Nistri-Lischi, 1983.

Scaparro, Fulvio, ed. *Volere la Luna. La crescita attraverso l'Avventura*. Milan: Unicopli, 1987.

Sewell, Elizabeth. *Principles of Education, Drawn From Nature and Revelation and Applied to Female Education in the Upper Classes*. New York: Appleton and Company, 1866.

_____. *Governess Life: Its Trials, Duties, and Encouragements.* London, 1849.

_____. *Hints to Governesses By One of Themselves.* London, 1856.

Spacks, Patricia Meyer. *Imagining a Self. Autobiography and Novel in Eighteenth-century England.* Cambridge, MA: Harvard University Press, 1976.

Stubbs, Patricia. *Women and Fiction. Feminism and the Novel, 1880–1920.* New York: The Harvester Press, 1979.

Thompson, Paul. *The Edwardians.* London: Weidenfeld and Nicolson, 1975.

Thompson, Thea. *Edwardian Childhoods.* London: Routledge & Kegan Paul, 1981.

Thomson, Patricia. "That Noble Body of Governesses." In *The Victorian Heroine, A changing Ideal*, 37–56. Oxford: Oxford University Press, 1956.

P. L. Travers, *Mary Poppins.* London: Collins, 1934.

_____. *Mary Poppins Comes Back.* London: Collins, 1935.

_____. *Mary Poppins Opens the Door.* London: Collins, 1943.

_____. *Mary Poppins in the Park.* London: Collins, 1952.

_____. *Mary Poppins in Cherry Tree Lane.* London: Collins, 1982.

_____. *Mary Poppins and the House Next Door.* London: Collins, 1989.

_____. *Friend Monkey.* London: Collins, 1972.

_____. *About the Sleeping Beauty.* London: Collins, 1977.

_____. *What the Bee Knows: Reflections on Myth, Symbol and Story.* Wellingborough: The Aquarian Press, 1989.

Vicinus, Martha. *Suffer and Be Still. Women in the Victorian Age.* Bloomington: Indiana University Press, 1973.

West, Katharine. *Chapter of Governesses. A Study of the Governess in English Fiction. 1800–1949.* London: Cohen & West, 1949.

Wilde, Oscar. *Complete Works.* London: Collins, 1966.

Wonderland Music Company Inc., ©,Walt Disney's *Mary Poppins* original motion picture soundtrack, 1963.

Wyatt, Jean. *Reconstructing Desire. The Role of the Unconscious in Women's Reading and Writing.* Chapel Hill: University of North Carolina Press, 1990.

INDEX